PORTFOLIO/PENGUIN

WORKING FOR YOU ISN'T WORKING FOR ME

Katherine Crowley, a Harvard-trained psychotherapist, and Kathi Elster, an executive coach, create the yin and yang of their company, K Squared Enterprises. Since 1989, they've combined their complementary expertise to develop a unique method for dealing with difficult people and challenging conditions at work. Their inside-out approach transforms the way businesses uncover and resolve their greatest interpersonal dilemmas.

Bestselling authors, educators, popular speakers, and veteran consultants, Katherine and Kathi are seasoned guides in the area of professional fulfillment through self-awareness and self-management. They use humor and a slew of engaging techniques to mediate solutions for individuals at every level of employment—from executives to managers to frontline employees.

Together they have written two other books: the business bestseller *Working with You Is Killing Me: Freeing Yourself from Emotional Traps at Work* and *Going Indie: Self-Employment, Freelance & Temping Opportunities.*

Contact Katherine Crowley and Kathi Elster at:

K Squared Enterprises
119 West 23rd Street, Suite 1009
New York. NY 10011
212-929-7676
info@ksquaredenterprises.com

And visit their Web site: www.ksquaredenterprises.com

D0047911

Working for You Isn't Working for Me

HOW TO GET AHEAD WHEN YOUR BOSS HOLDS YOU BACK

Katherine Crowley AND Kathi Elster

PORTFOLIO/PENGUIN

PORTFOLIO/PENGUIN
Published by the Penguin Group
Penguin Group (USA) Inc., 375 Hudson Street, New York, New York 10014, U.S.A.
Penguin Group (Canada), 90 Eglinton Avenue East, Suite 700, Toronto,
Ontario, Canada M4P 2Y3 (a division of Pearson Penguin Canada Inc.)
Penguin Books Ltd, 80 Strand, London WC2R 0RL, England
Penguin Ireland, 25 St. Stephen's Green, Dublin 2, Ireland
(a division of Penguin Books Ltd)
Penguin Books Australia Ltd, 250 Camberwell Road, Camberwell,
Victoria 3124, Australia (a division of Pearson Australia Group Pty Ltd)
Penguin Books India Pvt Ltd, 11 Community Centre,
Panchsheel Park, New Delhi – 110 017, India
Penguin Group (NZ), 67 Apollo Drive, Rosedale, North Shore 0632,
New Zealand (a division of Pearson New Zealand Ltd)
Penguin Books (South Africa) (Pty) Ltd, 24 Sturdee Avenue,
Rosebank, Johannesburg 2196, South Africa

Penguin Books Ltd, Registered Offices:
80 Strand, London WC2R 0RL, England

First published in the United States of America by Portfolio,
a member of Penguin Group (USA) Inc. 2009
This paperback edition published 2010

1   3   5   7   9   10   8   6   4   2

THE LIBRARY OF CONGRESS HAS CATALOGED THE HARDCOVER EDITION AS FOLLOWS:
Crowley, Katherine.
Working for you isn't working for me : the ultimate guide
to managing your boss / by Katherine Crowley and Kathi Elster.
p. cm.
Includes index.
ISBN 978-1-59184-275-0 (hc.)
ISBN 978-1-59184-368-9 (pbk.)
1. Managing your boss.   2. Psychology, Industrial.   I. Elster, Kathi.   II. Title.
HF5548.83.C77 2009
650.1'3—dc22   2009010628

Printed in the United States of America · Set in ITC New Baskerville
Designed by BTDNYC

This book is dedicated to

THELMA SOHN KRIEGER, 1918—2007,

a woman who taught us to set our sights high

and never lose focus

Contents

Introduction

WHOEVER YOU ARE and whatever kind of work you do, part of your job involves dealing with authority. You may have to report directly to a boss or supervisor, or you may work for a major account that demands large chunks of your time. You may be held accountable by a board of trustees, or perhaps there's an institution that provides you with funding or resources. We all answer to somebody. And your ability to manage these crucial relationships may just mean the difference between success and failure.

Some authority figures are easy to deal with. They are excellent communicators who know how to lead and inspire others to reach their full potential. Unfortunately, the untrained or inept leader seems to be a far more common occurrence. And then there are individuals who either abuse or misuse their power: supervisors who hire smart people only to micromanage their work; executives who encourage the free flow of ideas and then shoot the ideas (and the people who offer them) down; board members who are absent, complacent, or resistant.

Difficult bosses of any kind can make the experience of work miserable. Their erratic or unreasonable behavior makes the people they manage feel crazy. But because these bosses are in the power seat, the individuals who must adhere to their authority (you) often feel powerless to do anything about the situation.

Since 1989, we've used our combined expertise as a psychotherapist and business strategist to study and understand the root causes of pleasure and pain, success and failure in the workplace. Our research shows that the single greatest determinant of an individual's happiness at work is the quality of the relationship between that person and his or her boss. When that association is good, work is good; life is good. When it's bad, nothing else seems right. A difficult boss/employee relationship will wreak havoc on an employee's work life, home life, social life, and internal life.

With the international success of our last book, *Working with You Is Killing Me: Freeing Yourself from Emotional Traps at Work*, we gained entry into numerous government agencies, businesses, and not-for-profit institutions. We gave presentations to CEOs, vice presidents, department heads, managers, supervisors, administrators, and line staff. After each presentation, one or more participants would inevitably approach us and confess their specific painful struggles with the people who managed them:

"I love my job, but I hate my boss."

"My supervisor is half my age with none of my experience."

"My boss is nice, but when a conflict arises, she never takes a stand."

"My employer keeps giving me responsibility without giving me the authority to carry it out."

"His first response to any idea that I propose is *no*."

If any of these statements sounds familiar, or if you're working for someone whose words and actions make your work life difficult in other ways, this book is for you. You may be a CEO or an entry-level employee. It actually doesn't matter what your job title is or how much money you take home. What matters is the fact that you report to someone—a boss, a board member, a customer, or an investor—who behaves in ways that frustrate, irritate, block, challenge, unnerve, frighten, infuriate, disgust, or otherwise trouble you.

There *is* a way to manage even the most challenging boss or authority at work and to take back your personal power. The solution lies in your hands. It begins with managing your internal responses to his or her behavior and ends with taking positive business actions on your own behalf. *Working for You Isn't Working for Me* teaches you how to do just that. We're going to take you through a powerful, practical 4-step program that incorporates and emphasizes both self-care activities and self-management techniques. We promise that if you really apply the principles of this book to your relationship with the boss, you'll feel a greater sense of control and a huge sense of relief. Our process will help you feel and be more successful at your job.

For those of you who hold positions of authority, *Working for You Isn't Working for Me* will give you valuable insight regarding your own behavior. It will also provide you with an inside look at what your employees need from you and fear about you as they interact with you on a daily basis.

We've broken *Working for You Isn't Working for Me* into four sections. Each section builds upon the one preceding it. In Section I, you'll discover how you're currently coping with your boss's bad behavior and why those coping tactics aren't really working. We'll help you identify which phase of a toxic boss/employee relationship you may be cycling through. We'll introduce you to twenty inferior boss behaviors and help you pinpoint what your boss is doing that causes you to lose sleep.

In Section II, we show you how to detach from your boss's bothersome behavior and take back your personal power. You'll receive numerous practical techniques for restoring your energy, repairing your emotional state, and rebuilding your confidence.

Section III shows you how to take the emotional sting out of any boss/employee relationship. By taking our Boss Baggage Profile Assessment, you'll gain invaluable information about your unique style of relating to authority. You'll come away from the assessment understanding what you need, what you expect, and what you fear from any boss relationship. Upon obtaining this information regarding your orientation toward authority, you'll feel immediate relief. You'll know how to improve your current situation and what to look for in future employers. You'll be able to clear away the emotional debris that prevents you from feeling a sense of achievement and accomplishment at work.

Finally, Section IV provides actionable steps for dealing with your boss. We'll show you how to respond to the boss in the heat of the moment—when your manager is criticizing your work, when your supervisor can't admit being wrong, when the company president begins to yell at you. We'll also give you suggestions for managing the relationship in the long run while you successfully further your career.

The material in *Working for You Isn't Working for Me: The Ultimate Guide to Managing Your Boss* is not self-help lite. Get ready to engage in some challenging exercises. We'll be asking you to evaluate your boss and assess yourself. We'll invite you to try some new and sometimes counterintuitive tactics. But we promise that your hard work will deliver rich personal rewards and many professional benefits.

Reader's Advisory: For best results, please do *not* read this book cover to cover. (You'll thank us later.)

Working for You Isn't Working for Me is designed to help you identify the type of boss you're working for and then strategize ways to manage that particular relationship.

With that in mind, we've organized this book to target different scenarios in different sections, so you don't need to read the whole book to get the advice you need. Here's how we suggest you read it:

1. Read chapters 1 and 2 to identify the exact behavior your boss exhibits and how it is affecting you.
2. Read chapter 3 to learn about detaching from a difficult boss, then go straight to your boss's type in chapter 4.
3. Read chapter 5 and take the assessment (you'll be glad you did) to determine how your behavior may be helping or hurting your situation.
4. In chapter 6 go directly to your profile (personality type) and find out how to depersonalize from your specific boss.
5. Read all of chapter 7, and then use chapters 8 through 12, each of which has been tailored to a specific boss/employee combination to find concrete solutions that can help you.

Note: This book could drastically improve your health

Working
for You
Isn't
Working
for Me

SECTION 1

Reader's Alert: This section is designed to help you identify the exact behavior your boss exhibits and how it is affecting you.

CHAPTER 1

If You Can Detect It, You Can Correct It

I T'S ONE THING to have a difficult job. It's another thing to have a difficult boss who makes it nearly impossible for you to succeed. Most of us look to the leaders in our lives for direction, guidance, encouragement, and inspiration. We'd like to be treated with appreciation and respect. We'd like to know what's expected of us and feel confident that we can deliver.

Yet, far too often, the people placed in positions of authority are unable to manage, guide, or direct us adequately. In fact, the person in charge often becomes the biggest obstacle to his or her employees' success. Instead of feeling supported, guided, or encouraged, employees working for less-than-adequate managers begin to feel thwarted, persecuted, undermined, or trapped.

A common initial reaction to working for a difficult boss is to compensate for his or her weaknesses. If, for example, you perceive that your boss is well intentioned but disorganized, you may try to counterbalance that limitation by being more organized yourself. You may show up for meetings with a detailed agenda, outlining the important items that need your boss's attention. You may also find ways to remind your boss about important appointments and deadlines.

In the best of circumstances, your manager appreciates your efforts and tries to take advantage of your orderly ways. Such a response allows you to feel good about the systems you create and positive about the relationship. If, however, this same disorganized individual discards your agendas, ignores your reminders, and then complains that you aren't doing your job, you'll have a different set of reactions.

Most likely, you'll feel frustrated, annoyed, misunderstood, and mismanaged. When your boss accuses you of dropping the ball, your mind will work overtime retracing your steps: "I know I reminded him of that appointment three times." Or "I gave her a report on the status of that project last Monday, and now she claims she never received it." If your boss continues to undermine your attempts to create order and insists on blaming you for the results, you'll probably start to feel crazy inside.

We've found that there are certain boss behaviors that eventually leave people on the receiving end feeling angry, manipulated, confused, tormented, defeated, held back, set up, and generally out of control. We've compiled a hit list of ways that bosses behave badly. See if you can recognize any of the following infuriating behaviors:

HAVE YOU EVER HAD A BOSS WHO . . .

. . . *sends you mixed messages?*
"My supervisor said I could take the afternoon off, then screamed when he couldn't find me at 4:30 p.m."

. . . *is a chronic faultfinder?*
"My manager criticizes my performance, shoots down my ideas, critiques my appearance, and corrects my grammar."

. . . *has constantly changing priorities?*
"Last week, my boss insisted that the most important priority was generating sales. This week, she claims that the only important thing is reorganizing the office.

. . . *gives unwarranted criticism?*
"Our department head rebuked me for implementing a program that was his idea in the first place!"

. . . *delivers random verbal attacks?*
"I was horrified when I overheard our director yelling at the receptionist because we'd run out of milk in the kitchen."

. . . is a micromanager?

"If I'm not spending hours writing detailed reports of everything I've done, I'm waiting for my boss's approval on every decision."

. . . is incapable of hearing another point of view?

"I know that I could save the company thousands of dollars with my cost-cutting ideas, but my boss refuses to consider them."

. . . insists on (always) being right?

"We were driving to a sales call, and I knew we were lost, but my boss kept insisting that he knew the way. When we arrived at the client's office one hour late, I got the blame."

. . . takes credit for other people's work?

"After spending weeks developing an awesome ad campaign, I overheard my boss saying, "'Thank you. This campaign is one of my proudest accomplishments.'"

. . . pits employees against each other?

"Our art director has a habit of giving the same assignment to two designers and letting them fight their way to the top."

. . . constantly lies?

"My former employer hired me for a position that never existed, promised a salary increase that never happened, and fired me for reasons that were never made clear."

. . . blurs the lines of responsibility?

"My manager never gave me a job description, and since we downsized, I never know whether I'm being asked to do my job, her job, or someone else's job."

. . . chronically neglects the staff?

"It's March, and I haven't talked with my boss since the holiday party in December. He comes in for an hour in the morning, answers e-mails, and leaves."

. . . is incapable of making decisions?

"We've learned that the best way to handle our indecisive manager is to make the decision ahead of time and pretend it was his idea."

If you work for someone who engages in any of these practices on a regular basis, then you probably have moments when you wonder if you're losing your mind. You may feel frustrated, misunderstood, unappreciated, constantly disappointed, angry, or confused. You may wonder how your boss ever got promoted or why this person is allowed to hold a position of authority. You may wish that you could render justice and simply have your boss removed.

HOW WE COPE WITH BOSSES
WHO BEHAVE BADLY

Typically, when grappling with this kind of confusing boss/employee relationship, we resort to certain kinds of coping tactics. Each tactic is a normal response to stressful workplace circumstances. Each maneuver emerges out of a desire to take back power and control.

Unfortunately, these attempts to wrest back control rarely yield a feeling of empowerment or resolution. On the contrary, very often the more we resist or try to correct conditions using these tactics, the worse things become. And each coping mechanism comes with a price—a cost to you, your health, your reputation, or your job. Let's take a hard look at how these strategies actually play out.

TEN COMMON COPING TACTICS
Tactic #1: Obsession

On the outside, it looks as if everything is rolling along. But on the inside, you can't stop thinking about the mixed messages and conflicting commands you're receiving. Your mind works overtime trying to figure out what is happening and how to fix the situation: "Didn't my boss ask me to develop systems and handle the calendar? Why does this same person refuse to follow any of the procedures I'm trying to establish? Is this a setup? How can I convince him to work with me here?"

Sound familiar? Gloria couldn't stop thinking about a particularly disturbing conversation she'd had with her boss on Monday morning. It woke her up in the middle of the night. It ran through her mind during breakfast. It caused her to miss her exit on the way to the office—making her late for work.

The cost to you: Sleepless nights, lateness, forgetfulness, and an inability to focus drain your energy and erode your work performance.

Tactic #2: Avoidance

Unsure of the correct way to handle the boss, you take whatever actions you can to steer clear of any direct contact. You refrain from engaging in small talk, keeping friendly exchanges to a minimum. If this individual walks toward your desk, you look busy. Instead of delivering reports by hand, you e-mail them or put them into his or her box. Instead of actually speaking, you e-mail or text.

Sound familiar? Because his supervisor said no to every suggestion he made, Norman began to avoid contact with him and stopped offering any new ideas. Unfortunately, this strategy earned Norman a poor performance review. His supervisor described him as a weak performer who was unwilling to collaborate with the rest of the team.

The cost to you: You come off as uncommitted, uncooperative, not pulling your weight.

Tactic #3: Self-doubt

This is where you wonder if you are the root cause of your problems with the boss. You may ask yourself such questions as: What am I doing wrong? Am I too slow for this assignment? How could I make so many mistakes? Any fears or negative beliefs that you harbor about yourself come bubbling up to the surface. Your inner critic is unleashed and you think: "I'm not smart enough. I'm too spacey to hold this position. I can't compete. No one respects me."

Sound familiar? When the chairman of the board ripped Tara's annual report to shreds in front of the rest of the board members, she began to question her competence as the executive director of a struggling not-for-profit.

The cost to you: Feelings of low self-worth hurt your confidence and interfere with your ability to perform the job.

Tactic #4: Sulking

Being unappreciated and misunderstood by your boss, you begin to feel sorry for yourself. As you nurse your wounds, you want others to witness your pain. You walk around with your head hanging low, wearing a frown or pouting. You may respond to requests with single-word mutterings and deep sighs. Whatever your version of sulking looks like, the aim is to let everyone know that you are not happy by dramatizing your bad mood.

Sound familiar? When the construction foreman forced the entire crew to work overtime for the second week in a row due to poor planning, Marc showed his anger by sulking on the job site. The foreman responded to Marc's moody behavior by crowning him "Princess."

The cost to you: Others view your conduct as childish and petty.

Tactic #5: Wishing for the Boss's Demise

This is the business edition of a revenge fantasy. Your mind imagines everything from the boss keeling over with a heart attack to the authorities coming in and hauling this person away. You want this infuriating authority figure to be arrested and put on trial. You even imagine being called to the witness stand to testify about your harrowing experiences under his or her evil reign.

Sound familiar? It's Monday morning, and while Dennis fumbles with the snooze alarm, an image drifts into his mind—a screech of wheels as an SUV flattens that sleazy, lying VP of sales. Entering the company building, Dennis imagines that same miscreant pinned in the revolving door with no one willing to help. And so the work week starts. While one part of Dennis savors these scenarios, another part of him feels sick inside.

The cost to you: Toxic thoughts take up mental space and psychic energy. They also leave you with an emotional hangover.

Tactic #6: Gloating over the Boss's Failure

Because you are angry with someone who holds authority over you, you actively seek instances where he or she gets caught making a mistake, doing something foolish, or failing in some way. You are delighted every time the boss appears less than perfect to people both inside and outside of the company. In the back of your mind you're hoping that everyone will see the truth about this person and finally validate your point of view.

Sound familiar? When word got out that the company president failed to win a crucial account, Charles couldn't help but relish the news. He walked around smugly, wearing a grin on his face while other staff members registered sadness and disappointment.

The cost to you: First of all, you look like the lesser person; second, your boss's failure is frequently your failure as well.

Tactic #7: Bad-mouthing

In this all-too-common strategy, you covertly try to hurt the boss by tarnishing his or her reputation. You look for opportunities to complain and make disparaging remarks to anyone who will listen. You reveal both professional and personal information about the boss just to make him or her look bad.

Sound familiar? Kyle was so angry that he felt justified in revealing the sordid details of his manager's difficult divorce to coworkers, vendors, and anyone else within earshot. When he applied for a job in another department, Kyle was informed by HR that he wouldn't be considered for the new post due to his lack of discretion and professionalism.

The cost to you: You come across as a gossip—someone incapable of safeguarding confidential information.

Tactic #8: Confrontation

Here, you try to take matters into your own hands by going straight to the boss and stating your concerns: "I gave you that report, and I don't appreciate being falsely accused of not doing my job." Or, "It's not fair to blame me when you don't read the e-mails I send you." Or, even stronger, "You're setting me up to fail."

Sound familiar? After being unfairly accused of slacking on the job, Greta marched over to the chief financial officer and said, "I work twelve-hour days and rarely eat lunch. How dare you tell me I'm not working hard enough?" Her boss replied, "Well, Greta, all I can tell you is that I get complaints about your socializing with other members of the staff."

The cost to you: A frontal attack leaves you vulnerable to being misunderstood and attacked back.

Tactic #9: Retaliation/Acting Out

This line of attack involves taking calculated actions to even the score. You go to your boss's supervisor and report the problems you're having. Or you "accidentally" cc the higher-ups to expose your boss's ways. You may "forget" to remind him or her of a crucial appointment. Some people find public venues in which to vent their frustration.

Sound familiar? In an attempt to get back at her verbally abusive boss, Mona recorded one of his tirades and posted it on YouTube for all of her colleagues and former coworkers to see. As much as Mona delighted in the responses to her posting, her triumph was short-lived. She was severely reprimanded and informed that any promotions or pay raises were now on hold. She became a hero to her peers, but a trouble-maker to her superiors

The cost to you: Striking back could hurt your reputation, burn bridges, and even get you fired.

Tactic #10: Shutting Out

In this case, all interactions between employee and boss are strained and there is little hope of salvaging the relationship. Individuals in shut-out mode no longer engage in regular forms of communication. They refuse to make direct eye contact with the boss. If you've reached shut-out, you probably respond to questions with silence. You don't walk into the same room as the boss unless it's absolutely unavoidable. If you have to communicate, you do it through a third party: "Tell Mr. Q that his presentation is ready."

Sound familiar? After Diane's boss once again promised her a raise, then failed to secure it, Diane resorted to freezing her out. "I couldn't stand looking at her or sitting in the same room with her." Unfortunately, Diane's shutout resulted in a disciplinary meeting with HR and a warning that she must either correct her behavior or risk termination.

The cost to you: Giving your boss the silent treatment makes you appear emotionally immature and unreasonable; worse, it can lead to termination.

As you can see, almost all of these strategies yield negative results. And the tactics themselves appear immature and unprofessional to others.

Many of the coping techniques (such as bad-mouthing, shutting out, and avoiding) are habits that we picked up in grade school or junior high. These practices from the playground don't serve us well in adulthood. In an attempt to take back power, we end up creating bad feelings, negative outcomes, or both.

A Different Approach

There is another way to handle tough boss/employee relationships.

Our process is a practical four-step program that incorporates and emphasizes both self-care activities and self-management techniques. We call it the Four D's. Each D stands for a very specific set of actions that you can take to improve your relationship with the head honcho. The Four D's will require some work on your part. But chances are your current situation can't get much worse, and at least this process will give you concrete tools to take back your power.

The process looks like this:

1. **Detect:** Realizing that you are in a toxic boss/employee relationship and understanding how it's affecting you.
2. **Detach:** Accepting that you are not going to change the boss and finding ways to take back your power.
3. **Depersonalize:** Learning to take the boss's behavior less personally and discovering ways to get what you need in the workplace.
4. **Deal:** Devising a plan of protection to manage the relationship with your boss and creating a strategy for moving your career forward.

In this book we'll show you how to take back your power and manage the relationship with your boss so that you have a greater sense of satisfaction and control at work. As we take you through our four-step program, you'll see that you *do* have options, even if the person you report to behaves in ways that currently leave you feeling exasperated, drained, frustrated, or ready to quit.

Detect

We're going to start with the first D—*Detect*—by describing eight predictable phases that anyone caught in a distressing boss/employee situation is likely to cycle through. Being aware of these phases will help you identify where you may be in the cycle. Once you know where you are, you can begin to break free.

The eight phases are:

1. **Honeymoon Period**: Are you and your boss still on your best behavior? Do you ignore any early signs of potential conflict?
2. **Internal Alarm:** Has your boss done or said something that made you feel uneasy, anxious, or alarmed? Did this incident surprise you or catch you off guard?
3. **Restart, Try Harder:** In an attempt to reinstate the initial goodwill between you and the boss, are you working harder? Do you find yourself putting in extra time and effort to win back his or her favor?
4. **Disappointment:** Are you realizing that your boss is not who or what you expected? Do you find yourself avoiding contact with this person or complaining to others?
5. **Rehearsing and Rehashing:** Do you obsess about conversations, e-mails, and meetings with your boss? Is your mind constantly rehashing the last encounter?
6. **Anger and Blame:** Are you constantly feeling angry and resentful toward your boss? Do you bad-mouth, sulk, or wish for this person's demise? Does your mind focus on ways to retaliate?
7. **Emotional Pain Turns Physical:** Do you feel physically depleted and emotionally drained? Have you developed neck pain, back pain, ulcers, or other physical conditions in response to the boss?
8. **Burnout:** Do you feel trapped working for your boss, with no visible exit? Are you exhausted, depressed, and isolating from family and friends?

To illustrate what each phase looks like, let's drop in on Bryan, who is dealing with a new boss named Richard.

PHASE ONE: HONEYMOON PERIOD

Richard heads up the business loan division for a small branch of a national bank in the Midwest. The VP of business loans at the bank's Chicago branch retires, and Richard gets transferred to fill the position. Richard has a stellar reputation within the business loan community. He's young, forward thinking, innovative, and considered to be an expert in business service development.

At his new post in Chicago, Richard has a staff of forty. The business loan division of this branch is as big as the entire branch he came from. Members of the Chicago office are excited to have a new leader who is sharp, aggressive, and growth-oriented.

Bryan has been the acting director of the business loan division for three months. Upon Richard's arrival, Bryan returns to his previous position as assistant director. Bryan welcomes the new leadership. He knows that his team needs some fresh ideas and positive energy. He looks forward to the clear direction and new life that Richard can bring.

When Bryan arrives at the bank on Richard's first day, his new boss is already there, hard at work. Richard sits combing through a stack of reports that Bryan carefully set aside the night before. Bryan extends his hand to greet Richard, who smiles, shakes his hand, and says, "Thanks for holding down the fort all these weeks. It looks like you've done a great job. I look forward to cashing in on your wealth of experience."

Bryan quickly responds, "Thank you, Richard. We're really glad you're here. Would you like me to explain any of these reports to you?" Richard shakes his head, "I'm good for now. Why don't we catch up later in the week?" Bryan feels a little disappointed, but understands that his boss needs time to acclimate to the new position.

We've just witnessed a snapshot from the first phase of a boss/employee relationship. The Honeymoon Period begins in a number of ways: at the start of a new job, following a promotion, after a transfer or a change in management. Honeymoons can last anywhere from one day to one year. In rare cases, the honeymoon period lasts a few years.

During this phase of the boss/employee relationship two things happen:

1. Each person is on his or her best behavior.
2. Each person naturally dismisses certain early warning signs that the other person may be problematic.

What does an early warning sign look like? In Bryan's case, the cues were subtle—his new boss just brushed him off. Instead of making time to meet with Bryan to benefit from his experience, Richard waved him away.

A warning sign could be the fact that your potential boss keeps you waiting for an hour and a half before your first interview. Or perhaps you witness an ostensibly cordial executive address the receptionist in a biting, sarcastic tone. Other examples include smelling alcohol on a new boss's breath at midday, having your boss confess his or her personal troubles early in the relationship, or noticing that your newly appointed supervisor interrupts you every time you speak.

Why do we dismiss these early indicators? The simplest answer is that we don't want to spoil the honeymoon. Generally speaking, we walk into a boss/employee relationship with a strong desire for it to work out. We have no history with the person and no baggage. The position may look promising, and we'd like to succeed. That desire for a good experience, coupled with the hope of financial and professional success, often leads to a certain form of denial: we put blinders on our perceptive abilities.

PHASE TWO: INTERNAL ALARM

> The end of the week comes and goes, and Bryan does not hear from Richard. Bryan assumes that Richard must be busy adjusting to his new position. There's an important compliance meeting that Bryan has been attending—reporting for the business loan department. He gets a confirmation notice that he's expected to be present at the next meeting.
>
> As Bryan walks toward the conference room, Richard's secretary, Ann, intercepts him, and says, "Richard says there's no need for you to attend this meeting anymore." Bryan is surprised, but quickly collects his thoughts. "Does he want me to brief him regarding what's been happening at these meetings?" Ann replies, "I'll find out."
>
> A minute later, Ann returns. "He says he's got it under control." Bryan's stomach drops. He feels himself blush in front of the secretary. As he walks back to his cubicle, he's not sure what happened. All he knows is that he feels marginalized and dismissed.

Now we've entered phase two: Internal Alarm. This phase is also known as the Uh-oh, Oh No, or Sinking Feeling stage. Pick the term that speaks to you. During this second phase, something strange happens. What began with great promise now seems to have taken a downward turn. You haven't changed, but your boss's behavior toward you is markedly different.

The person who initially seemed eager for your ideas now shoots holes in your first proposal. The boss who expressed great confidence in your judgment aggressively questions every decision you make. The executive who once called your input "invaluable" suddenly excludes you from important meetings.

After such an incident sets off an internal alarm, your body reacts. You may feel a crater forming in your gut. Your thoughts may begin to race, and your heart may beat faster. You may find yourself obsessing about or avoiding interactions with the boss. You don't want to admit it, but some part of you knows and is telling you that the honeymoon is over.

Because you still want to believe that things can go well with this person, you tend to play down the incident. You may tell yourself it was a one-time event, a misunderstanding, or a situation where you were being too sensitive. Still, there's another part of you that's wondering what just happened. Maybe your internal alarm is trying to alert you to impending interpersonal hazards.

PHASE THREE: RESTART, TRY HARDER

> Even though Richard always offers a cheery greeting to Bryan when they pass each other on the floor, Bryan is beginning to feel uneasy about his status with the new boss. He wants to find out what's expected of him and he's eager to have Richard clarify his responsibilities as the assistant director.
>
> Bryan decides to ask for a meeting with Richard. He tries to schedule an appointment through Ann, Richard's secretary. Ann tells Bryan that Richard will get back to him. Bryan then steps up his campaign to secure an appointment with his new boss, sending a copy of his calendar to Ann and suggesting several times when he and Richard could meet. Bryan also attaches a copy of his job description to clarify what he'd like to discuss during this meeting.
>
> Despite his exertions, Bryan doesn't hear anything for a few days. On Friday, he runs into Richard and asks, "Have you figured out a time when we could meet?" Richard snaps back, "I'm swamped right now. You know your job. Just do it." Later that day, Bryan receives an e-mail from Ann, giving him an appointment with Richard two weeks later. While this is not ideal, Bryan feels relieved.

When faced with the changing tide, it's natural to try and steer the relationship back to its positive beginning. Thus begins the third phase, Restart, Try Harder. As the employee, you focus your energy on reinstating yourself with the boss. You hope that by increasing your efforts you'll prove that the Internal Alarm moment was a glitch—not an emerging pattern.

For example, you may redouble your efforts to be agreeable, helpful, and cooperative. You may try to wow your boss with even more productivity and dazzling results. Or you may quietly do your work and stay out of the way, hoping that lying low will mitigate the situation.

While you're putting your best foot forward on the outside, your mind is working double time on the inside. It's trying to make sense of your boss's bewildering behavior. Why am I being misunderstood? What misconception does my boss have about me? What might I be doing wrong? Have I done something inadvertently to fall out of favor? These obsessive thoughts run day and night, and with them come some uncomfortable sinking feelings as well.

PHASE FOUR: DISAPPOINTMENT

Two weeks later, Bryan is sitting in Richard's office. He has come to the meeting fully prepared to discuss his job and to clarify the performance goals that his new boss wants him to achieve. While Bryan tries to guide the conversation toward his job description, Richard wants to go in a completely different direction. He pulls out photos of the house he just bought and expounds on what a momentous transition moving from the suburbs to the city has been for his family.

After fifteen minutes, Bryan pipes up, "Why don't we talk about some of the plans you have for this department?" Richard's face becomes serious; he shakes his head and says, "We've got to get leaner here. I don't know how you justify your salary. Where I come from, we don't pay these kinds of salaries."

Bryan isn't ready for that kind of conversation. He's floored. He's able to blurt out, "I understand that you may be used to seeing lower pay scales, but this is Chicago. The cost of living is high, and we work very hard here." Richard shrugs his shoulders and responds, "Well, I'd better see some superhero results for this kind of pay."

Once Disappointment sets in, you have to admit that the boss you have is a far cry from the boss you expected. A number of unsettling things have happened. The honeymoon is a distant memory. Now, if your boss says one thing and does another, you interpret that behavior as his or her management style—instead of an innocent mistake. You may discover that the boss who excluded you from important meetings has also removed you from his e-mail list. Perhaps the supervisor who lost her temper weeks ago gradually emerges as a chronic berater. Or the executive who failed to confront an unruly member of his staff in one instance now appears to be generally spineless.

In Bryan's case, the disappointment is multilayered. First, he expected some appreciation for the work he did before Richard arrived. Second, he wanted an explanation of his new position. Third, he expected to hear a future plan and a vision from his new leader. Basically, he hoped for a different meeting with a different kind of boss. Now, Bryan realizes that he's dealing with a dismissive, somewhat self-absorbed manager who minimizes his contribution and delivers a thinly veiled threat regarding his job.

During the Disappointment phase, you can expect to feel angry, hurt, confused, betrayed, and generally let down. You may feel a strong urge to bad-mouth the boss. You may wish for his or her demise. You may also find yourself avoiding contact with this individual and gloating over any news of his or her failure.

PHASE FIVE: REHEARSING AND REHASHING

After that meeting, Bryan is truly shaken. He can't believe that his new boss went from thanking him for his efforts to challenging the value of his job. He starts to rehash the few exchanges they've had. He wonders whether the reports that he left for Richard were adequate. He describes the series of events to his wife, who seems surprised and perplexed. As he lies in bed, he keeps combing over the details of the past few weeks, trying to figure out what went wrong.

While Rehearsing and Rehashing, you're trying to gain control over your circumstances by running events through your mind over and over again. In an attempt to figure out what went wrong, you ask yourself (and others) a lot of questions: What did I do to deserve this kind of treatment? Does this story make sense to you? What would you do if your boss acted that way? Am I crazy? Who can work under these circumstances?

If you're caught in Rehearsing and Rehashing, you'll spend hours obsessing about events at work. You'll revisit and review conversations, e-mails, meetings, and other interactions with the boss in great detail. Frequently, people caught in Rehearsing and Rehashing share their frustration, pain, and confusion with friends, family members, and anyone else who will listen. During this phase, you may question your sanity and be plagued with self-doubt.

PHASE SIX: ANGER AND BLAME

As the weeks pass, Bryan becomes more and more frustrated. Richard continues to keep him out of the loop. Bryan performs the most basic duties of his job—he still oversees the work of several loan officers—but he is no longer involved with strategic planning or decision making. Instead, Richard sends him the same e-memos he sends to everyone announcing departmental initiatives and policies. With each memo, Bryan becomes increasingly incensed.

One day, Bryan is in the midst of changing a five-gallon water cooler bottle, and Richard walks by. As he passes, Richard says, "Is *this* what I'm paying you for?" Bryan smiles and turns back to finish the task, but inside he is furious. He says to himself, "No, you creep. You're actually paying me to salvage this department where everyone wants to quit because they feel totally undervalued by you."

By the time you reach Anger and Blame, you may be acting out in a number of ways. Feeling victimized by your circumstances, it's easy to sulk and let others see how unhappy you are. Many employees in this phase grab every opportunity to bad-mouth the boss and gloat over his or her failures. You may try confronting your persecutor with less-than-positive results. You may retaliate in some way. Because you have been hurt and disappointed a number of times, it's very difficult to see your employer in anything but a negative light. In fact, in this phase it's common to wish for (and imagine) the boss's demise.

PHASE SEVEN: EMOTIONAL PAIN TURNS PHYSICAL

By now, Bryan has developed a physical condition in response to his boss. He's grinding his teeth at night and seems to have chronic neck pain. He's popping Tylenol on a far too regular basis. When he sees an e-mail from Richard, he automatically starts massaging the back of his neck.

When Bryan goes for a medical assessment, his doctor says, "I think you are suffering from some*one*, not some*thing*. What's going on at work?"

At this point, the mental and emotional anguish resulting from interactions with the boss convert into physical pain. In the Emotional Pain Turns Physical phase, it's common to develop back pain, headaches, chronic indigestion, TMJ, ulcers, insomnia, chronic fatigue, or high blood pressure. Some people gain or lose weight. If you've hit this stage in the boss/employee relationship, you probably feel physically depleted and emotionally drained. Just getting out of bed in the morning may seem like a major accomplishment.

PHASE EIGHT: BURNOUT

After several months with Richard at the helm, Bryan is in bad shape. He now dreads going to work. He has trouble getting up in the morning. Whenever he sees Richard talking to another bank employee, he immediately imagines the worst—that his new boss is saying negative things about him. Once happy to share information, Bryan has become withdrawn and depressed.

Burnout is a state of chronic mental, physical, and emotional exhaustion. If you reach this phase, you're likely to feel depressed and angry. Your self-esteem is at a low point. Your health is in jeopardy. You may be overeating or undereating, drinking, or smoking excessively. Your sleep patterns may be disturbed. In Burnout, it's not uncommon to sleep long hours yet still feel tired when you get out of bed.

Many people who hit this stage go into isolation mode. In addition to shutting out the boss, they also withdraw from family and friends. They stop participating in hobbies, sports, and community events that once gave them pleasure. This adds to the problem.

Another aspect of this phase is a tendency to be argumentative and to entertain paranoid thoughts. If you're feeling paranoid, then any time you see the boss talking quietly to someone, you assume the conversation is negative and about you. You may suspect that the boss is invading your e-mail account or tracing your phone calls

Although you may desperately want to quit your job, the state of Burnout has left you in poor condition to find another one. You are exhausted and defeated and daunted by the prospect of beginning a job search. The overall feeling is one of being trapped with no visible exit.

Bryan's story is not an isolated incident. There are many people who cycle through these eight stages of a toxic boss/employee relationship in their positions at work. You might be feeling just like Bryan right now. Or you may be in a different but equally uncomfortable state.

You may find yourself engaging in one of the ten coping behaviors: obsessing, avoiding, doubting yourself, sulking, wishing for your boss's demise, gloating in your boss's failure, bad-mouthing, confronting, retaliating, or shutting your boss out.

Take another look at the eight phases of a toxic boss/employee relationship:

- Are you still in the honeymoon phase?
- Has an internal alarm gone off?
- Are you trying to restart the relationship by working harder?
- Has disappointment set in?
- Do you find yourself rehearsing and rehashing interactions with your boss?
- Are you angry at your boss? Do you blame this person for the problems you're having?
- Has the emotional and mental anguish from this relationship turned into some form of physical pain?
- Do you think you've reached a state of burnout?

If you identify with any of the eight phases or ten coping behaviors, it's safe to say that you've taken the first step: you've detected that you're in a difficult boss/employee relationship and that it's taking a negative toll on you. Consider Detection the entry point to taking back your power; if you can see where you are in the cycle, you can also map your way out. Congratulations! You've completed the first of the four D's.

In the next chapter, we'll take detecting to a deeper level by describing twenty of the most common difficult bosses you're likely to find in the workplace. We'll explain how each kind of authority figure behaves and how that behavior affects the people who work for him or her.

You'll be able to recognize whether you've got a boss who plays head games or a boss who always has to be right. You might realize that you're working for someone who blurs the lines of authority by confiding too much personal information and demanding too much emotional support. If your boss is a reluctant leader, you'll be able to pinpoint how he or she avoids making tough decisions—leaving you and your co-workers to fend for yourselves. Or you may verify that your difficult boss/employee relationship is the result of unwelcome circumstances such as a change in management or a politically based promotion.

First, we'd like to give you an overview of the three remaining D's (steps) of our Four D's process. You've just learned about the first D, Detect. Now, using Bryan as our guide, we'll show you how to Detach, Depersonalize, and Deal.

Detach

If you're caught in a distressing boss/employee relationship, you know what it feels like to be held hostage by someone else's behavior. Interactions with this person drain your energy and consume your mind. The stress of working under his or her authority wreaks havoc on your mental and emotional state. Because you're preoccupied and obsessed with the relationship, you can easily neglect yourself physically, mentally, and emotionally.

If you detect that you're caught in a harmful association with a difficult boss, then your next step is to Detach—to find ways to separate yourself from the problematic relationship. *Detaching* requires refocusing your mind and your efforts. Instead of focusing on the boss—trying to get the response you want, or correct his or her behavior—you focus on taking back your power. How? By taking charge of the things that you do have control over.

Stay with us here. We know that this doesn't seem fair. The boss is the problem, right? Still, trying to control someone else's behavior is like trying to control the weather—it's out of your hands. The best you can do is face the reality of the kind of person you are working for (the boss) and get to work on regaining a sense of control.

Detaching is a two-part process. Part one involves accepting that you are not going to change the boss. This means, for example, that instead of trying to stop your angry boss from exploding, you recognize and acknowledge that you work for someone with anger issues and that this person is sure to blow up again. (We'll explain more about this in Chapter 2.)

Part two of the detaching process involves taking actions to restore your energy, repair your emotional state, and rebuild your confidence. A typical plan may involve exercising three times a week (to restore energy), returning to a favorite hobby (to feel better emotionally), and writing down your successes every day (to rebuild confidence).

Let's see how detaching works for Bryan.

In search of practical advice regarding his situation, Bryan calls Ray—his former boss, who recently retired. "I hate to admit it, Ray, but I'm having a tough time with your successor." Ray agrees to meet him for breakfast the following Monday.

As Bryan confides in Ray regarding Richard, Ray says, "It sounds like you're dealing with someone who doesn't know how to build a team. I've seen guys like him—they're very bright, but not very good at bringing the best out in others. And they don't know how to give credit for a job well done."

Ray continues, "I bet you've tried everything you can to forge a connection with this guy, right?"

Bryan sighs. "Yep. No matter what I do, he still keeps me out of the loop."

Ray smiles. "For now, I suggest that you stop trying to get a different response from Richard and start taking control of yourself."

Together, they create a Personal Recharging Plan: Bryan trades in his morning sugar doughnut for a granola bar and yogurt, Ray agrees to meet weekly with Bryan as his unofficial mentor, and Bryan returns to swimming—something he loves to do.

Within a couple of weeks, Bryan feels much better. Reducing his morning intake of sugar helps stabilize his energy level at work. By meeting with Ray, Bryan receives practical guidance from someone who believes in him. Swimming three times a week has two payoffs: Bryan is able to release negative energy and return to a sport he truly enjoys.

Richard has not changed, but Bryan's reaction to Richard is starting to shift. By focusing on himself and taking steps to recharge, Bryan is able to reestablish a sense of personal power.

Don't get frustrated if it takes a while to really detach from your boss/employee situation. Learning how to detach is similar to losing weight. You can't lose twenty pounds in one week—especially if it took you a year to put on the weight—and you can't fix in one hour a relationship that took weeks to deteriorate.

Depersonalize

Once you've detached from the relationship, you can move on to step three: Depersonalize. By *depersonalize*, we mean understanding two things that will take the emotional sting out of your experience. First, whatever your boss is doing, you didn't cause it. Second, his or her actions may be triggering your worst fears—making it even more difficult to manage the relationship effectively.

Let's start with the first point: whatever the person in authority is doing to make your work life miserable, you can trust that there were people before you who experienced the exact same thing. The yelling boss yelled at many people before you arrived on the scene. The last-minute delegator has always dished out assignments at the end of the day. The executive who avoids all confrontation has been dodging disputes for many years.

Then why, you may be asking, does it feel so personal? Why do I think I created this situation? The short answer is that people who behave badly in the workplace are usually very skilled at making their behavior appear to be someone else's fault. So the yeller may say, "Look how angry you've made me!" The last-minute delegator may say, "I'm able to adjust my priorities in the moment, you should be able to do the same." The conflict-avoiding executive may say, 'I'm sorry, but my hands are tied. You'll have to work it out on your own."

These statements add to the confusion and leave you feeling responsible for the problems in the relationship. If you can really understand that the authority figure is doing what he or she *always* does (whether it's yelling, avoiding, or making impulsive decisions) and you just happen to be the current target, then you are on your way to depersonalizing his or her behavior.

The second part of depersonalizing the boss's behavior involves taking a look at what you are bringing to the relationship. Most of us approach anyone in a leadership position with certain expectations, needs, and fears. These attitudes influence the way we relate to the boss. More important, they shape our internal reactions to the boss's behavior. In Chapter 5, we'll show you how to uncover the expectations, needs, and fears that you may have when dealing with people in positions of authority. In the meantime, let's see what depersonalizing looks like for Bryan.

One Tuesday, Bryan gets a call from a senior loan officer at Richard's old office. The caller is inquiring about an account transfer. As the call comes to a close, the officer says, "Good luck with your new boss. We used to call him Tricky Ricky because you never knew where you stood with him. He has a unique management style—he keeps everyone in the dark."

As Bryan gets off the phone, he feels strangely relieved. He realizes that he's just one of many people who have been closed out by Richard. He contacts Ray and reports, "I just found out that Richard has a history of keeping his employees in the dark. That's exactly what's happening here!"

At their next weekly meeting, Ray commends him. "Nice work, Bryan. So now you know that Richard's behavior is not about you." Then Ray continues. "Let me ask you a few questions that may clarify why Richard's behavior drives you crazy."

"Okay."

"What did you expect from Richard as your new boss?"

"I expected him to appreciate and value my experience. I held his position before he arrived, so I thought he'd be interested in what I have to say."

"He hasn't met your expectations, right?"

"Right."

"Next question: What do you need from Richard as a boss?"

"I need some direction. I wish he'd tell me his goals for the department. I'd like to know what he wants me to accomplish."

"Okay. So he's not giving you what you need from a boss?"

"Correct."

"Okay, last question: What's your greatest fear with any boss?"

"I fear being dismissed and marginalized."

"Uh-huh. So when Richard keeps you at a distance and excludes you from all decision making, he triggers your worst fears, right?"

"Exactly."

"All right," Ray says. "So here's your challenge. You've got a boss who fails to meet any of your expectations or needs and whose behavior triggers your worst fears. You've got to figure out a way to *deal* with him."

"You got it. So how do I turn this situation around?"

Now that Bryan has detected, detached, and depersonalized, he's ready for the final step. Bryan is ready to *Deal*.

Deal

Dealing involves constructing a strategy for working with the boss in a way that works for you. To *deal*, devise a plan of protection that adjusts your expectations, addresses your needs, and alleviates your fears. The goal here is to convert the boss/employee relationship from intolerable and upsetting to acceptable. In some cases, your actions may even result in establishing a positive relationship with the boss.

Let's start with expectations. If you expect the boss to praise you for your hard work, and he or she is not comfortable giving praise, you'll be disappointed again and again. If, however, you adjust that expectation, then you can stop looking to this authority figure to give you what he or she cannot give. Instead, you can seek that praise and recognition from other sources.

Bryan manages his unmet expectations by organizing a monthly out-of-office lunch for all assistant directors in the bank. During this lunch, colleagues discuss what initiatives they're working on. They acknowledge one another for goals achieved and progress made in each department. In addition, Bryan and Ray create a list of his accomplishments, past and present, which Bryan can refer to whenever he needs to be reminded of his value.

When it comes to the workplace, if you determine that the things you need or want from an authority figure are not available, then "dealing" involves finding alternative ways to get those needs met. This is a proactive step. Rather than deny your needs (or plan the boss's demise), you can take actions to fulfill them through other avenues in the workplace. For example, let's say you need a job description, and your boss is not forthcoming. To fulfill that desire, you may do one of several things: draft your own job description and have the boss approve it (our favorite option), request a copy of your job description from HR, or go to someone in another department who holds a similar position and adapt his or her job description to your circumstances.

To address his need for a clearer understanding of his responsibilities, Bryan writes out his own job description and drafts his own performance goals. He submits these documents to Richard. He asks his boss to review, correct, and sign off on both items. He welcomes any changes or corrections that Richard makes.

Alleviating your fears may be the most challenging part of dealing. First, know that everyone has certain internal fears that get triggered in difficult boss/employee relationships. It may be fear of being held back, fear of making a mistake, fear of being dismissed, or some other worry. Your job is to identify the fears that flare up in tough times and dispel them. *Fears are not facts.* Yet fear is a very powerful emotion. It can create distortions in what we see, hear, and experience. Some people refer to fear as False Evidence Appearing Real. For this reason, we suggest you enlist the assistance of others to dispel your fears. Depending on the severity of the fear, you can lean on a friend or hire a professional to help you out. (For more on this, see Chapter 7.)

> To dispel his fear of being dismissed and marginalized by Richard, Bryan seeks the support of a colleague who is also working under Richard's supervision. The next time Richard makes a disparaging remark, Bryan can go to his buddy, describe the incident, and get a reality check reminding him that Richard talks down to everyone and that Bryan's role as the VP of business loans remains important to other members of the staff.

Bryan may never feel great about working for Richard, but he can continue to practice the Four D's so that he feels some sense of control at his job. As he builds his self-confidence, he can see other options for himself and new directions to take his career.

WORK IT OUT
Detect
If You Can Detect It, You Can Correct It

WHEN YOUR BOSS'S BEHAVIOR DRIVES YOU CRAZY, WHICH COPING TACTICS DO YOU TURN TO? (CHECK ALL THAT APPLY)

❏ Obsession

❏ Avoidance

❏ Self-doubt

❏ Sulking

❏ Wishing for His or Her Demise

❏ Gloating over His or Her Failure

❏ Bad-mouthing

❏ Confrontation

❏ Retaliation/Acting Out

❏ Shutting Out

WHICH PHASE OF A DISTRESSING BOSS/EMPLOYEE RELATIONSHIP ARE YOU CAUGHT IN? (CHECK YOUR PHASE HERE)

❏ Honeymoon Period

❏ Internal Alarm

❏ Restart, Try Harder

❏ Disappointment

❏ Rehearsing and Rehashing

❏ Anger and Blame

❏ Emotional Pain Turns Physical

❏ Burnout

CHAPTER 2

Detecting Twenty
Boss Behaviors
(That Drive Us Bonkers)

V ERY FEW BOSSES are all good or all bad, but many bosses have specific traits that drive us crazy. For example, your manager may be very encouraging, but lack the ability to hold anyone accountable. Perhaps your department head is an excellent communicator, but has a habit of constantly changing the rules. Maybe you have an easygoing boss who never moves forward on initiatives. Or your supervisor could be extremely smart yet extremely critical of your work.

In the last chapter you learned to Detect signs that you are being driven around the bend by your boss's behavior. Now, we're going to focus on the other side of the equation, by examining five categories of boss behaviors that are sure to cause distress. The categories are:

1. Head Game Players
2. Big Shots and Mother Superiors
3. Line Crossers
4. Ambivalent Leaders
5. Delicate Circumstances

Under each category, you'll find a rogue's gallery of specific boss behaviors that are challenging to work under. Read each profile and see if you can match your experience to the boss behaviors that we describe.

CATEGORY 1: HEAD GAME PLAYERS

If you work for an authority figure who engages in head games, his or her behavior often causes you to question your reality. A head-gaming boss may build you up one day only to tear you down the next. He or she may ask you to perform a certain task in the morning, then chastise you for doing it that same afternoon. Head Game players have a knack for making other people look responsible for their mistakes. Because these bosses are very good at confusing the people who work for them, most employees spend a lot of time rehearsing and rehashing the interactions they have with these authority figures. Let us introduce you to the Chronic Critic, the Rule Changer, the Yeller, and the Underminer.

Chronic Critic

A Chronic Critic is able to find fault with just about anything you do. It may be the way you look, the report you wrote, the meeting room you reserved. Whatever the situation, this individual can find and state the flaw. These are the workplace perfectionists who feel it is their duty to point out any and all deficiencies in others. If you work for a Chronic Critic, the constant criticism, coupled with a refusal to acknowledge your hard work, starts to take a toll over time. You feel as if you can never win.

- "I came back excited after I closed a big account only to hear my manager say, 'That's great, but can you do it again?'"
- "As I proudly placed our department's annual report on the director's desk, he looked up and said, 'How long am I going to spend rewriting this?'"
- "I showed up early at the client's office for a major presentation. My boss walked in, pulled me aside, and said, 'You're wearing *that?*'"

You know you work for a Chronic Critic if . . .

1. You feel as if you can never do anything right in his or her eyes.
2. Even when you succeed, it's never enough.
3. You find yourself checking and rechecking your work to avoid mistakes.

4. You spend a lot of time preemptively predicting what flaws the boss might find in your work, your words, or your appearance.
5. You start avoiding your boss to evade his or her judgment.

Rule Changer

The Rule Changer sees rules as fluid, mere guidelines to be adjusted as needed—without notification. A rule-changing boss may tell you to take a lunch break, then be surprised when you aren't at your desk during lunch hour. He or she may state that the two of you will have weekly meetings, only to cancel those appointments time after time. Employees who work for Rule Changers feel as if they are battling policy amnesia—their bosses always forget the very rules that they established. Working for a Rule Changer is very confusing. You never know exactly what is expected of you.

- I spent hours working on a project, only to have my boss say, "Didn't I tell you? We put that project on hold."
- I agreed to attend a weekly Monday meeting with my manager, only to learn that he's never in the office on Mondays.
- At my supervisor's encouragement, I submitted my overtime hours to payroll. One week later, she reprimanded me, "We don't have the money for this. What were you thinking?"

You know you're working for a Rule Changer if . . .

1. You feel confused by your boss's constantly changing commands.
2. You start questioning your memory and your hearing.
3. In an attempt to make sense of your situation, you rehash and rehearse previous conversations, e-mails, and meetings.
4. You feel immobilized because you receive so many mixed messages.
5. You start to mistrust everything the boss tells you.

Yeller

Bosses who yell have the advantage of being easy to identify. This is the one kind of head game that presents itself very clearly. The part that's tricky is that you don't always know what will set this person off. Most Yellers have unresolved rage, which they let out at both predictable and unpredictable moments. You may be the target if you deliver bad news (predictable). Or you may have done everything right one day, only to have the Yeller zero in on an incident from the past and blow up anyway (unpredictable). Those on the receiving end of this behavior often cycle through the eight phases of a toxic relationship at a rapid pace. They usually end up in burnout—avoiding the boss, keeping their heads down, and cringing whenever they feel an explosion brewing.

- I approach my boss only after a positive staff meeting because that is the safest time to say anything.
- Everyone in my office meets at the local bar after work to help each other recover from our supervisor's daily verbal attacks.
- When my manager starts pounding the table, I brace myself because I know that in ten seconds the fireworks begin.

You know you're working for a Yeller if . . .

1. You're constantly taking your boss's emotional temperature.
2. It's common to find someone crying or sullen after a meeting with the boss.
3. You spend a lot of time deciding when and how to approach the boss to minimize the chances of an explosion.
4. You feel intense anxiety and an impending sense of doom the night before a big meeting with the boss.
5. You avoid the boss whenever possible (to preserve your self-esteem).

Underminer

Undermining bosses will ask for your help and then make it impossible for you actually to assist them. You may be assigned to complete a special project and discover that your boss has given this same assignment to three other people. Your boss may ask you to oversee a department, but fail to inform the staff within that department that they now report to you. Or you may be given the authority to make certain decisions, only to have the boss override every decision you make.

Because your employer is not clear regarding who is in charge of what, coworkers end up fighting over territory and vying for attention. The people who work for Underminers often feel confused and frustrated. Over time, they feel set up to fail.

- Before my boss went on vacation, he put me in charge of the store. But because he failed to inform the rest of the staff, no one would listen to me.
- I was excited when my boss gave me a "top secret" assignment. Then I discovered she'd assigned the same project to a junior associate. Didn't she think I could do it?
- By overriding the decisions I make, my boss has trained my staff to second-guess my directives.

You know you work for an Underminer when . . .

1. Your boss gives you responsibilities, only to take them away.
2. You frequently find out that the boss has been less than honest with you.
3. You are often surprised to discover that the boss has said one thing to you and another thing to someone else.
4. You learn not to trust what your boss says.
5. You feel as if you are constantly set up to fail.

CATEGORY 2: BIG SHOTS AND MOTHER SUPERIORS

A second category of bosses covers those leaders who are fiercely competitive. These individuals view everyone as a potential opponent, including members of their staff. If you work for a Big Shot or a Mother Superior, your only job is to make him or her look good. Should you question or challenge this kind of boss, he or she will have to retaliate and punish you in some way. You may be ridiculed, put down, or made out to be wrong in front of others. Employees who work for Big Shots and Mother Superiors frequently end up exhibiting a number of unproductive coping behaviors: bad-mouthing the boss, wishing for his or her demise, or gloating over his or her failure. This category of boss is the opposite of a team player. The cast of characters includes "I'm Always Right," "You Threaten Me," Grandiose, and the Control Freak.

"I'm Always Right"

Bosses who are "always right" may initially be very attractive. They have a self-assured attitude and exude great confidence. They give the impression that their ideas and policies are always correct—even when there is substantial evidence to the contrary. If you work for this kind of person, you soon learn that he or she must always come out on top. So, for example, if you present a clever initiative to your boss, it may be met with lukewarm enthusiasm. Should the department eventually implement your idea, this same boss will say, "I knew it was the only way to go." Because this kind of leader is so invested in being right, your attempts to offer a differing opinion or viewpoint may be treated as attacks. Discussions often turn into verbal battles that the Always Right boss must win.

Should this authority figure make a blatant mistake, he or she will look for others to take the blame. In the face of his or her unwillingness to admit any wrongdoing, it's common for employees to feel oppressed and resentful.

- I've learned that the only responses my boss wants from me are, "You're right" and "I agree with you."
- The last time I tried to correct my boss in a staff meeting, he quickly turned toward me and said, "I think you'd better check your facts before you mouth off like that again."
- When I suggested a faster, easier way of managing our database, my boss refused to test it. She insisted on retaining her complicated, laborious, time-consuming method.

You know your boss must always be right when . . .

1. Any discussions with the boss turn into situations where he or she must prove a point.
2. You begrudgingly agree with your employer because it takes too much energy to disagree.
3. You begin to resent your boss's certainty and self-assuredness.
4. You have fantasies of your boss being forced to admit that he or she is wrong.
5. You and your colleagues frequently roll your eyes when this person speaks during staff meetings.

"You Threaten Me"

A boss who feels threatened may take a while to show his or her true colors. Typically, this kind of person will encourage employees to perform at their highest level. All is well when you make the boss look good. Problems arise when you outperform or outshine him or her. This can happen in a number of ways. A senior executive may single you out for outstanding performance in the company, or your work may receive accolades from a professional association. Should the boss sense that you're stealing some of the glory, he or she will take immediate action to keep you down. When you are on the receiving end, the boss's negative reaction to your stellar accomplishments is very confusing—especially since he or she was so encouraging at the outset.

- I was exceeding my district sales goals when my manager suddenly transferred me to a remote area where I had no contacts.
- Initially, my boss called me the shining star of our package design department. Then one of my designs got nominated for an industry award. She quickly reminded me that there were more prestigious awards—and I shouldn't be too impressed with myself.
- After ten years of working long hours and making huge profits for the law firm, I asked to be considered for partnership. The senior partner looked at me in disbelief. "Where is this coming from?" he asked. "Aren't you being a bit presumptuous?"

You know you work for someone who is threatened by you when . . .

1. Your boss suddenly shifts from acknowledging and encouraging you to undervaluing your accomplishments.
2. You notice that when you're recognized by higher authorities or outside institutions for a job well done, your boss tries to minimize it.
3. You go from being included and valued by your employer to being shut out and dismissed.
4. Requests for promotions or pay raises are viewed as bold and overly ambitious.
5. Your boss gives you the most difficult, least accomplishable assignments.

Grandiose

A Grandiose boss is easy to identify. Whatever he or she does is *the best*. These individuals consider themselves to be experts—top in their field. They are quick to put down anyone who claims to have knowledge in their areas of expertise. Grandiose bosses have one favorite topic—themselves. They love telling stories about their earlier experiences, their great successes, the obstacles they've overcome, and the people they know. They don't mind repeating these narratives either. If you work for a Grandiose boss, you can probably recite certain anecdotes verbatim. While Grandiose bosses can be charming and generous, they are also energetically exhausting. You may find that you are constantly the recipient of lectures, stories, and rants. Good at talking, this kind of boss often has trouble listening.

- I admire my boss's years of experience. I just wish I didn't have to listen to the constant retelling of that experience.
- Staff meetings are painful. Instead of discussing present challenges, we have to hear tales about past successes.
- We should be learning from our competitors, but my boss can only focus on putting them down.

You know you're working for a Grandiose boss when . . .

1. Your boss's experience is the only one that counts.
2. Conversations incvitably go to, "That reminds me of the time I. . . ."
3. No one is as smart, as accomplished, or as deserving of recognition as your employer.
4. You often find yourself listening to stories rather than addressing immediate business issues.
5. You sometimes imagine telling your boss to shut up and listen for a change.

Control Freak

In order to feel in control, this kind of boss needs to know *everything* that is going on at all times. Because they don't like looking bad or being caught off guard, Control Freaks take every precaution to make sure that they are informed and aware of all activities under their domain. A Control Freak boss will want to know the status of every project at all times. He or she wants to approve every decision. The worst thing you can do to these authority figures is surprise them. If you work for a Control Freak, you've probably learned that you must secure approval on everything and that this approval process creates a bottleneck. But if you dare to make decisions without the Control Freak's consent, you'll get reprimanded.

- I spend a lot of time waiting around for my boss's approval. If she's running late or out of the office, projects just sit there . . . and so do I.
- I ordered office supplies the other day, and my boss told me not to spend company money again without his permission—even though it's the same order every month.
- I wish my boss would allow me to make some decisions without questioning me. It would make work much more interesting.

You know you're working for a Control Freak if . . .

1. You frequently find yourself waiting in line for a meeting with the boss because you can't move forward without his or her authorization.
2. You question every decision you make, fearing that the boss would do it differently.
3. Instead of thinking for yourself, you start trying to imagine how the boss would approach any problem.
4. You can't give anyone a direct answer without running it by the boss first.
5. You grapple with feelings of frustration and boredom because the boss's management style is so limiting.

CATEGORY 3: LINE CROSSERS

There are certain people in positions of authority who have blurry interpersonal boundaries. Line Crossers have a hard time understanding what constitutes appropriate behavior between themselves and their employees. If you work for a Line Crosser, you've probably experienced a number of uncomfortable situations: You may have received unwanted sexual advances. You may have witnessed unethical behavior. Your boss may share the intimate details of a dark personal secret. In some cases, a line-crossing boss will lie and expect you to lie as well. Many Line Crossers lean on their staff for emotional support—trying to convert employees into confidants and friends. Whatever the situation, you'll feel as if you have two jobs—one is the job you were hired to do and the other is managing your boss's inappropriate behavior. Line Crossers include Love-Struck, Calculating Confidant, Tell-All, and Liar, Liar.

Love-Struck

This kind of situation crops up when the boss is hungry for emotional or sexual intimacy. The early signs include casual flirting and a desire to impress you in some way. Over time, you may be asked to work late nights or be chosen as his or her "companion" for important business functions. Your employer may begin to compliment you—noticing what you're wearing, your latest haircut, or a new pair of shoes. You may catch the boss gazing at you in an admiring way. All of this attention may feel good on one level, but it can also be intimidating.

First, you may not share your boss's amorous feelings. In this case, you fear that by rejecting your employer's advances, you risk being fired or punished. Second, if you welcome your boss's advances, you may still fear that getting involved could jeopardize your job and your reputation. "If the relationship doesn't work out," you wonder, "how can I continue to work for this person?"

- As soon as I saw how attractive my boss was, I knew I was in trouble.
- I could tell that my boss wanted more than a professional relationship when he left a Valentine on my desk.
- It makes me uncomfortable when my boss winks at me during staff meetings.

You know you work for a Love-Struck boss if . . .

1. You are often called in for long meetings that turn into casual, flirty conversations.
2. Coworkers tease you regarding the boss's crush on you.

3. You seek outside advice about managing your supervisor's affections.
4. Your boss calls you at home to talk about business, and the conversation quickly turns personal.
5. You feel intense pressure, and fear saying or doing the wrong thing.

Calculating Confidant

This kind of boss can be difficult to detect initially because he or she acts friendly, caring, curious, and charming. These individuals appear to be compassionate and trustworthy. During conversations, they are able to draw you out and uncover things about your background, your home life, and your personal pressures. Their kind demeanor and ability to listen can lead you to reveal confidential information about your finances, your health, and your closest relationships. To put you at ease, Calculating Confidants make it a point to share some private tidbit regarding their past as well. You may find out that your boss is a recovering alcoholic, a war veteran, or a former high-school dropout. These "secrets" give the semblance of a balanced relationship. Problems arise when your employer uses the personal information you've shared as a weapon against you. Suddenly, the personal relationship becomes a professional liability.

- My boss used to have me to her house for dinner. Little did I know that the stories I shared about my coworkers would be repeated to the wrong people.
- Shortly after I confided to my boss about the problems I was having in my marriage, the company president approached me and asked if I needed time off.
- Ever since I confessed that I'm feeling some financial pressure, my boss scolds me every time I walk into the office with a shopping bag. "You don't have money to waste like that, do you?"

You know you're working for a Calculating Confidant if . . .

1. You find yourself confiding in-depth, non-job-related personal information to your employer. It could involve home life, family members, health concerns, or financial pressures.

2. You leave meetings with your manager feeling as if you just had a counseling session, not a business meeting.
3. Your boss invites you to his or her home, weekend house, or social club as a means of getting closer to you outside of the workplace.
4. After revealing a personal story to the boss, you have a sinking feeling that you've said too much.
5. There are moments when the boss uses some piece of information about your personal life to either discount your opinion or devalue your behavior.

Tell-All

Also likable characters, Tell-Alls believe that part of being a boss is sharing all kinds of personal information about themselves. Unlike the Calculating Confidants who pull information out of you, these authority figures don't really need to know anything about your private affairs. Instead, they need your ear, your attention, and your emotional support. Sharing personal information is their way of soliciting sympathy and protection from others. They see employees as their trusted servants who enjoy hearing about their very interesting lives. Early on, you'll learn intimate details about family members, sexual escapades, failed relationships, and problems with food, alcohol, and other substances. You'll be told the history behind their most enduring friendships and their worst relationships. At first, serving as your boss's BFF (Best Friend Forever) can be fun and interesting. Over time, however, witnessing and hearing about the constant dramas becomes exhausting. Instead of doing your job, you spend the bulk of your time holding the boss's emotional hand. Some employees who work for Tell-All bosses actually end up doing their employer's job—especially when the boss becomes too emotionally distraught to make decisions.

- Initially, I found my boss's candor touching. Now, when she starts to tell me about another personal problem, I feel overwhelmed.
- I really like my boss, but his life is a mess. He talks about his last failed relationship more than he talks about business.
- After telling me about her family's scandal, my boss begged me to cover for her while she met with the lawyer.

You know you work for a Tell-All boss if . . .

1. You put a lot of extra time into listening to his or her personal stories and problems.
2. Your boss often thanks you for listening and being such a great friend.
3. You feel drained over time because your boss's personal problems never seem to lessen.
4. To compensate for the emotional strain your boss is under, you end up doing parts of his or her job.
5. You find yourself explaining or making excuses for your boss based on the knowledge you have of his or her personal challenges.

Liar, Liar

This kind of boss takes a while to uncover. Lying bosses may appear friendly and congenial at first; their deceitful ways usually emerge over time. The degree to which this kind of authority figure tampers with the truth or acts in unethical ways varies. A less severe Liar, Liar boss may hire you with the promise that you'll get a raise in three months when the truth is that the company has a freeze on all raises. Should you later confront this employer, he or she will confess, "I knew about the freeze, but I hoped it would be lifted by now." A more severe version of this boss might say, "I never told you that," denying the previous statement and dismissing your concerns. The first time you catch an authority figure in a lie, you may give that person the benefit of the doubt. The second time you detect a falsehood, you probably feel confused, betrayed, and a little sick. By the third duplicitous statement, you may start to wonder whether you can believe anything coming out of your boss's mouth. It's challenging to work for this kind of boss because you never know what the truth is and you fear uncovering blatantly unethical behavior. People who work for Liar, Liars also spend a great deal of time unraveling the fabrications and false promises that their bosses communicate to vendors, clients, and colleagues.

- I sat at a meeting while I heard my boss make promises to a potential account that I knew we couldn't deliver. I felt sick inside.
- It's gotten to the point where I know the facial expressions and hand gestures that indicate my boss is lying.
- My boss has broken so many promises that I can barely stand to be in the same room with him.

You know you're working for a Liar, Liar boss when . . .

1. You realize that what your boss says and what actually happens are rarely the same.
2. You often hear your boss denying statements that you *know* came out of his or her mouth.
3. You find yourself going to other sources to uncover the truth about any issue because you can't trust what your boss tells you.
4. You spend a lot of time repairing business relationships after your boss makes empty promises to other people.
5. You find yourself smirking at everything the boss says.

CATEGORY 4: AMBIVALENT LEADERS

Ambivalent leaders have mixed feelings about being in charge. On the one hand, they like being held in high esteem by others. On the other hand, they don't like all that is entailed in being a strong leader. First, most ambivalent bosses don't like to do anything that could cause a negative reaction in others: They don't like making tough decisions. They don't like giving tough feedback. They don't like saying no to certain requests and they don't like holding people accountable for their work. These are the bosses that secretly wish employees could just get along, do their jobs, and manage themselves. Second, ambivalent leaders rebel against their responsibilities passively. Instead of admitting that they don't want to settle a dispute between two coworkers, for example, ambivalent leaders simply find a way to avoid the conflict altogether—leaving the employees feeling angry and unprotected. The ambivalent leaders are the Sacred Cow, Checked Out, Spineless, and the Artful Dodger.

Sacred Cow

These are the people in organizations who get promoted because of longevity, loyalty, personal connections, or family ties. They don't make waves and they always comply with company policy. Eventually, Sacred Cows rise up through the ranks into positions of complete incompetence where their only defense is to maintain existing systems and to coast. Sacred Cows can be very frustrating to work for because, while they may encourage you to be innovative and creative, they are risk-averse. These bosses are not willing to try anything new. In fact, you'll be hard-pressed to get a Sacred Cow boss to take action of any kind—even on existing projects. If you work for one of these authority figures, you may engage in coping behaviors such as bad-mouthing and wishing for his or her demise. Anytime you try to get direction, encouragement, or support for a project, the Sacred Cow blocks it: "Now is not a good time." "That's not the way things are done here." "Upper management won't like it." These statements stop you in your tracks, triggering disappointment and unleashing feelings of anger and blame.

- There's no point in presenting any idea to my boss. She sees only the barriers to doing it.
- If I hear my boss say "That won't fly here" one more time, I'll scream.
- My boss spends most of the workday tracking his retirement funds on the Internet.

You know you work for a Sacred Cow boss if . . .

1. He or she is very invested in the established way of doing things on the job.
2. Your boss encourages fresh ideas, but balks at trying anything new.
3. You wonder what your boss does all day.
4. You can't imagine why your boss hasn't been fired yet.
5. Your predominant feelings toward this person are frustration and disdain.

Checked Out

This is sometimes a temporary condition caused by a life crisis. It could be that your boss is grappling with a medical problem, a family problem, an extramarital affair, or a situation involving substance abuse. A close relative may be ill, a marriage could be falling apart, or your boss may be struggling as a new parent. In each of these cases, overwhelming outside circumstances cause the boss to be distant, out of touch, physically absent, and disengaged. The challenge for people who work for a

Checked Out boss is to figure out what is expected of them and who is in charge. Checked Out bosses don't hold meetings, don't give direction, and don't make decisions. Projects under their leadership either stall or die out. The workplace environment becomes lackluster because there is no driving force. And coworkers often become argumentative and territorial. Without leadership, it's every man for himself.

If you work for a Checked Out boss, you may find yourself acting out in a variety of ways. You may confront the boss to get a reaction out of him or her. It's common to create emergencies that require the boss's attention. Another tactic is to break the rules (arrive late, leave early, slack off) just to see if anyone is watching.

- When I go to my boss with a question, he's either totally preoccupied with personal phone calls, working behind a closed door, or not there.
- My boss shows up for work wearing a pained expression. She's physically here, but mentally somewhere else.
- Without any leadership, our department is falling apart. No one is driving the bus!

You know you're working for a Checked Out boss if . . .

1. The boss seems unavailable and unresponsive to you and other members of the staff.
2. You feel frustrated by a lack of leadership and direction.
3. There is constant infighting among staff because no one is in charge.
4. You wonder if or when "the old boss" will check back in.
5. You question how long your department/business/division can go on like this.

Spineless

This brand of boss cannot take a stand regarding any issue. Charming and likable, they are so afraid of being disliked that they cannot say no or rock the boat. If you work for this kind of authority figure, you'll wish that he or she could just take decisive action. You may go to him or her with complaints about a disruptive coworker, suggestions for improving office procedures, or requests for better working conditions. Your boss will listen, nod, and do nothing. Over time, you'll become increasingly angry, frustrated, and disappointed. You may come to the conclusion that you are working for an invertebrate.

The most painful aspect of working for this kind of authority is the fact that he or she will never step in and protect you. Spineless bosses are not able to defend their staff against the attacks of upper management, coworkers, vendors, or customers. In an attempt to make the boss take a stand, you end up confronting this person—usually with no success. You feel helpless and unprotected.

- Because my boss refuses to intervene, she allows bad behavior in our department to continue.
- I wish my boss would just spell out what he expects of us, instead of leaving us guessing.
- I couldn't believe it when a client screamed at me in a meeting and my boss didn't come to my defense.

You know you work for a Spineless boss when . . .

1. You notice that any sticky issue you bring to the boss's attention goes unaddressed.
2. You and your colleagues are constantly complaining about the boss's wishy-washy behavior.
3. You hope that your boss will take a course in management.
4. When a colleague misbehaves, you end up taking matters into your own hands because you know the boss won't.
5. You want to yell, "Don't just sit there, *do something*!"

Artful Dodger

Like Spineless, Checked Out, and Sacred Cow bosses, Artful Dodgers avoid confrontation. Unlike the other ambivalent leaders, however, these authority figures get a lot accomplished by using other people to do their dirty work for them. Artful Dodgers do whatever it takes to establish and maintain an untarnished image. Their primary goal is to look good at all costs. They want to be respected and admired both inside and outside of the company. Employees who work for this type of manager find out that the boss is unhappy with their performance only through secondhand sources. To your face, Artful Dodgers will always appear positive, encouraging, and congenial. What is said after you leave the office, however, is another matter. To avoid appearing mean or harsh, the Artful Dodger will have someone else deliver any unpleasant news to members of the staff. If your boss finds fault with a proposal you write, for example, you'll receive the negative feedback from another staff member on the boss's behalf. If you are one of the people assigned to deliver these unpleasant messages, you know what it feels like to be set up. The recipient may challenge you and go directly to the boss for verification. The Artful Dodger boss will then either evade responsibility for his or her statements or avoid that employee altogether, waiting for the issue to blow over. You are stuck in the role of bad guy.

- My boss said that after three months on the job, I was doing a great job. So I was confused when I got a warning from HR stating that this same person was unhappy with my attendance record.
- I saw my boss tell a roomful of software developers that he loved their product ideas. As they proudly walked out of the room, he turned to me and said, "We can't use any of those concepts."
- It got to the point that I never knew when my boss was being honest with me.

You know you work for an Artful Dodger if . . .

1. Your boss cannot confront, correct, or fire anyone, but manages to find other people to carry out those tasks.
2. You've seen your boss act friendly toward certain employees in public settings, then criticize their behavior in private.
3. Your boss is very concerned with his or her public image—always wanting to appear charismatic, kind, and caring.
4. Over time, you catch glimpses of a cold and calculating side of the boss, which seems contradictory to his or her polished image.
5. Eventually, you see the boss as manipulative and controlling.

CATEGORY 5: DELICATE CIRCUMSTANCES

There are certain boss/employee relationships that are particularly delicate. These are the situations where the boss is someone you wouldn't normally imagine in a leadership position. You may have to work for a supervisor who is significantly younger than you. Perhaps a close friend and colleague suddenly becomes your boss. Or you may report to a manager who unconsciously discriminates against you. If you work for a family business, you may wind up working under a relative who inadvertently puts you down. These delicate circumstances can be emotionally stressful and mentally draining. They feel inherently unfair. The bosses who come with these delicate circumstances are Junior, Former Colleague, Unconscious Discriminator, and Persecutor.

Junior

These are the bosses who have a great deal of talent, drive, and energy, but very little management experience. Junior bosses are usually very bright; technology is second nature for them. They like to investigate and apply the newest devices to whatever they are doing. Because they tend to value ideas and people who are on the cutting edge, Junior bosses tend to feel uncomfortable around their more mature employees. Rather than embrace the experience of a veteran staff member, these managers tend to be impatient with old or traditional ways. The result is a tense relationship between the old and the new. A Junior boss may discount or block out his or her senior staff's suggestions. At the same time, this kind of leader will be intolerant of the difficulty older employees have adapting to new technology. Further tension is created because the two generations have different communication styles. What the Junior boss sees as casual conversation may be experienced as immature or unprofessional by his or her mature employee. If you work for a Junior boss, you may revert to a number of coping tactics including avoidance, gloating in his or her failure, and wishing for his or her demise. It's common to feel disappointed by the lack of respect you receive, and eventually to get caught in anger and blame.

- My boss introduced me to our new database with a two-minute tutorial, then expected me to know everything about it.
- I approached my boss with a suggestion about doing a survey of our customers to gauge their satisfaction. She just smiled at me and said, "That's not the way our generation does things."
- I wish my boss could write an e-mail without typing "*C u ltr*" at the end.

You know you work for a Junior boss if . . .

1. You can't believe that you have to take orders from someone that young.
2. You wish the boss were a little more open to the value of your experience.
3. You start to feel that your age is your greatest handicap.
4. You have a hard time taking the boss seriously.
5. You feel a constant pressure to "keep up" with your boss's initiatives.

Former Colleague

While you may initially be happy for a colleague when he or she gets promoted, that happiness may turn into remorse once you realize that your chummy coworker is now the boss. The person you once laughed with, gossiped with, and sometimes partied with is now in a position of authority. He or she must monitor your performance and hold you accountable for your work. Most people take on a different attitude when they move up the corporate ladder. With added responsibility comes a different way of interacting with the staff. Now your Former Colleague is privy to information from the top that he or she can't share with you, and his or her job is to make sure that you do yours. It's not uncommon to experience your friend-turned-manager as cold, formal, secretive, or distant. You may feel as if you're being watched or judged in a way that you hadn't experienced previously. In response to these changes, you may avoid, obsess, or sulk. Initially, it's common to restart and try harder to get the old, friendly association back. Eventually, disappointment sets in, and you realize that you and your Former Colleague are in a new relationship for good.

- We used to go out after work and talk about everything and everyone in our department. Now he doesn't have time.
- My colleague and I used to laugh so hard at the antics of upper management. Now that she's one of them, she's lost her sense of humor.
- Josh turned into everything we both disliked about our other bosses. I wish I could tell him.

You know you work for a Former Colleague when . . .

1. You're happy for your friend, but sad about the loss of a peer relationship.
2. You're surprised to see how power and authority affect this person.
3. You react with anger and indignation when your former buddy orders you around.
4. You find yourself feeling jealous of your colleague's promotion—what did he or she do to deserve it?
5. You long for the days of fun and friendship that are gone due to your coworker's promotion.

Unconscious Discriminator

The workplace has people of different sizes, shapes, religions, ethnicities, races, genders, and sexual orientations. You may have a boss who inadvertently discriminates against you due to one of these factors. If you are a woman, you may be shocked when a man with less experience is promoted above you. If you are of Asian descent, you may feel disturbed when your boss playfully imitates a Chinese accent. An African American man may feel slighted when he realizes that his boss holds lower expectations of his performance—and therefore offers him fewer opportunities to shine. If you are a Muslim, you may notice your manager's discomfort when you ask for time off for religious observances.

Should you be overweight (relative to your colleagues), you may experience your boss's prejudice when you are excluded from important meetings and presentations with new clients. Many bosses are unaware of the ways in which they discriminate against employees in the workplace. If you are a target of unconscious discrimination, you'll probably cycle through a wide range of reactions, including shame, anger, confusion, self-doubt, and blame.

- I felt embarrassed and humiliated when I heard my boss imitating my accent as I passed by her office.
- I was shocked when my boss said that out of his concern for my health, he was willing to pay for a membership to Weight Watchers.
- When we had the company picnic, my boss asked me to bring fried chicken because "my people" make the best.

You know you work for an Unconscious Discriminator when . . .

1. You find yourself wondering whether you misheard or misread a prejudiced statement.
2. You notice that your boss seems uneasy with some aspect of your race, creed, or appearance.
3. Your boss acts friendly toward you at work, but excludes you from social outings that include other members of the staff.
4. It seems like the boss promotes only his or her kind.
5. One part of you wishes you could change the boss's mind, while another part of you just feels defeated.

Persecutor

Perhaps the most delicate circumstance of all occurs when you feel persecuted by your boss. It's not clear what you did to warrant the negative attention. For some reason, your manager decides that you are a problem employee and sets out to make you look bad. You may go to a staff meeting and suddenly become the focus of your boss's harsh criticism. You may catch the boss talking negatively about you to others. Try as you may, your boss will not adjust his or her opinion of you. Even your attempts at meeting with the boss to find out what you've done to warrant such treatment prove fruitless. Your boss treats you with aloof indifference and refuses to answer your questions or address your concerns. Your mind races back in an attempt to pinpoint the moment when this relationship went sour. The cruel treatment doesn't seem rational or fair. For some odd reason, you've become a target—the departmental scapegoat.

- I knew there was a problem when my boss began questioning the relevance of everything I said at staff meetings.
- It seems as if I can't do anything right in my boss's eyes. He's just decided to dislike me.
- It's weird to hear my boss joke with my colleagues about their weekends, then have her walk by me in silence.

You know you work for a Persecutor boss if . . .

1. You feel you can do nothing right in your boss's eyes.
2. Your boss is outwardly hostile toward you.

3. The more you try to remedy the situation, the worse it gets.
4. You keep wondering what you did to warrant this kind of treatment.
5. You feel unfairly ostracized for mistakes that other people make without incident.

Now that we've introduced you to twenty boss behaviors, you should have a much better understanding of the specific things that your boss says and does that drive you bonkers. Congratulations, you've successfully completed the first step of our process—Detect. Take a few minutes to read one more time the list of twenty behaviors that follows and check off the behaviors that pertain to your situation. Then, come with us to the next section, where you'll learn how to Detach and take back your personal power from the boss.

WORK IT OUT
Detecting Twenty Boss Behaviors (That Drive Us Bonkers)

**CHECK OFF YOUR BOSS'S BEHAVIORS
THAT DRIVE YOU BONKERS**

❏ Chronic Critic: finds fault with everything you do

❏ Rule Changer: keeps changing and rearranging what he or she originally decided

❏ Yeller: explodes without notice and says incriminating things about you

❏ Underminer: will set you up to fail

❏ "I'm Always Right": needs to be considered infallible

❏ "You Threaten Me": takes credit when it's not due

❏ Grandiose: can't see past his or her own ego

❏ Control Freak: micromanages uncontrollably

❏ Love-Struck: can't manage his or her own emotions

❏ Calculating Confidant: has a hidden agenda

❏ Tell-All: makes you his or her captive audience

❏ Liar, Liar: can implicate you in his or her lies

❏ Sacred Cow: not going anywhere; if you challenge, you will lose

❏ Checked Out: preoccupied with non-work-related personal matters

❏ Spineless: incapable of defending anyone

❏ Artful Dodger: afraid of tarnishing his or her perfect image

❏ Junior: may not value your experience

❏ Former Colleague: the balance of power has changed

❏ Unconscious Discriminator: unintentionally expresses bias

❏ Persecutor: targets and torments you

SECTION II

Detach

Reader's Alert: Chapter 3 will show you how to detach from a difficult boss. After you read it, move on to chapter 4 to learn more about your boss's type.

CHAPTER 3

Getting Out from Under Your Boss

JOYCE IS A medical copywriter assigned to a line of pain relievers at a large pharmaceutical company. She enjoys her current job, but feels ready for the next challenge in her career. A senior editor position opens up in the most successful division of the company—diabetes medication. The job entails more responsibility and a significant increase in salary. It's the kind of position Joyce has always wanted—her dream job.

When Joyce stops by the HR department to apply for the posting, Callie, the recruiter, is courteous but cautious. "Do you know anything about the head of this division, Rhonda Steeleman?" she inquires.

Joyce responds, "I know she runs a tight ship."

Callie smirks and says, "That's an understatement."

Two days later, Joyce walks into Rhonda Steeleman's large and elegantly furnished office. She sits on the leather couch that faces Rhonda's antique Italian desk. Joyce is impressed. Ms. Steeleman is impeccably dressed and engaged in an animated phone conversation with one of her press contacts. She waves hello to Joyce and continues talking for ten minutes.

After completing her call, Rhonda glances at Joyce's résumé, scans her outfit, and says, "HR finally sent me someone presentable. I'll have them push you through." With that, Rhonda gives Joyce a firm handshake and dismisses her.

Joyce walks away elated. It seems odd that her potential manager didn't ask for writing samples or inquire about her past work experience, but Joyce assumes there will be plenty of time for them to get acquainted.

Her first day on the job, Joyce arrives early. Mary, the receptionist, leads her to a nearby cubicle. At 8:42 a.m., Rhonda Steeleman enters the office suite, zips by the reception area, and almost passes Joyce. "Are you a temp?" Rhonda asks.

Joyce is stunned, but manages to say, "No, Ms. Steeleman, I'm the senior editor you just hired."

Rhonda raises her eyebrows. "That's strange," she replies, "I remember a much more polished person." With that, Rhonda goes into her office and closes the door.

Let's stop here.

Before we discuss Detachment, the second step in our process, let's review the first D: Detect. As you may recall, you can detect that you're caught in a challenging boss/employee relationship in one of two ways: by identifying which coping tactics you're employing in response to the boss's behavior or by recognizing which phase of a distressing boss/employee relationship you are caught in.

If we were to apply detecting to Joyce's situation, we could say that she's already in phase two—internal alarm. Her honeymoon period with Ms. Steeleman was short-lived. Rhonda's demeaning tone toward her new employee surprises and concerns Joyce. Just one hour into her dream job, Joyce is already nervous and full of self-doubt. With each day, Joyce continues to move through the predictable phases of a distressing boss/employee relationship. Let's return to her story to see what happens next:

> Over the next few weeks, Joyce works hard to familiarize herself with the responsibilities of her job. She has a heavy workload, which includes overseeing all of the communications associated with two different kinds of diabetes drugs. She manages two copywriters and top-edits Web copy, advertising copy, medical pamphlets, and patient brochures. Everything Joyce edits must receive final approval from Rhonda.
>
> Joyce's first experience of Steeleman's review process is harsh. After

leaving the copy for a new brochure in Rhonda's box, Joyce comes in the next morning to find the document back on her desk. On top is a Post-it note that says, "You call this writing???" Underneath the Post-it, Joyce sees large red *NO*s scribbled on top of every sentence that Rhonda doesn't like.

That afternoon, Joyce approaches her new boss to try to gain a better understanding of what Ms. Steeleman wants. Joyce knocks gently on Rhonda's office door. Without looking up from her desk, Rhonda says, "If you want to know what decent copy looks like, read your predecessor's last efforts." She then shoos Joyce away with a wave of her perfectly manicured hand.

That night, Joyce combs through the previous senior editor's documents. She begins to decipher the style and tone that Ms. Steeleman favors. Joyce takes the brochure copy and completely reworks it. After a second submission, she finds the corrected pamphlet on her desk, this time minus Post-its and red marks. Instead, Joyce receives a one-sentence e-mail from Rhonda: "You should have gotten it right the first time."

As Joyce closes the e-mail, she slumps in her chair. She *detects* that she's in the disappointment phase of a stressful boss/employee relationship. She realizes that her glamorous new boss is extremely judgmental and very demanding. Callie's subtle warning when Joyce first applied for this job now makes complete sense. Just a few weeks into her job, Joyce finds herself obsessed with and frightened of Rhonda.

"If I don't figure out how to handle this woman," she thinks to herself, "this great career move is going to give me a nervous breakdown."

Joyce is right. If she wants to make it with Steeleman, she's got to do more than simply perform the functions of her new job. To survive under the supervision of her cold, insensitive, and highly critical boss, she needs to learn how to *Detach*.

DETACHING: THE ULTIMATE SKILL FOR CHALLENGING RELATIONSHIPS

If you're caught in a draining association with a difficult boss, then that relationship probably has you in its grip. Once you detect where you are in the cycle, the next step is to break out of its hold. How do you break out of a situation that is consuming you? By practicing the art of detachment.

To *detach* is to separate yourself mentally and emotionally from the problematic relationship. You know you've successfully detached if you can observe, listen to, or communicate with your boss without feeling tense, angry, frustrated, worried, resentful, paranoid, anxious, depressed, betrayed, or trapped.

When you truly detach from another human being, you can participate in the relationship without feeling consumed or controlled by his or her behavior. You are able to maintain a healthy distance between yourself and the other person. Here's what it looks like:

> Maria was proud of herself when she could sit in a staff meeting and watch her unceasingly angry manager yell at everyone without feeling terrified.

> Doug knew he'd detached when he realized that his boss's need to micromanage him had nothing to do with his competence.

> Tyler felt relieved when the company president's condescending tone rolled off his back.

It may be hard to believe that it's possible to work with a difficult boss and actually achieve a state of detachment. You may fear that being detached would require you to become cold or uncaring. We promise that it is possible to detach and still be true to yourself. You won't become uncaring; you'll just learn to see the other person for who he or she is without reacting so strongly to the behavior.

Why bother to detach? Why is it worth the work? When a boss/ employee relationship turns sour, it colors your experiences inside and outside of the workplace. Thoughts and feelings about the boss invade your mind whether you're punching the clock or sitting at a dinner party. Social events may suddenly feel like tiresome chores because your brain is buzzing with the last conversation, e-mail, or meeting. The injustice of your workplace situation rules your internal life and becomes all-consuming.

Until you detach, you're allowing someone else's negative behavior to invade and control your life. Perhaps the boss's disparaging words constantly ring in your ears. Or a department head's contradictory commands keep swirling around in your mind. Maybe the COO's glares haunt your dreams. Whatever it is, the boss's behavior will continue to dominate and define your reality until you are able to detach from it.

Detaching is a two-part process. Part one is *accepting* that you are not going to change the boss. Part two involves finding ways to *take back your personal power* despite the boss's poor behavior.

Acceptance: The Most Daunting Part of Detachment

Practicing acceptance is simply the fastest way to detach from a boss whose behavior drives you crazy. But acceptance does not equal approval. To accept is to realize and come to terms with certain facts about the boss. These facts name the boss's problematic behaviors. They clarify the reality of your situation.

For example, if you work for someone who is chronically disorganized, can you accept the fact that he or she is likely to lose important documents and forget crucial appointments? If you know that your boss bends the truth, can you accept the probability that he or she will continue to prevaricate? If your boss has an eagle eye for the slightest flaw in your output, can you accept the reality that you work for a faultfinder? What if your supervisor happens to be moody? Can you accept the fact that, no matter what you do, his or her moods will still swing?

We know this is a tall order. You read these questions and think, "You're asking me to condone my boss's bad behavior? That's ridiculous!" But before you throw this book across the room, hear us out. Sure, you're right—in theory. In a theoretical (perfect) world, no one would have to tolerate chronic disorganization, blatant lies, faultfinding, or moodiness. But being right in theory won't change your reality. On the contrary, your insistence on being right keeps you stuck in a power struggle, an interpersonal tug of war with the person whose behavior you deem unacceptable.

Accepting that the boss behaves a certain way is not approving of, agreeing with, or condoning the behavior. Acceptance allows you to take the person at face value and not get emotionally charged by his or her actions. If, for example, your boss is habitually late, and you can accept this fact, you'll find ways to deal with it. But if you resist reality, if you insist that the boss should not be tardy and demand better time management from this person, you'll become increasingly frustrated and angry.

Let's see how to apply acceptance to Joyce's situation:

> After just one month in her new position, Joyce is in bad shape. She's eating too much ice cream, watching too much reality TV, and talking incessantly to her friends about Rhonda Steeleman. At one point, her best friend says, "If you're so miserable, why don't you just quit?"
>
> Joyce reaches out to Callie in HR for guidance. Callie says, "I know this is a tough assignment, but you can learn a lot from Steeleman. You just have to accept who she is and find ways to recharge yourself outside of the workplace. If you can do those two things, you can use this experience to further your career."
>
> As Joyce hangs up the phone, she still feels frustrated, but she knows that Callie's advice is right. Joyce reminds herself that she's not a quitter. She senses that learning how to work with her difficult boss is something that will help her grow personally and professionally. If she can figure out how to work with Rhonda without feeling emotionally battered, she'll benefit from Rhonda's wealth of knowledge and improve as an editor.

How can you tell whether you're on the road to detachment? Successful detachment begins when you no longer expect the other person to change his or her behavior for your benefit. You accept that this individual will continue to do and say things that you don't like; you accept that you cannot alter his or her personality.

Practicing Acceptance

Try this exercise: create a log of your boss's annoying traits. Write a sentence about each thing that irritates you. Here are some examples:

- My boss will stretch the truth to suit her purposes.
- My boss is quick to notice my mistakes, but won't admit his own.
- My boss's moods are unpredictable.
- My boss is disorganized.
- My boss takes credit for other people's work.

Jot down as many of your boss's foibles as you can think of. Then take each item and write the phrase, "I accept the fact that . . ." in front of it.

Here's what that looks like:

- I accept the fact that my boss will stretch the truth to suit her purposes.
- I accept the fact that my boss is quick to notice my mistakes, but won't admit his own.
- I accept the fact that my boss's moods are unpredictable.
- I accept the fact that my boss is disorganized.
- I accept the fact that my boss takes credit for other people's work.

Now for the really challenging part of this exercise: read each statement on your list out loud and see how it feels. Don't worry if you don't really *feel* accepting at this moment. Remember that this is a *practice* session. You must practice acceptance as you would any other skill you want to master. By recording each item and reciting the sentence "I accept the fact that . . . ," you begin the acceptance process.

Notice which traits feel easy to come to terms with and which traits remain difficult for you. We can promise that, for every fact about your boss you can accept, you'll experience some degree of relief. With that relief, you'll gain clarity. You'll be able to see and experience the boss with more objectivity and less emotion. Eventually, you'll be able to come to terms with the other things about this person that drive you crazy.

Reminder: Acceptance (as we are using it) is *not* approval. Acceptance is the recognition of reality—the sobering truth about the person whom you call boss.

Joyce goes home that night, polishes off the remaining chocolate ice cream in her freezer, and sits down to write her own acceptance list. It looks like this:

- I accept the fact that I work for a woman who is uncaring toward her staff.
- I accept the fact that Rhonda says mean things to me and to my colleagues at work.
- I accept the fact that my boss cares only about impressing the client.
- I accept the fact that Rhonda is highly critical of any mistakes.
- I accept the fact that Rhonda judges people on their appearance.

- I accept the fact that my boss doesn't give me any credit when I do a good job.

Joyce finishes her list and reads it out loud. Now she understands why she's had such a tough time adjusting to her new position. "My last job was fun, and my boss was friendly. Now, I'm working for the Ice Queen. No wonder it's so uncomfortable." She's not sure if she can accept all of these facts about Rhonda right now, but she's willing to give it a try.

After writing and reviewing your initial acceptance list, you may notice that certain items trigger very strong reactions in you. There may be certain things about your boss that you just can't stand. In that case, try adding your feelings about this person and your situation to your acceptance list. Here's what Joyce did:

- I accept the fact that I don't like Rhonda very much.
- I accept the fact that I wish she were different.
- I accept the fact that I miss my old boss.

Once you've made your acceptance list, we suggest you read it daily for a while. Keep it in a place where you can review it on a regular basis. It's not enough just to write about acceptance. You eventually want to believe it. It's not until you can truly accept something that you can work with it.

After you've begun the acceptance process, you can start to reclaim your personal power—the second part of detaching.

TAKING BACK YOUR PERSONAL POWER

Without even realizing it, we give the people who oversee our work a great deal of power. If the boss is in a good mood, we feel good. If he or she is in a bad mood, we feel bad. If the boss likes and appreciates us, we feel good about ourselves. If that same person focuses on our faults and shortcomings, we feel bad about ourselves. If the boss ignores or neglects us, we may interpret that as an indication that we are worthless.

The second part of detaching involves taking back any power that you may have unwittingly bestowed upon the boss. For example, if you've developed back pain as a result of working for someone, then your boss has power over your physical state. If you have sleepless nights, your boss exerts undue influence over your thoughts. If you feel depressed and defeated, the boss may be dominating your emotional condition.

Taking back your power requires concerted effort on your part. It begins with exercising impulse control. When dealing with a stressful relationship, it's natural to want to isolate yourself and engage in self-comforting habits. You may eat more than usual, drink a few extra cocktails, smoke more cigarettes, watch more TV, play more video games, or engage in other forms of distraction and gratification. While these activities help in the moment, they don't help you release or resolve your problems.

In fact, these attempts at self-comfort usually leave you feeling worse over time. Overeating may provide immediate relief, but you'll eventually put on unwanted pounds. Drinking a few extra cocktails may feel good in the moment, but you'll wake up feeling hungover and irritable. Think of these activities as forms of self-medication rather than self-empowerment.

Instead of resorting to your usual habits, we're asking you to delay instant gratification and choose from a stockpile of healthful, tried-and-tested recharging activities, which we'll discuss in a moment. These recharging activities are designed to restore your energy, repair your emotional state, and rebuild your confidence.

What follows is a catalog, or curriculum, if you will, of fifty or so action steps to recharge yourself, body and soul. We've divided these remedies into things you can do outside of work and those you can practice on the job. We don't expect you to have the time or energy to do all of these things. In the next chapter, we will discuss how to use these techniques strategically to counter the harmful effects of the particular challenging boss/employee situation you're in.

RESTORING YOUR ENERGY

Challenging boss/employee relationships tend to be energy drainers. Tangoing with an unmanageable boss leaves the employee feeling exhausted, tapped out, fed up, or wound up. Many people develop physical problems—neck pain, back pain, stomach problems, sleep disorders.

To combat these conditions, you need to take concrete actions that replenish your energy. Energy-restoring activities also help release negative emotions such as anger, frustration, fear, and anxiety. As you let go of toxic energy, you also rebuild your immune system.

RESTORING ACTIVITIES

After work hours

- **Exercise** Tennis, anyone? Try walking, running, swimming, dancing, playing sports, weight training, aerobic exercise, hiking, boxing, kickboxing, biking, roller skating, ice skating, skiing, martial arts, yoga, Pilates.
- **Mind/Body Remedies** Zen out! Mind/body remedies help release negative energy and relax both body and mind. They include massage, acupuncture, reflexology, Alexander Technique, biofeedback, and moving or sitting meditation.
- **Medical Attention** Check it out! If this relationship has taken a toll on your body, then seek the help of a professional. Go for physical checkups, start physical therapy, invest in a nutritionist for assistance with your diet.
- **Healthy Escapes** Take a hike! Contact with nature can be healing. Take day or half-day trips to local gardens, forests, trails, beaches, bodies of water, landmarks. Treat yourself to a weekend getaway. Book and follow through on a sports vacation, spa vacation, "chill" vacation, or sightseeing trip.
- **Hit the Sack** Never underestimate the restorative effects of a good night's sleep. If you're sleep-deprived, make it your business to get more "restful" sleep. That means turning off the television, computer, BlackBerry, cell phone, iPod, radio, lights, and any other distractions. It also means going to bed at a decent hour.

During work hours

- **Breathe** Try this very simple breathing exercise: sit in a chair with your back straight and your feet planted comfortably on the ground. Place your hands in your lap. As you inhale deeply and gently, say to yourself,

"I am." As you exhale slowly and gently, complete the phrase: "Relaxed."
Repeat this exercise several times until you feel yourself truly relaxing.

- **H_2O Cure** Water is a cleanser. It washes away toxins both inside and outside the body. Wash your hands, splash your face with water, drink cold
water, sip hot water.
- **Scentsational** If you're someone who responds positively to certain
scents, keep an object on your desk (scented candle, essential oils, flowers) that has a smell you really like.
- **Change Your Environment** Step away, whether it means going for a quick
walk outside or visiting another floor.
- **Reduce Your Body's Energy Spikes** Limiting your intake of sugar and
caffeine will decrease the chemical highs and lows you experience. Get
off the roller coaster and switch to decaf; replace candy with fresh fruit.
Instead of eating three cookies, substitute a yogurt or a granola bar.

Here's what works for others . . .

"Whenever I have to meet with my boss, I focus on my breathing. Taking a
few slow, deep breaths as I listen to him helps me relax."

"I recently returned to playing tennis. A weekly game with good
friends helps me feel much better physically and gives me a great outlet
for my frustration."

"I love to drive, so I've begun restoring my energy by going on short
escapes after work. I drive to my favorite bridge and watch the sunset."

REPAIRING YOUR EMOTIONAL STATE

When you are grappling with a difficult boss, your emotional state
usually takes a beating. It's common to feel anxious, angry, frustrated,
scared, misunderstood, betrayed, persecuted, or depressed. You may
walk around with a cloud over your head, feeling stuck in an emotional
haze that you can't break out of. As you take actions to restore your
energy, you'll also want to purge negative emotions and reconnect with
positive feelings.

REPAIRING ACTIVITIES

After work hours

- **Pursue a Passion or Pastime** Get back to a favorite hobby or find a new one. Read mystery novels, take an art class, go fishing, study a foreign language, tend to a garden, take a cooking class, or knit. Do something you take pleasure in.
- **Reach Out and Reconnect** Counter the tendency to isolate (which will exacerbate your situation) with some kind of outreach campaign. Reconnect with positive professional acquaintances; look up friends whose company you enjoy; spend time with family members who energize you; consider doing your energy-restoring activities with a partner.
- **Turn to a Pro** Seek professional help. Go for short-term counseling, find a career coach, or join a support group. Working with a trained professional can help you quickly and objectively disentangle emotionally from your boss.
- **Get on the Soul Train** Depending on your personal preference, you may derive comfort from prayer, meditation, attending services, reading literature, or joining or rejoining a religious or spiritual community.
- **Clean House** If you can't improve your work environment, then focus on creating a home environment that appeals to you. You can do this with music, visual art, candles (scented or unscented), flowers, aromatherapy, or simply by decluttering.
- **Get Inspired** What inspires you? Everyone is different. Is it books, music, sports, museums? Read books, articles, and magazines that inspire you. Attend concerts, plays, movies, and sports events that entertain and give you hope. Go to museums and exhibits that embody greatness.

During work hours

- **Comic Relief** Enlist someone—a colleague or friend—in the cause of helping you release stress. Your ally may be someone who is an excellent listener, a constructive problem solver, or simply someone who makes you laugh. Make a pact to offer each other perspective, humor, and healthy distractions, and otherwise assist each other during tense times.

- **Photo Therapy** Have pictures of nature, your favorite escape, good friends, your children, your pets—to remind you of what's really important.
- **Game Break** Spend a few minutes playing an online de-stressor game, such as solitaire, Sudoku, or a shoot 'em up video game. Pick something that distracts and relaxes you.
- **Take a Quick Reality Check** Write your answers to these questions: What's happening here? What are the facts? What's the boss's part? What's my part? What are my options?
- **Call a Time-out** If emotions run high, excuse yourself and go to a private place until you are able to cool off.
- **Lucky Charm** It could be a special stone, worry beads, a family heirloom, or a religious symbol of some kind. Wear or carry an object that gives you strength, comfort, and a sense of control.

Here's what works for others . . .

"Instead of falling asleep in front of the television, I'm taking a pottery class. Being creative feels great!"

"I have a stone that says LET GO. I keep it on hand at all times as a reminder to detach."

"I became so depressed at work that I sought short-term counseling. The cloud that hung over my head is finally lifting."

REBUILDING YOUR CONFIDENCE

Confidence is self-assurance or the belief in your ability to succeed. Many people who work for difficult bosses start out feeling confident; they may have years of solid success behind them. But a bad experience with authority at work can erode anyone's confidence within weeks or months. If you are someone whose self-confidence was shaky to begin with, a toxic boss/employee relationship will really wreak havoc.

When you have self-confidence, you can see options for yourself and your career. Without self-confidence, it's hard to imagine that you deserve or can find a better situation.

Rebuilding your confidence is an inside job. Like restoring your energy and repairing your emotional state, it takes a conscious effort. The best way to regain a sense of confidence is to engage in activities that let you *feel* successful. These activities can take place inside or outside of the workplace. We suggest you start with small actions and build.

REBUILDING ACTIVITIES

After work hours

- **Find a Mentor** A mentor is somebody older and more experienced who can advise and guide you. You can ask someone inside the company whose expertise you respect, or go to your high-school or college alumni association. Mentors can sometimes be found within professional or trade associations.
- **Make a List of Your Successes Every Day** Your log can range from simple successes such as "Got up on time; worked out when I didn't want to; cooked a healthy meal" to larger achievements such as "Helped a colleague complete her project; repaired the copier; surpassed our sales goal by 10 percent."
- **Spend Time with People Who Support You** Reconnect with past friends, colleagues, or bosses who think highly of you.
- **Make a Difference** Contribute your time to a group or cause that you care about. This may involve helping people less fortunate than you (soup kitchen, literacy program), raising money for a cause you care about (medical research), or giving your time to an organization you respect (professional or civic group).

During work hours

Use these devices for creating a positive internal dialogue.

- **Workplace Proverbs** Post quotes or statements that inspire you in places where you can easily see them, and refer to them often. Here are some of our favorites.
    "No one can make you feel inferior without your consent."
    —ELEANOR ROOSEVELT
    "Slow motion will get you there faster."
    —HOAGY CARMICHAEL
    "If you want to be great, hang out with greatness."
    —ROBERT FRITZ

"Insanity: doing the same thing over and over again, and expecting different results."
—ALBERT EINSTEIN

- **Gratitude Inventory** When you're working with a difficult boss, it's easy to feel as if you're playing a losing game. Gratitude helps you see what you do have, which helps with the rebuilding process. When you feel as if you can't win, write down three things you are grateful for. They can be simple: health, friends, family, a good cup of (decaf?) coffee, minimal traffic on the way to work.
- **Aim for Small Achievements** Clean out a desk or file drawer, declutter your computer files, respond to an e-mail, complete that item on your to-do list that haunts you.
- **Find Ways to Be Useful Outside of Your Department** Sit in on a task force to solve a specific problem at work, help plan a conference, contribute your skills to a company campaign (working green, saving energy) or special event.

Here's what works for others . . .

"I began making a list of my successes every day. I was amazed to discover how much I manage to accomplish–despite my boss's comments to the contrary."

"Now that I have a mentor, I have someone who can see my capabilities and who suggests realistic, constructive ways of handling my boss."

"When I joined the planning committee for this year's technology conference, I had people from every department telling me what a good job I was doing."

HOW JOYCE TAKES BACK HER POWER

Let's check back in with Joyce to see how she takes back her personal power from Rhonda. . . .

As Joyce looks at her situation, she begins to construct a personal power recharging plan. She decides to restore her physical energy by contacting a former running partner and asking if they can begin to jog together again. She begins to repair her emotional state by focusing on her home environment. Joyce buys some new plants for her living room and repaints her bedroom a soothing shade of blue. She rebuilds her confidence by writing down her successes every day. On day one, she records: "Paul [one of Rhonda's copywriters] brought me a cup of coffee this morning. Completed second draft of information pamphlet. Got copy back from Rhonda with only four NOs."

By the end of the first week, Joyce has gone for a run, made some small improvements to her home, and started to feel better about the work she's doing for Rhonda. She's able see that the more she learns to accept her new boss and take care of herself, the better she feels about going to work.

DETACHMENT DON'TS

Just as there are certain activities that will help you detach, there are others that will exacerbate your situation.

The following is a list of detachment no-no's:

- **Don't increase your intake of caffeine, sugary drinks, or sugary foods at work.** These substances will heighten your mood swings and make you feel more frenetic.
- **Don't isolate.** When faced with a difficult boss/employee relationship, it's tempting to hide out and nurse your wounds rather than reach out and get support. Fight the urge to climb into bed and pull up the covers. Reach out instead.
- **Refrain from bad-mouthing, chronic complaining, or gossip.** It may feel good in the moment, but this kind of communication only gives more power to the problem. If you want to vent, find someone who will help find the solution.
- **Don't overuse the substance of your choice.** Whether it's alcohol, prescription drugs, television, video games, shopping, gambling, or another form of escape, too much of any mind-altering activity will create more problems—not less stress.

- **Try not to take out your workplace frustration on others.** Spouses, children, small pets, and in-laws are easy targets, but not the real culprit when the boss is giving you a hard time.
- **If you're feeling truly miserable, don't hesitate to seek professional help.** When working for a very difficult boss, it's not uncommon to experience depression, self-loathing, and destructive thoughts. Don't keep these feelings and thoughts to yourself. Find counsel and possibly medical support.

WORK IT OUT
Detach
Getting Out from Under Your Boss
Practice Acceptance

WHAT DO YOU HAVE TO ACCEPT ABOUT YOUR BOSS?
(WRITE DOWN WHAT YOU HAVE TO ACCEPT)

I accept the fact that _____

I accept the fact that_____

I accept the fact that_____

I accept the fact that_____

Taking Back Your Power

HOW WILL YOU RESTORE YOUR ENERGY AFTER WORK?
(CHECK AS MANY ACTIVITIES AS YOU LIKE)

❏ Exercise

❏ Mind/Body Remedies

❏ Medical Attention

❏ Healthy Escapes

❏ Sleep

HOW WILL YOU RESTORE YOUR ENERGY AT WORK?
(CHECK AS MANY ACTIVITIES AS YOU LIKE)

❏ Breathe

❏ H_2O Cure

❏ Scentsational

❏ Change Your Environment

❏ Reduce Your Body's Energy Spikes

HOW WILL YOU REPAIR YOUR EMOTIONAL STATE AFTER WORK?
(CHECK AS MANY ACTIVITIES AS YOU LIKE)

❏ Pursue a Passion or Pastime

❏ Reach Out and Reconnect

❏ Turn to a Pro

❏ Get on the Soul Train

❏ Clean House

❏ Get Inspired

HOW WILL YOU REPAIR YOUR EMOTIONAL STATE AT WORK?
(CHECK AS MANY AS YOU LIKE)

❏ Comic Relief

❏ Photo Therapy

❏ Game Break

❏ Take a Quick Reality Check

❏ Call a Time-out

❏ Lucky Charm

HOW WILL YOU REBUILD YOUR CONFIDENCE AFTER WORK?
(CHECK AS MANY AS YOU LIKE)

❏ Find a Mentor

❏ Make a List of Your Successes Every Day

❑ Spend Time with People Who Support You

❑ Make a Difference

**HOW WILL YOU REBUILD YOUR CONFIDENCE AT WORK?
(CHECK AS MANY AS YOU LIKE)**

❑ Workplace Proverbs

❑ Gratitude Inventory

❑ Aim for Small Achievements

❑ Find Ways to Be Useful Outside of Your Department

CHAPTER 4

Detaching from Twenty Boss Behaviors: Giving In Without Giving Over

I N THE LAST CHAPTER, we gave an overview of the process of detaching. In this chapter, we'll lay out specific strategies for detaching. Let's revisit our twenty boss behaviors and discover what detachment looks like in each situation. We'll offer specific attitudes and concrete actions anyone can take to effectively get out from under each difficult boss's thumb.

We recommend that you scan through this chapter to find the boss behavior that most closely matches your situation and read the accompanying summary and strategies. Or, if you would like, read through them all. The situations are classics; there are lessons that each of these challenging leader types have to teach us.

CATEGORY 1: HEAD GAME PLAYERS

These are the bosses who control the people who work for them through intimidation, mixed messages, and manipulation. Initially welcoming and positive about the contribution you can make to the company, Head Game bosses ultimately make it very difficult for you to succeed. Because these authority figures are extremely competitive, their games are designed to ensure that they always come out on top.

Your best bet is to become well versed in the specific head game that your boss practices.

- **Chronic Critics** find fault with everything you do.
- **Rule Changers** keep changing and rearranging what they originally decreed.
- **Yellers** explode without notice and say incriminating things about you.
- **Underminers** will set you up to fail by asking for help and then making it impossible for you to assist them.

Detaching from this brand of boss takes real diligence and skill. You have to identify and accept the specific head games that they play. Only then can you change your reaction and lessen the negative impact of their behavior.

Detaching from a Chronic Critic

WHAT YOU HAVE TO ACCEPT

1. You can never fully please this person.
2. Your boss must find the flaw, mistake, shortcoming, or imperfection in anything that you do.

Detaching from a Chronic Critic boss begins with accepting the fact that you are not going to change their faultfinding ways. Chronic Critics are perfectionists. They are on a quest for the unobtainable. The flip side is that they are as hard on themselves as they are on everyone else around them. You can do your best to get them to be less critical, but it will get you only more frustrated. This person *must* find the flaw in every situation. Your moment of freedom from a Chronic Critic comes when you can listen to your employer deliver yet another critique without feeling bad inside. Instead of reacting with anger, embarrassment, or humiliation, you take this person's verbal barbs in stride.

"Once I came to terms with the fact that my boss is a fundamentally negative person, I stopped trying to make him happy and put the focus back on doing my job."

"When I finally accepted that my boss must find fault with every project, I stopped taking her criticism to heart."

"It took a while, but after I realized that my supervisor truly was a Chronic Critic, I started to have compassion for him."

Suggestions for Taking Back Your Power

Over time, the constant faultfinding of a Chronic Critic can take a heavy toll on your confidence. To take back your power, it's best to focus on confidence-building activities.

AT WORK

1. **Aim for Small Personal Wins** The idea is to experience success on a micro level. Take one item from your to-do list that you've been putting off and complete it. It may involve researching a new product idea, completing an expense report, updating your résumé, or clearing off your desk. Whatever it is, give yourself credit for tackling it.

2. **Find Ways to Be Useful Outside of Your Department** While your critical boss can't give you credit, there are people outside of your department who will. To regain your confidence, look for opportunities to get involved with events, committees, task forces, or sports teams.

AFTER WORK

1. **Write Down Your Successes Every Day** So your boss can't acknowledge your successes at work. That doesn't mean they don't exist. Take a minute to write down three work-related accomplishments each day. Initially, this may seem difficult, but notice and list simple things, such as:
   • Helping a colleague solve a technical problem
   • Completing a project on time
   • Catching a bookkeeping error that saves the company money

2. **Spend Time with People Who Support You** When you work for a Chronic Critic, it's important to remind yourself of your positive qualities. This can be accomplished most easily by seeking the company of coworkers, alumni, and friends who know and believe in your capabilities.

Detaching from a Rule Changer

WHAT YOU HAVE TO ACCEPT

1. Your boss is not consistent; he or she does not want to be pinned down, hemmed in, or held to any fixed commitments.
2. The rules, plans, decisions, and policies under this person will always change.

Rule-changing bosses have a strong need for flexibility and adaptability in everything they do. These are the original individualists, who like to go with the flow according to the circumstances of their lives. A rule-changing boss may say, "Let's meet every Monday at ten a.m." You agree and prepare accordingly. Should your boss spot a better business opportunity during that time slot, however, your 10:00 a.m. meeting will be shelved without hesitation. When pressed for an explanation, this boss will say, "Something came up." Working for a Rule Changer can be frustrating and infuriating. Your moment of freedom comes when you stop expecting the decisions he or she makes to be carried out as planned.

"I've learned to insert the word *maybe* in front of every plan my boss makes. It helps."

"When I accepted that my boss was a Rule Changer, I started to write everything down in pencil."

"Now I understand that nothing is set in stone with my boss, so I arrive at work ready to adjust to his shifting priorities."

Suggestions for Taking Back Your Power

The most frustrating aspect of a rule-changing boss is the lack of control you feel over your work life. For that reason, we encourage you to focus on activities that repair your emotional state.

AT WORK

1. **Comic Relief** Find someone (colleague or friend) who is aligned in helping you relieve stress. Call on this person to provide humor, support, and perspective when your Rule Changer acts out.

2. **Take a Quick Reality Check** Each time your boss changes the rules, quickly write answers to the following questions: What's happening here? What are the facts? What's the boss's part? What's my part? What are my options?

AFTER WORK

1. **Pursue a Passion or Pastime** Whether it's reading meaningful books, returning to tennis, taking a writing course, or fly-fishing, do something you truly enjoy. It will give you a sense of control and mastery.
2. **Clean House** By putting the focus on improving your home environment in some way, you gain a sense of order in your life. You may want to declutter, redecorate, or renovate.

Detaching from a Yeller

WHAT YOU HAVE TO ACCEPT

1. Your boss has unresolved rage that you didn't cause, but that you also can't control.
2. He or she will continue to erupt at both predictable and unpredictable moments.

Of all of the Head Game bosses, Yellers are the most challenging to detach from. When this kind of authority figure explodes, the accusations that he or she flings seem very personal: "I'm surrounded by idiots!" "Can't you do anything right?" "I never should have hired you!" These verbal lashings are demeaning and painful—even if you aren't the direct recipient. The irony is that Yellers usually have no idea about the impact of their behavior. After the explosion, this kind of boss may apologize and assume that all is well. You walk away feeling beat-up and humiliated. Your moment of freedom with a Yeller comes when you are able to watch the flare-up and understand that it has nothing to do with you. The goal is to become a cool observer who is able to witness the event without absorbing the toxic energy.

"When I realized that my boss was going to explode no matter what, I actually started taking the outbursts less seriously."

"It took a while, but once I accepted that my manager yells on a regular basis, I began to watch her as if she were possessed—like a demon from a low-budget horror film."

"I used to put a lot of time and energy into preventing my boss from getting mad, but he always found something to be angry about. Now I put that same energy into looking for another job."

Suggestions for Taking Back Your Power

When a Yeller explodes, he or she releases both cutting words and negative energy. To take back your power from this kind of authority figure, it's important to both restore your energy and rebuild your confidence. We encourage you to refer back to Chapter 3 and look at all of the energy-restoring activities listed there. Utilize as many as possible. In the meantime, here are a few must-do ideas.

AT WORK

1. **Breathe** When working for a Yeller, it's natural to brace yourself and stop breathing in preparation for an attack. Your best antidote is to focus on taking deep, calm inhalations and long, gentle exhalations. Breathing deeply and gently for two minutes at a time will make a world of difference in how you feel.

2. **Workplace Proverbs** Post quotes or statements that inspire you in places where you can see them—especially before or after meetings with your boss—like the following from Eleanor Roosevelt: "No one can make you feel inferior without your consent."

AFTER WORK

1. **Exercise** Physical release is the goal here. Find any kind of exercise that suits you. Walk, run, work out at the gym, lift weights, play competitive sports, practice yoga, or do Pilates at either end of your day.

2. **Find a Mentor** Look for someone older and more experienced who can advise and guide you. A mentor will have the wisdom to help you take your volatile boss's behavior less personally. At the same time, this seasoned professional can give you tips for building your career—whether you continue working for your yelling boss or decide to move on.

Detaching from an Underminer

WHAT YOU HAVE TO ACCEPT

1. You are working for someone who will continue to give you responsibility and then take it away.
2. Your boss is incapable of truly trusting others to effectively carry out his or her plans.

Undermining bosses are often very charming and personable. Of all of the Head Game bosses, they are probably the least offensive. At the same time, working for this kind of boss can be extremely frustrating. When Underminers approach members of their staff asking for help, they have every intention of letting those individuals take on more responsibility. Problems arise shortly *after* the boss delegates a project, task, or responsibility to the care of someone else. He or she then gets nervous and takes back the controls without notification. If your boss is an Underminer, you know what it's like to have a special project assigned to you then reassigned to someone else. Your boss may override the very decisions that he or she asked you to make. Your manager may ask you to be in charge of the department during his or her absence, then "forget" to inform your colleagues.

Your moment of freedom from the frustration of working for an Underminer comes when you accept that your boss's fickle ways are due to his or her trust issues and need for control. This person's compulsive habit of asking for your help, then obstructing you, says nothing about your capabilities.

"Once I realized that my boss has serious trust issues, I stopped taking her habit of overriding my decisions personally."

"When my boss hands me a 'special project,' I now know to ask other members of the staff if they are 'special,' too."

"I've learned to take my boss's directives with a rock-size grain of salt."

Suggestions for Taking Back Your Power

Working for an undermining boss can literally be crazy-making. The tendency to say one thing and do another is very disconcerting. To take back your power, focus on the area of emotional repair.

AT WORK

1. **Comic Relief** The best way to handle the constant confusion and scrambling that result from working for an Underminer is to find a "partner in crime" who can listen, sympathize with your situation, and make you laugh. This person's job is to give you perspective and act as a sounding board regarding your well-intentioned-but-undermining boss.

2. **Take a Quick Reality Check** Whenever you feel as if your boss may be undermining you, take this pop quiz: What's happening here? What are the facts of the situation? What's the boss's part? What's my part? What are my options?

AFTER WORK

1. **Seek Professional Help** To deal effectively with this kind of boss over the long run, it's best to have professional guidance and support outside the workplace. You can join a support group, hire a coach, or go to a career counselor. The idea is to have a place where you can sort out the mixed signals that your boss gives.

2. **Get Inspired** To stay positive about your own career and repair your state of mind, it's always useful to read books, listen to music, watch motivating programs on TV, and go places that inspire you. Underminers unknowingly sabotage the people who work for them. Taking in positive images, fresh ideas, and hopeful messages will help alleviate the self-doubt and insecurity that get triggered under this style of management.

CATEGORY 2: BIG SHOTS AND MOTHER SUPERIORS

Detaching from Big Shots and Mother Superiors is difficult, but not impossible. Let's review the characters in this category.

- **"I'm Always Right"** bosses need to be considered infallible.
- **"You Threaten Me"** leaders take credit when it's not due.
- **Grandiose** authority figures can't see past their own egos.
- **Control Freaks** micromanage uncontrollably.

Each boss in this category is irritating from the perspective that you constantly have to service his or her ego. This second, unofficial job takes energy and self-discipline. It is humbling. The most important thing to accept with these authority figures is the fact that they must always be the top dog. This need prevents them from letting you truly excel or stand out on your own. At best, you can be one of their loyal disciples. If you threaten their sense of power and control, you quickly lose favor. The payoff with Big Shots and Mother Superiors is their willingness to train and teach the people who work for them.

Detaching from an "I'm Always Right" Boss

WHAT YOU HAVE TO ACCEPT

1. This person must believe that his or her ideas, opinions, decisions, and policies are always correct.
2. Consequently, your boss will never admit to being wrong.

Although an "infallible" boss may be charming at times, he or she is very challenging to work for. No one can be right all of the time. Working for someone who insists that his or her perspective is the only valid one can be frustrating and emotionally draining. While it may be tempting to judge this kind of boss as arrogant, pigheaded, or uncooperative, those labels won't help you address or improve the situation. Your moment of freedom comes when you accept that your boss is constitutionally incapable of admitting that he or she could be wrong.

"I quickly realized that if I wanted my boss to hear me, I had to start by agreeing with everything he said."

"My boss can do no wrong, and I let her think that's true."

"When I truly understood that my boss couldn't handle being wrong, I felt less defensive if he blamed a mistake on me."

Suggestions for Taking Back Your Power

Because you constantly have to swallow your ego and your pride with this kind of boss, it's important to take back your power by rebuilding your confidence.

AT WORK

1. **Find Ways to Be Useful Outside of Your Department** One way to get out from under the heavy-handed leadership of an Always Right boss is to venture outside of your department and find a project or event where you can participate, contribute, and be heard. It could be a task force, a company campaign (like going green), or a community-related event.

2. **Aim for Small Achievements** Small personal successes that have nothing to do with your boss will give you a sense of ownership and self-esteem. Set up a filing system, rearrange your workspace, take a new employee under your wing and act as a mentor.

AFTER WORK

1. **Find a Mentor** This could be a past boss, a college alumnus, a friend, or a family member who is older and successful. Spending time with someone who believes in your ability and encourages your professional growth will help combat self-doubt and provide constructive feedback regarding your work life.

2. **Make a Difference** Contributing your time to a group or cause that you care about puts your difficult situation in perspective. It also provides you with a specific venue for building relationships, displaying your skills, and feeling good about yourself. Coaching a Little League team, helping with a fund-raising car wash, participating in a com-

munity cleanup campaign—these and similar activities will give you a sense of accomplishment that you can take back to work.

Detaching from a "You Threaten Me" Boss

WHAT YOU HAVE TO ACCEPT

1. You can never outshine the boss.
2. Should you attract too much positive attention to yourself, your boss will take actions to hold you back.

This kind of boss feels threatened whenever employees receive recognition for individual accomplishments outside of his or her domain. It's okay when you land an account and the outside world attributes that win to the boss; it's not okay if the outside world gives you sole credit for the accomplishment. The rule is, "Do not take any credit for things that you accomplish under my leadership." Your moment of freedom comes when you understand that success with this person depends on making the boss (not you) look good.

"When I came to terms with the fact that my boss needs to be the star, I made it a point to share the credit for every successful project I completed."

"After I accepted that my boss truly feared anyone outshining her, I stopped pushing so hard for personal recognition."

"In order to be successful with my boss, I make sure that everything we do is in his best interest."

Suggestions for Taking Back Your Power

An easily threatened boss is very skilled at using his or her position to strip you of any credit for the successful results of your efforts. These individuals insist that the people who work for them would be nowhere without their leadership and the opportunities that they provide. For this reason, you want to focus on repairing your emotional state and rebuilding your confidence.

AT WORK

1. **Find Ways to Be Useful Outside of Your Department** If you feel squelched by your boss's fear of being overshadowed, go outside of the department and get involved in projects, committees, or task forces where you have permission to contribute and shine.

2. **Take a Quick Reality Check** The next time your boss says something that seems devaluing, competitive, or otherwise upsetting, ask yourself the following questions: What's happening here? What are the facts of the situation? What's the boss's part? What's my part? What are my options?

AFTER WORK

1. **Pursue a Passion or Pastime** Pick up or return to a hobby, from knitting to skydiving. The idea is to engage in something that you enjoy, where you can experience success without threatening your boss.

2. **Spend Time with People Who Support You** To reinforce positive feelings and boost self-confidence, seek out the company of colleagues, friends, classmates, and other people who think highly of you.

Detaching from a Grandiose Boss

WHAT YOU HAVE TO ACCEPT

1. Part of your job involves reinforcing your boss's ego with compliments, acknowledgment, and respectful treatment.
2. Your boss must be recognized as the best in any situation.

Grandiose bosses have the advantage of being fairly transparent. They make it very clear that they need and thrive upon compliments and flattery. Their egos require constant stroking. Because Grandiose bosses are emotionally needy, listening to them and working for them can be exhausting—both physically and emotionally. Your moment of freedom with this kind of authority figure comes when you accept the fact that before you can get down to business, you must pay tribute to your boss's wealth of knowledge and self-proclaimed greatness. Only then can your boss listen to your concerns.

"I've built in listening to my boss's tales of glory as part of my work-day. I just added 'listening to stories' to my job description."

"If I want to make a point with my boss, I first take a moment to mention her undisputed expertise in the field."

"It became easier for me to deal with my manager when I willingly set aside the first half hour of every meeting for his war stories."

Suggestions for Taking Back Your Power

Because Grandiose bosses are energy vampires, your best approach to taking back your power is through energy-restoring activities.

AT WORK

1. **Breathe** Sometimes just remembering to breathe in and out deeply and gently can recharge your batteries and give you a sense of relief.
2. **Reduce Your Energy Spikes** The more balanced you can keep your energy, the better you'll be able to handle your boss's neediness. Drinks and snacks that are high in sugar, caffeine, or fat will rev you up, then bring you down. Stick to healthy snacks and drinks—substances that won't aggravate your situation.

AFTER WORK

1. **Exercise** The more you engage in activities such as walking, running, swimming, sports, or yoga, the more energized and relaxed you will feel.
2. **Hit the Sack** It takes energy to listen to your boss's stories and patience to deal with his or her immense ego. Instead of falling asleep at your desk, make sure to get a good night's sleep at home.

Detaching from a Control Freak

WHAT YOU HAVE TO ACCEPT

1. Your boss has a very hard time trusting anyone to carry out his or her directives properly.
2. No decisions can be made without the boss's direct approval.

This kind of boss is plagued by his or her own perfectionism. Because the fear of making a mistake is so great, these individuals tend to obsess over every decision. Their need for control is not a reflection on you. Control Freaks don't like surprises and can't tolerate the notion that anything is happening within their territory that they aren't aware of. The prospect of losing control makes this kind of boss extremely anxious. While it may be time-consuming to keep your boss constantly updated, informed, and involved with your activities, Control Freaks are not the worst bosses to work for. Over time it is possible to win your boss's partial trust. He or she may eventually allow you to perform certain tasks without interference. Your moment of freedom with a Control Freak boss comes when you accept that he or she must be informed and alerted regarding every action you take.

"The day I understood that my boss's controlling methods were an attempt to stave off anxiety, I was able to fill out the detailed report forms without feeling resentful."

"In response to my boss's need to know exactly what I'm doing on behalf of his department, I've learned to be more methodical and detail-oriented."

"When I go to my boss regarding a decision that needs to be made, I always offer my approach to the problem. My boss is learning to trust my judgment."

Suggestions for Taking Back Your Power

Because they need to know everything that's going on, Control Freak bosses are high-maintenance. Taking back your power requires a commitment to restoring your energy and repairing your emotional state.

AT WORK

1. **Take a Game Break** Take a few minutes out to play an online de-stressor game. A few minutes devoted to this healthy distraction may help to relieve your immediate frustrations with a very controlling boss.
2. **Comic Relief** Sometimes the best antidote to this kind of manager is to see the humor in your situation. See if you can find a coworker who can serve as a stress reliever and make you laugh.

AFTER WORK

1. **Exercise** Physical activity after work (running, walking, swimming, biking, dancing, competitive sports, or yoga) is always a great tool for clearing out the frustrations of the day and purging negative energy from your body. Exercise can also be an area where you feel a sense of control and mastery.
2. **Healthy Escapes** Restore your energy by taking quick getaways to favorite places in nature, quiet retreats, or cultural activities that you enjoy.

CATEGORY 3: LINE CROSSERS

It's normal to look to your boss for guidance, leadership, and direction. It's confusing when that same person blurs the professional lines between the two of you. As you'll recall, this is the lineup of Line Crossers:

- **Love-Struck** bosses can't manage their own emotions.
- **Calculating Confidants** have a hidden agenda.
- **Tell-Alls** make you their captive audience.
- **Liar, Liars** can implicate you in their webs of deception.

Believe it or not, Line Crossers are often oblivious to how inappropriate their behavior is. Whether you find yourself deflecting the boss's affections, covering up your manager's lies, or holding your supervisor's hand during a messy divorce, these individuals will often act surprised if you call them on their line-crossing conduct. In addition, there is little training for the correct way to set limits within these unwanted circumstances. How do you gently reject the department head whose heart flutters when you walk into the room? What do you say when your leader tells a blatant lie, then asks you to cover for him or her? Detaching from Line Crossers takes courage and emotional restraint. You want to clearly identify and acknowledge the inappropriate behavior to yourself first. Eventually, you can craft a strategy for fending off the boss without harming your career.

Detaching from a Love-Struck Boss

WHAT YOU HAVE TO ACCEPT

1. You cannot control your boss's feelings of affection for you.
2. You will eventually have to set a limit.

The first thing to understand about a Love-Struck boss is that, whatever is happening, you did not cause it. On a rare occasion, the two of you may be soul mates whose lives are destined to come together. In general, however, Love-Struck bosses are emotionally hungry and professionally dangerous. Their longing gazes are an attempt to receive emotional and sexual nourishment from you. While it may be flattering to receive this kind of attention, deciding how to manage the relationship can be overwhelming. Your moment of freedom with a Love-Struck boss comes when you accept the fact that this person has strong feelings for you, and those feelings don't have to be acted upon.

"After I accepted that my boss was interested in me, I simply said, 'I don't mix business with pleasure.'"

"It really helped me to find out that my boss has had serial crushes on new employees. I was just the most recent arrival."

Suggestions for Taking Back Your Power

Dealing with a Love-Struck boss can be very confusing and emotionally draining. To take back your power, you want to focus on activities that help you repair your emotional state.

AT WORK

1. **Take a Quick Reality Check** The next time you feel uncomfortable
   with your boss's amorous attention, ask yourself the following questions: What's happening here? What are the facts? What's my boss's
   part? What's my part? What are my options?
2. **Call a Time-out** If emotions run high, excuse yourself and go to a
   private place until you are able to cool off.

AFTER WORK

1. **Reach Out and Reconnect** Spend time with friends, family, and colleagues who energize you. You want to know that you have healthy,
   stimulating relationships and a personal life outside of work so that
   you don't feel trapped in your confusing situation.
2. **Get on the Soul Train** Make sure you stay connected to your values.
   Whether you engage in prayer, meditation, or religious services, a return to your core ethics and values will help you make the best decisions regarding the boss.

Detaching from a Calculating Confidant

WHAT YOU HAVE TO ACCEPT

1. These bosses will use your personal information for their own professional gain.
2. Your boss does not truly care about your personal problems.

When faced with an authority figure who appears personable,
charming, and easy to talk to, it's hard to believe that his or her hidden agenda is to obtain information that gives him or her the upper
hand. These are the bosses who present themselves as concerned,
parental, and wise. No matter how busy they are, they always have
time to talk. Calculating Confidants don't single out just you. They
usually have the goods on a number of people. Your moment of
freedom comes when you accept that your boss cannot be trusted
with personal information. You can then continue to be friendly

toward the boss without offering any potentially damaging details of your private life.

"When I accepted the fact that my boss misused private information, I learned to describe my personal life in vague, positive terms."

"I refrained from telling my boss anything about my divorce until it was complete, because I knew he might use it against me in my review."

"At a casual dinner after work, my boss revealed intimate details of a coworker's life to everyone else at the table. I realized that she could do the same thing to me."

Suggestions for Taking Back Your Power

It takes extra effort to detach from a Calculating Confidant. To avoid telling your boss too much, you need to restore your energy at work and repair your emotional state after hours.

AT WORK

1. **Breathe** Breathing gently and deeply will help you get centered and collect your thoughts before meetings with the boss.
2. **Reduce Your Energy Spikes** Calculating Confidants have a knack for catching people at their vulnerable moments and getting them to spill the beans. When dealing with this kind of boss, you want to stay even-keeled physically—not revved up, tired, or drained.

AFTER WORK

1. **Reach Out and Reconnect** Cultivating and maintaining relationships outside of work will guarantee that you have people to safely confide in—rather than your boss.
2. **Seek Professional Help** If you feel overwhelmed by personal problems and need additional support, enlist the help of a paid professional, rather than confessing your difficulties to the boss.
3. **Exercise** and **Mind/Body Remedies** The best defense with a Calculating Confidant is to reinforce your mental and physical health so that you can regain your sense of power. For this reason, exercise and mind/body practices such as massage, meditation, and yoga can be extremely beneficial.

Detaching from a Tell-All

WHAT YOU HAVE TO ACCEPT

1. Your boss is self-centered and obsessed with his or her own problems.
2. Sharing stories about personal dramas is this person's way of seducing you into taking care of him or her.

When you first start working for a Tell-All boss, his or her friendliness and warmth may be a welcome change from more formal authority figures in the workplace. Very soon, however, you find out more than you need to know about many aspects of your boss's complicated and dramatic life. Health concerns, extramarital affairs, family dramas, financial issues—listening to the sordid details of each personal problem becomes part of your daily routine. Tell-All bosses feel overwhelmed and distracted by the circumstances of their lives. They want the people who work for them to compensate for them on the job so that they can focus on their emotional distress. Your moment of freedom with a Tell-All boss comes when you accept the fact that these dramas will never go away, and you don't have to compensate for your boss at work.

"Once I realized that my boss had 'emergencies' on a regular basis, I stopped working overtime to cover for her absences."

"At one point I decided that just because my manager had many personal problems, I didn't have to make them mine."

"I've learned to listen to the drama and say, 'I'm sure it will all work out.'"

Suggestions for Taking Back Your Power

Tell-Alls are energy drainers. To take back your power, you want to focus on restoring your energy and recharging yourself.

AT WORK

1. **Breathe** Breathing deeply and gently will help you stay centered in the midst of the Tell-All's emotional storm. The more grounded you are, the less likely you are to get sucked into the Tell-All's drama.
2. **Take a Quick Reality Check** The next time your boss dumps his or her personal problems at your feet, stop and refer to your job description. Does it include "emotional hand-holder"? If not, try asking yourself the following questions: What's happening here? What are the facts? What's my boss's part? What's my part? What are my options?

AFTER WORK

1. **Exercise** Because Tell-Alls are serious energy drainers, exercise is one of the primary ways for you to recharge and reenergize.
2. **Hit the Sack** In addition to working out, playing sports, or engaging in some other form of physical activity, it's important to restore your mind and body with a good night's sleep. Try going to bed at a decent hour. Make sure you have the full amount of slumber that your body needs.

Detaching from a Liar, Liar

WHAT YOU HAVE TO ACCEPT

1. You work for someone who feels comfortable altering the truth.
2. Your boss is not trustworthy.

If you are an honest person who works hard to do the right thing, it's probably hard for you to believe that certain bosses are comfortable making false promises and stretching the truth. Extreme lying bosses are capable of cheating and stealing from the company as well. Whether they are truth-stretchers or outright thieves, these individuals have a different relationship to truth-telling than you do. For Liar, Liar bosses, all truth is relative. The most important thing is getting what they want. Once you discover that your boss has mendacious tendencies, you may have a hard time continuing to show up for work with a good attitude.

It's common to lose respect and feel trapped in your job. Your moment of freedom comes when you accept that you work for someone who stretches the truth and you cannot trust what he or she says.

"I learned to brace myself at client presentations because I knew my boss would guarantee things we couldn't deliver."

"After I met with my boss, I went around the department and conducted a fact-check regarding everything he told me."

"I've come to terms with the fact that part of my job is apologizing to customers for the false promises my boss makes to them."

Suggestions for Taking Back Your Power

AT WORK

1. **Breathe** It's common to tighten up and hold your breath around someone whose behavior disturbs you. To stay centered and calm, remember to take several deep, gentle breaths— inhale and exhale— before and after interactions with your boss.
2. **Take a Game Break** The idea here is to distract your mind and relax your body. Find a game that you can play for a few minutes to calm your system down.
3. **Photo Therapy** When faced with a Liar, Liar boss, you can remember what truly matters to you by referring to photos of friends, family, and beautiful places that inspire you.

AFTER WORK

1. **Exercise** Physical activity is a constructive tool for working out your frustrations and feeling more in control of your destiny. Run, walk, play sports. Do something that clears your mind, releases toxins, and puts you in a better state.
2. **Seek Professional Help** or **Find a Mentor** Dishonest bosses tend to bend the truth and tamper with reality. Working with a psychological counselor, a career coach, or a mentor can help you decipher the truth of your situation. You can receive guidance and support for dealing with your unethical leader.

CATEGORY 4: AMBIVALENT LEADERS

Ambivalent leaders don't like getting their hands dirty. They may like the status of managing people, but they do not want to handle any interpersonal difficulties between their employees. Ambivalent leaders are skilled avoiders of confrontation, disagreement, argument, and other forms of conflict. The roster of reluctant leaders includes:

- **Sacred Cows** don't take action and won't get fired.
- **Checked Out** bosses are preoccupied with non-work-related personal matters.
- **Spineless** bosses can't defend anyone, including themselves.
- **Artful Dodgers** avoid any interactions that could tarnish their reputation.

The bosses in this club are friendly and congenial, but unable to protect, guide, or stand up for their staff. Detaching from this brand of boss requires accepting that these individuals will not do anything that makes them emotionally or professionally uncomfortable.

Detaching from a Sacred Cow

WHAT YOU MUST ACCEPT

1. Your boss may not be competent, but he or she isn't going anywhere.
2. If you challenge the Sacred Cow's authority, you will lose.

Most people who work for this kind of boss spend a lot of time in disbelief. They ask themselves: How did my boss get promoted to this level? Why doesn't someone fire this person? How does anyone get away with doing so little?

While these questions are understandable, they do little to address your situation. The truth is that most Sacred Cows have one great skill—they know how to foster connections and build loyalty with people in higher positions. It could be that your boss worked for the company during its earliest stages. Perhaps he or she is a distant relative to an important executive. Your Sacred Cow boss may have bailed someone out in a time of need. Whatever happened in the past, this person is now secure. Your moment of freedom comes when you accept the fact that your boss isn't going anywhere. For you to succeed, you'll have to figure out how to work with your protected leader.

"Once I realized that my boss was a permanent fixture at the company, I had to let go of all hopes that he would be fired."

"I've gotten good at pushing things through by acting as if I respect my boss and value her input."

"Because I give my boss full credit for my work, he's letting me do more and more."

Suggestions for Taking Back Your Power

Focus on restoring your energy and rebuilding self-confidence.

AT WORK

1. **Breathe** Working with a Sacred Cow is often extremely frustrating, so taking time throughout the day to sit calmly and focus on breathing in and out for a few minutes can make a big difference.
2. **Aim for Small Achievements** Because this kind of boss often holds up your bigger projects, aiming for small achievements such as clearing out your e-mail box or completing an expense report can give you a sense of accomplishment and control.

AFTER WORK

1. **Exercise** To release tension and pent-up irritation, engage in exercise three to four times a week.
2. **Spend Time with People Who Support You** Friends, family members, and former colleagues who think highly of you can help you remember your capabilities and talents.

Detaching from a Checked Out Boss

WHAT YOU HAVE TO ACCEPT

1. Your boss is preoccupied with non-work-related personal matters.
2. He or she is not capable of managing you or anyone else effectively.

There are many factors that might cause a boss to "check out." Sometimes, his or her preoccupation and lack of awareness are triggered by a personal crisis—a life-threatening illness, the birth of a child, a death in the family, marital difficulties, or a chemical addiction. Sometimes, the individual has been absent mentally and emotionally for a long period of time. Whatever the situation, it can be very distressing for you, the employee. While your boss misses meetings and looks at you with a vacant stare, you feel the anxiety of working for an oblivious leader. What's more, nothing you do or say can shake your preoccupied boss out of his or her stupor. Your moment of freedom comes when you realize that you have to function without your boss's guidance or attention. For the time being, you work in a leaderless environment.

"Because my boss was often MIA during his messy divorce, I just started making decisions without him."

"After my boss's husband died, I realized that she was too depressed to make decisions of any kind. I started sending reports letting her know what I was doing and sought guidance outside of my department."

"When I realized that our manager was truly checked out, I organized a departmental meeting where we assigned specific responsibilities to each member of the staff."

Suggestions for Taking Back Your Power

The primary experience when working for someone who is checked out is neglect. Your boss is too preoccupied with personal problems to give you the time and attention you need. To take back your personal power, begin by paying attention to your physical and emotional well-being. Focus on restoring and repairing yourself.

AT WORK

1. **Breathe** Though your boss may be absent, you don't want to check out as well. When you start your day, take a few minutes to catch your breath—through deep and gentle inhalations and exhalations. Return to breathing exercises throughout the day when you feel wound up and frustrated.
2. **Take a Quick Reality Check** This will help you decipher what is happening and figure out what your options are. Your best option

must be not to feel victimized by your boss's absence, but to take control.

AFTER WORK

1. **Seek Professional Help** Sign on a career counselor, a mentor, or a coach. Get some professional guidance on how to handle your situation.
2. **Healthy Escapes** Because you've taken on additional responsibilities that you didn't bargain for, it's important to give yourself breaks in settings that relax and inspire you. It may be a bike ride, a drive to the beach, a weekend away with a friend. Find small ways to restore your energy and return to work refreshed.

Detaching from a Spineless Boss

WHAT YOU HAVE TO ACCEPT

1. Your boss is not capable of defending anyone—including him- or herself.
2. This person will never enforce a rule or policy that may incur someone else's wrath.

This kind of boss generates a great deal of unhappiness and anger among the staff. Why? Because employees who work for a Spineless leader know that their boss's inability to take a stand produces numerous unresolved problems and a chaotic work environment. For example, if a customer unfairly rails against a member of the staff, the Spineless boss will not intervene, defend the employee, and settle the dispute. Instead, he or she will either watch the interaction passively or avoid it altogether. Staff members learn that no one is protected, and the workplace is unsafe. Your moment of freedom comes when you stop expecting the boss to come to your defense or stand up to anyone else's unruly behavior.

"Although my boss is a nice person, I've learned that I have to settle any workplace disputes on my own."

"It used to drive me crazy when my coworker never got reprimanded for being late. Now I see that my manager isn't capable of enforcing even the simplest rules."

"Whenever I want a raise, I have to supply my boss with the ammunition and lobby for myself on the side."

Suggestions for Taking Back Your Power

Because your boss can't defend you or take a stand on any important issue, you'll tend to experience a great deal of anger and frustration. To regain a sense of control, concentrate your efforts on activities that release the anger and strengthen your self-esteem. Focus on restoring your energy and repairing your emotional state.

AT WORK

1. **Change Your Environment** The next time your Spineless boss fails to take a stand, try changing your environment. It's a constructive way to cool off in the heat of the moment. Whether it's going to the restroom and splashing cold water on your face or taking a brisk walk outside of the office, removing yourself from your workspace for a few minutes and shifting your energy will help.

2. **Comic Relief** To gain a better perspective and relieve stress, it's great to have a friend or colleague who can make you laugh. Find someone you can trust to see the humor in any situation. Draw on each other at those moments when your boss's behavior doesn't seem very funny at all.

AFTER WORK

1. **Seek Professional Help** It's very hard to know how to deal effectively on your own with this kind of boss. A career counselor, life coach, or mentor can offer valuable experience and advice regarding the best way to achieve your career goals in spite of your boss.

2. **Mind/Body Remedies** Massage, yoga, acupuncture, and meditation all help relieve stress. The idea is to get your energy back in balance so that you can handle your boss's wishy-washy behavior through strategy, not anger and frustration.

Detaching from an Artful Dodger

WHAT YOU HAVE TO ACCEPT

1. Your boss will always avoid delivering any kind of information that may tarnish his or her image.
2. Underneath the friendly exterior lies a calculating and manipulative person.

It takes a while to uncover most Artful Dodgers. These bosses present themselves as refined, caring, charming, and ingratiating. You learn about the dark side of this authority figure only when you are informed, through a second party, that he or she is unhappy with some aspect of your performance. Initially, the negative feedback is both surprising and disorienting. "Isn't this the same leader who just told me what a stellar job I'm doing?" You'll become further confused when your employer acts as if there's nothing wrong the next time you meet. Your moment of freedom with an Artful Dodger comes when you accept the fact that he or she is incapable of being truly honest with you (or anyone else). Out of the need to be respected and admired, these authority figures will withhold any news or feedback that could tarnish their perfectly crafted image.

"It took a while, but I eventually realized that my boss was incapable of delivering honest feedback. I now go to her second in command to find out the truth."

"I enjoy my manager's positive spin on everything, but when I want to know where I really stand, he's not going to 'fess up."

"Every time our executive director sends me to deliver bad news to an unsuspecting staff member, I accept the fact that part of my job is acting as the bad cop."

Suggestions for Taking Back Your Power

This person has a way of tampering with your reality and distorting the truth. While his or her words sound positive and appreciative, you grow to suspect that behind the pleasant veneer lurks judgment and unspoken criticism. To combat the effects of an Artful Dodger manipulation, engage in any activity that repairs your emotional state.

AT WORK

1. **Comic Relief** With an Artful Dodger boss, you want to keep your sense of humor and perspective alive. Look for a friend or colleague who seems to have a good grasp on reality and takes life's blows with a grain of salt. Turn to that person anytime you feel confused or disturbed by your boss's shifty behavior.
2. **Photo Therapy** Photos of family, friends, and favorite places or trips offer an important visual reminder of the things that really matter—no matter what is happening at work.

AFTER WORK

1. **Pursue a Passion or Pastime** Hobbies such as gardening, fishing, antiquing, or painting provide a venue for enjoyment and success outside of work.
2. **Get on the Soul Train** Prayer, meditation, reading, or religious services can offer spiritual comfort and a fresh outlook regarding your situation.

CATEGORY 5: DELICATE CIRCUMSTANCES

As workplace diversity increases, the number of delicate circumstances that can potentially crop up between a boss and an employee also rises. There's a good chance that you could work for someone much younger than you. Perhaps your boss is of a different race, gender, culture, or religion. A former friend and colleague may jump to manager status—putting a strain on your relationship. Whatever the circumstance, detaching from it requires a willingness to go beyond your comfort zone in dealing with one of the following bosses:

- **Junior** may not value your experience.
- **Former Colleague** treats you differently because the balance of power has changed.
- **Unconscious Discriminator** unintentionally expresses bias.
- **Persecutor** targets and torments you.

Detaching from a Junior Boss

WHAT YOU HAVE TO ACCEPT

1. Although your boss is young and inexperienced, he or she has valuable skills that you don't possess.
2. Your boss may not appreciate or value your years of experience.

Junior bosses are usually fairly new to management and might feel as if they have a great deal to prove. While older employees may be alarmed at their manager's obvious lack of experience, a Junior boss may feel equally intimidated by the prospect of managing someone twice his or her age. The result is an awkward relationship where both parties have trouble understanding or appreciating what the other party is bringing to the workplace table. Your moment of freedom with a Junior boss comes when you can accept the fact that you're working for someone who has different values, expectations, and skills than you do. While you may have more life experience, your manager may have more ease with technology and the most current approaches to solving workplace problems.

"It took a while, but I eventually grew to appreciate my young boss's facility with technology. Instead of resisting her instruction, I've learned to value her knowledge."

"The more I accept my boss and appreciate his energetic leadership, the more he seems interested in my experience."

"When my boss says something inappropriate, I write it off to his lack of experience."

Suggestions for Taking Back Your Power

Focus on repairing your emotions and rebuilding your confidence.

AT WORK

1. **Find Ways to Be Useful Outside of Your Department** While your younger boss may have a hard time recognizing your value, you can build successes in other ways. Venture outside of your department

and assist with projects, events, or conferences where your efforts can be recognized and appreciated.

2. **Photo Therapy** or **Lucky Charm** Whether it's a picture of the people who matter most or a lucky talisman that gives you strength, draw on these symbolic images for inner strength and reassurance.

AFTER WORK

1. **Reach Out and Reconnect** Take time to spend time with people your own age. As an antidote to the negative bias you may feel directed toward your own age group, relish the experience, wisdom, and humor of friends and colleagues who share cultural references.

2. **Make a Difference** Contributing your time and energy to causes you care about reminds you that you have skills, information, and ideas that can benefit others. You are still a vital member of society.

Detaching from a Former Colleague

WHAT YOU HAVE TO ACCEPT

1. Your former relationship with this person will never return.
2. Your colleague's new position requires that he or she hold you accountable.

It's common to be happy and excited for a colleague who receives a promotion. It isn't until he or she steps into the new position that you experience the personal ramifications of this kind of change. Interactions with your colleague-turned-boss remain cordial, but less chummy. Your former associate is less accessible now for casual chats and friendly exchanges. No longer one of the rank and file, he or she is not able to joke, gossip, or socialize with you in the same way. What's more, your old friend/new boss may have to address performance issues with you—putting an additional strain on the relationship. The primary experience for employees whose colleagues become their managers is loss. Your moment of freedom comes when you truly accept that the balance of power between the two of you has changed.

"I had to learn to schedule appointments to speak with someone who used to hang out at my cubicle on a regular basis."

"It took me a while, but I've grown to appreciate that my former colleague shoulders more responsibility (and pressure) than I do."

"We eventually found a way to be friends outside of work by practicing 'Don't ask; don't tell,' when it comes to the office."

Suggestions for Taking Back Your Power

The toughest part of a former colleague becoming your boss is the loss of peer camaraderie. What once was a comfortable relationship now has restrictions. To fill the void, focus on repairing your emotional state. Take steps to expand your circle of friends and adjust to the new reality.

AT WORK

1. **Take a Quick Reality Check** This fast mental exercise can take the emotional sting out of any situation where your former colleague treats you differently because of his or her new position. Ask yourself the following questions: What's happening here? What are the facts of the situation? What's the boss's part? What's my part? What are my options?

2. **Call a Time-out** When you feel your emotions running high and you're tempted to yell at your former colleague, take a moment to cool off by calling a time-out. Go to a quiet place, take a few deep breaths, and calm down.

AFTER WORK

1. **Reach Out and Reconnect** When you've lost a good workplace friend, you'll need to fill the gap by building new friendships outside of work and reinforcing current relationships on the job.

2. **Pursue a Passion or Pastime** While you watch your friend advance on the work front, you may want to progress in other areas of your life. Is there a skill you'd like to acquire, a language you'd like to learn, or an interest you want to resurrect? Take steps to make it happen.

Detaching from an Unconscious Discriminator

WHAT YOU HAVE TO ACCEPT

1. Your boss is unintentionally treating you unfairly.
2. He or she is uncomfortable with the differences between the two of you.

Most people approach a new job hoping to be judged by their performance—not their size, shape, race, nationality, or religion. When a boss treats you unfairly due to his or her unconscious prejudice, it can trigger strong feelings of anger, sadness, and shame. The temptation is to take this person's insensitive behavior personally and want to attack back. While mounting an aggressive counterattack may be tempting, it will not improve your situation. Your moment of freedom with an Unconscious Discriminator comes when you can see your boss as misinformed, not malicious.

"I knew my boss was uneasy about my religion, so I brought her a sampling of holiday sweets that she really enjoyed."

"When my boss made an insensitive remark about my country, I chalked it up to his lack of knowledge."

"Once I got the sense that my boss equated heavy people with laziness, I made it a point to dress professionally and produce impeccable work."

Suggestions for Taking Back Your Power

No matter how innocent the infraction, it's painful to be the recipient of someone's discriminating behavior. To take back your power, you will want to draw on actions that repair your emotional state and rebuild your confidence.

AT WORK

1. **Workplace Proverbs** In the face of prejudicial treatment, the wisdom of others can offer consolation and perspective. You can draw on quotes you've already posted or find new statements online.
2. **Photo Therapy** and **Lucky Charm** Because Unconscious Discrimina-

tors inadvertently put you down, you may want to use photographs or a lucky charm as reminders of what is important to you. Whether it's a picture of your kids, a religious symbol that you wear, or an inherited family heirloom, these items can provide comfort, connectedness, and strength.

AFTER WORK

1. **Spend Time with People Who Support You** It's important to have a support network. Instead of withdrawing or isolating in reaction to discrimination, spend time with the people who will honor your character, background, and appearance.
2. **Get on the Soul Train** Engaging in spiritual practices—prayer, meditation, reading literature, or attending religious services—can alleviate feelings of persecution. Eventually you can see the bigger picture and develop compassion for your misinformed boss.

Detaching from a Persecutor

WHAT YOU HAVE TO ACCEPT

1. For reasons you may not understand, your boss has decided to target you as a recipient of negative feedback.
2. There is very little you can do to change this person's mind.

Individuals who work for persecuting bosses are in a difficult situation from the onset. Even if you receive cordial treatment early on, you may do or say something that suddenly turns the tables. It may be a statement you make in an e-mail, a question you pose at a meeting, an offhand remark that your boss misinterprets, or a perceived slight of some other kind. This kind of boss is a tinderbox of unspoken expectations waiting to flare up in disappointment. While you may not know it, you aren't the first person that he or she has targeted for negative treatment, and you won't be the last. Your moment of freedom comes when you realize that your boss singles out and persecutes individual employees on a regular basis. You are simply the most recent target. This individual has an unconscious need to attack and derail others at work.

"At first I kept trying to figure out what I'd done wrong. Then I realized that my boss simply needed a workplace punching bag and I was it."

"The head of HR warned me that my manager's department had the highest turnover in the company. Now I understand why."

"After a particularly rough staff meeting, a coworker approached me and whispered, 'I was the target last month. Ignore it, and he'll move on to someone else.' "

Suggestions for Taking Back Your Power

Persecuting bosses affect their employees on every level—physical, mental, and emotional. To take back control, you may need to draw on tools from all three of the personal power areas—restoring your energy, repairing your emotional state, and rebuilding your confidence.

AT WORK

1. **Breathe** Being the target of an authority figure's negative attention is extremely uncomfortable. A normal reaction is to walk around in a state of constant fear, frustration, and agitation. To keep your feet on the ground, make it a point to help your body calm down by breathing. Whenever you can, remember to inhale and exhale, gently and deeply—at your desk, during meetings, and traveling to and from the job.

2. **Take a Quick Reality Check** If your persecuting boss gives you the cold shoulder or speaks to you in a derogatory manner during a meeting, help yourself recover from the interaction by answering the following questions: What's happening here? What are the facts of the situation? What's the boss's part? What's my part? What are my options?

3. **Call a Time-out** Whenever the pressure of being the target of your boss's disdain becomes too great, give yourself a break. Walk to another floor of the building, go outside for a moment, or find a private room where you can collect your thoughts and catch your breath.

AFTER WORK

1. **Exercise** There is nothing like exercise to purge toxins. If you work for a Persecutor, you can use physical movement—walking, running, biking, aerobics, contact sports, and other activities—as a healthy release of the negative energy you absorb from the boss.

2. **Seek Professional Help** Persecuting bosses tend to do a number on their employees' self-esteem and self-confidence. You'll wonder what you did to deserve such treatment. You may spend hours trying to unravel the mystery. To help you find your professional bearings, enroll the assistance of a counselor, career coach, or human resources expert. This experienced guide can offer valuable emotional support and help you map out a strategy for moving ahead.

3. **Find a Mentor** In tough times, it's especially helpful to have a role model and guide who can understand your workplace challenges and give you wise counsel for building you career. Look to alumni groups, professional associations, or older family friends for strategy and support.

SECTION III

Depersonalize

Reader's Alert: The next two chapters provide more tips on overcoming your toxic boss relationship. Be sure to take the Boss Baggage Assessment in chapter 5 to determine how your behavior may be helping or hurting your situation.

After that, find your specific profile in chapter 6 to find out how to depersonalize from your specific boss.

CHAPTER 5

It's Not About You . . . or Is It?: Assessing Your Boss Baggage Profile

L ET'S START WITH a quick recap. You've now become familiar with the first two D's in our Four D's process. You know how to **Detect** that you're in a toxic boss/employee situation and find which phase of the relationship you're in. After reading about the twenty top boss behaviors that drive us bonkers, you've also identified the particular boss profile that's causing you pain.

In Chapters 3 and 4, you studied how to **Detach** from your boss. You saw the importance of accepting your boss's behavior—rather than insisting that he or she change. You also established a personalized action plan, based on the specific boss behaviors that you're grappling with. This plan helps you regain a sense of personal power by restoring your energy, repairing your emotional state, and rebuilding your confidence. Now that you've been able to detach and gain some emotional distance from your boss, you can move to the third D, **Depersonalize.**

By *depersonalize*, we mean learning to take the boss's behavior less personally. To begin depersonalizing, you have to understand one very important fact: no matter how offensive, insulting, infuriating, or generally inappropriate your boss's behavior and remarks may seem, you are not the first person who has experienced this and you won't be the last. *It's not about you.*

When, for example, a Chronic Critic finds fault with everything you do, it's not because you are hopelessly flawed. It's because this person is engaging in what he or she does best—zeroing in on the error, mistake, or flaw in every situation. If you work for a Sacred Cow who blocks your ideas at every turn, it's not because your plans and projects lack merit. Your cautious boss simply fears taking *any* action that could attract negative attention. You are one in a long line of employees who've been stymied by your stonewalling superior's risk-averse, do-nothing management style.

Depersonalizing can ease the sting of the hurtful words or harmful actions that your challenging manager cluelessly inflicts on you. The more you can see the other person's conduct from an objective viewpoint, the less power it has over you.

To depersonalize effectively, you have to understand two important points.

1. You did not cause your boss's behavior. It existed long before you entered the scene.
2. This person's actions may be triggering your worst fears.

Ironically, the Depersonalize step involves a good deal of introspection. In this chapter, we're going to introduce an extremely valuable tool for self-reflection that will help you depersonalize your relationship with any authority figure whose behavior causes you distress. This tool gives you crucial information for understanding and managing any "bad boss" situation. It will help you uncover what you need from the people who hold authority over you at work and clarify why your boss's behavior gets under your skin. But before we start, let's go over some basic concepts.

BOSS BAGGAGE

Everyone comes to the boss/employee relationship with a certain amount of baggage. Baggage isn't all good and it isn't all bad. It's the historical, habitual way we relate to, have expectations of, and harbor fears about someone who can make decisions that affect us. Wherever we go, we carry our Boss Baggage with us.

You started packing your Boss Baggage many years ago during your formative years as a child. At that time, "the boss" consisted of your parents, your teachers, grandparents, babysitters, clergymen and clergy-women, and anyone else who served as an authority figure in your life.

Through those relationships, you learned certain ways of behaving and you probably adopted certain ideas about yourself. If, for example, you were a quiet child who was rewarded for needing little attention, you may have decided that you get the best results when you stay out of the way and accomplish things on your own. Today, you may relate to any new authority by maintaining a low profile and performing your job with minimal fanfare.

If, on the other hand, you were a gregarious child who served as mother's little helper, you may have decided that your greatest value is as a happy nurturer. When you have a new boss, you automatically introduce yourself and begin tending to that person's basic needs—you bring food, water the plants, and offer to help out when any problem arises.

Or maybe you were raised in a large, boisterous family where you fought to be heard. In that case, you may believe that the first person to speak up in any situation wins. You may then approach all people in positions of authority with an urgent need to voice your opinion.

Just as the luggage you wheel to the airport contains miscellaneous objects packed together, likewise your Boss Baggage holds many com-mingled emotions and attitudes. Boss Baggage can include the hope of being appreciated and the fear of being devalued. It can contain a friendly initial attitude toward someone in power, as well as a healthy skepticism toward that person's initiatives. Boss Baggage may consist of a wish to be led and inspired, coupled with a desire to be left alone.

The mix of emotions, thoughts, and motives that get stirred up in each of us when dealing with people in positions of authority is com-plex. It's also extremely valuable to uncover. Why? Because although it's natural (and convenient) to blame the boss when we don't feel sup-ported or acknowledged at work, it's more helpful to address the situa-tion by starting with *you*. Regaining a sense of power and control in the boss/employee relationship begins with knowing and managing *your* reaction first.

Don't worry. We aren't saying that your boss isn't culpable. You wouldn't be reading this book if you weren't dealing with an authority figure whose behavior is problematic. You may be grappling with someone who is unreasonable, unavailable, unfair, unkind, unreliable, undermining, or emotionally unstable. Still, no matter how deplorable your boss's conduct may be, your greatest point of power comes from identifying and deactivating the negative feelings, thoughts, or actions that his or her misbehavior triggers in you.

Consider this scenario:

Teresa is the newly assigned director of a local Health and Human Services Center for Disease Control and Prevention. Her assistant, Phillip, has worked at the CDCP for ten years. Teresa is his second boss. When Phillip and Teresa start working together, he's impressed with her confident air and can-do attitude. Problems arise as he tries to help her devise the department's annual budget.

With his previous boss, Phillip played an important role in estimating the costs of running the department and offering adjustments. With Teresa, however, every suggestion he makes is challenged. Teresa responds to his ideas and calculations by saying, "That can't be right." She then insists that each member of the department provide her with his or her financial estimates from previous budgets so that she can develop her own plan.

Phillip is angry and frustrated with his new boss. He feels dismissed and disrespected. When Teresa gives him the final budget to send out, he sees that practically every figure on her proposed budget is identical to the estimates that he'd suggested. This makes Phillip furious. "I'm working for someone who doesn't respect my input and won't listen to my suggestions." Stung, he complains, "Why does she even need my assistance?"

We could argue that Phillip's current boss is dismissive and inconsiderate of her experienced assistant's knowledge. We could approach Teresa and try to explain that Phillip produces great work when given responsibility. But any new boss has the right to delegate work carefully and to question the established ways of doing things. Teresa may need time to assess Phillip's strengths and weaknesses so that she can trust his input.

If Phillip wants a better relationship with his new boss, he has to refrain from assuming that her resistance to his suggestions is an indictment of his character. If he can take Teresa's behavior less personally,

Phillip can set about discovering how his new boss differs from the previous one, what her management style looks like, and what kind of help she actually needs from him.

Knowing your own Boss Baggage gives you immediate options when dealing with someone in a position of authority. If interactions with a boss turn sour, you can quickly determine how you may be adding to the problem. You want to be able to answer these questions:

- Which of my *expectations* aren't being fulfilled?
- What *needs* of mine aren't being met?
- What *fears* are being triggered in me?

By *expectations*, we mean assumptions you have about what you will experience or receive from the boss. For example, you may expect your manager to treat you with respect. Or, you may expect your employer to explain what he or she wants from you. Many employees expect their bosses to give them feedback. Once you realize that a certain expectation is not going to be met, you can adjust it.

Needs, on the other hand, are personal requirements or strong wants. In order to be productive, you may need clear direction. If you happen to be shy or withdrawn, you may need a boss who can speak up on your behalf and defend you. Needs differ from expectations because they aren't adjustable or flexible. For you to thrive at work, your needs must be met. So, if your boss isn't able to give you clear direction, you may still need to find ways to receive clear instructions from someone else.

Fears are those phantom thoughts and feelings that arise when our emotional safety is threatened. Fears are very different from needs and expectations because they can be triggered without your even realizing it. For example, if your boss walks in with a frown on his face, you may fear that you've done something wrong—even if he or she hasn't said anything to indicate displeasure with you. We all have fears that lie dormant inside of us. If you can determine which fears are triggered by the boss, you can defuse them.

If you can decipher those things, then you can adjust your expectations, assuage your fears, and find ways to get support from someone other than the boss. In other words, you can figure out how to neutralize your part in the negative equation.

Returning to Phillip, he may *expect* his boss to trust his experience and go along with the established way of doing things; he may *need* to feel valued and respected by his boss; and he may *fear* not being needed by his employer.

If Phillip understands these things about himself, then he has a choice. The next time Teresa challenges his suggestions, rather than collapsing into his fear of being dismissed or devalued, Phillip can adjust his approach. As Teresa rebuffs his ideas, Phillip can pause, manage his internal reactions, and ask, "How would you like me to help in this situation?"

As Phillip gets a grip on his own Boss Baggage, he is able to work with his doubting director from a less emotional place. He can see real options for managing the relationship.

Understanding your Boss Baggage takes you out of acting automatically from a fear-based position and into discovering a reality-based approach to handling your boss.

ASSESSING YOUR BOSS BAGGAGE

Are you ready to examine what's in your Boss Baggage? To help you depersonalize, we've devised a Boss Baggage Assessment. Based on your responses to our questions, you can develop your Boss Baggage Profile. These are powerful tools. We've found that most people grappling with a difficult boss/employee situation are unaware of their internal reactions. They know they're unhappy, but they don't know what's being triggered in them. We promise that once you identify your unmet needs and expectations, and once you uncover your fears, you'll immediately begin to feel relief.

Knowledge *is* power. Knowing your Boss Baggage will allow you to reclaim control. By understanding what you aren't getting from your boss, you can take back the power that you bestowed upon this person and find other ways to have your needs and expectations fulfilled. You can also learn how to manage your fears so that they do not plague you at work.

For instance, if you take the assessment and discover that you are a Star, you'll know that one of your primary needs at work is to *shine*. You'll understand why you're unhappy with a boss who keeps giving you lackluster projects where your contributions are not visible. You can take back control by joining an organization outside your boss's purview that allows you to excel and be seen as a stellar member.

If you determine that you are a Harmonizer and you work for a hypercritical, angry boss, you'll grasp why your need to have amicable relationships at work can never be realized with this person. You can then take your bullying boss's angry outbursts less personally and find the cooperation and appreciation you need elsewhere.

Get Ready . . .

We've identified ten basic Boss Baggage Profiles, in five categories. Each of these basic profiles describes a specific orientation toward authority— and each contains a set of behaviors, needs, fears, and expectations that emerge in the presence of authority figures. The ten profiles are: Nurturer, Harmonizer, Star, Challenger, Observer, Worker Bee, Storyteller, Disarmer, Coaster, and Low Beamer.

As you read each description and answer the questions, you may find that you possess a few characteristics of each profile. That is normal. Chances are, however, that there's one profile that fits you better than the rest, and two or three others that have a familiar feel. Rather than try to match yourself, in all your complexity, to one profile, we suggest that you read every profile, answer the questions, and rank your top three. Following the basic profiles, the Boss Baggage Assessment continues with a checklist that will help you arrive at your Boss Baggage Profile.

Get Set . . .

You may still have reservations about taking this assessment. We know. The problem is the boss, not you. Where is the solution? Just give our Boss Baggage Assessment a try. We promise that the insight you'll gain will help you manage any boss/employee situation. Grab a pencil. Keep notes. We'll refer to the profiles as we tackle specific boss/employee quandaries in the next chapters and learn to Depersonalize and, finally, Deal with these situations.

Go . . .

Here's how to determine your Boss Baggage Profile.

Read the description of each profile below. Then simply answer the questions that follow each description with a yes or no. Tally the number of yes responses you have at the bottom of each profile. When you've gone through all of the profiles, see which ones you scored highest on. Rank your top three orientations. You will then compile a list of your top fears, needs, and expectations, based on the fears, needs, and expectations associated with your top matches.

Remember: be honest in your answers. Keep in mind that one profile is not better or worse than another. The point is to get to know your baggage, not to trade it in for a better set. You need to understand your basic orientation to authority as part of the Depersonalize step of the Four D's process.

Important note: Don't be alarmed if you have tying scores. For example, you may have the same score for Evader and Disarmer. If that's the case, just put both profiles on the same line.

CATEGORY 1: THE CAREGIVERS

These are the employees who feel emotionally responsible for making the boss and others feel good at work.

The Nurturer

Nurturers are the unpaid social workers at work. They send congratulatory e-mails, bring food to staff meetings, and give cards to coworkers for holidays, birthdays, and special events. These are the people who embody care and concern for others.

Nurturers naturally tune in to their boss's physical and emotional needs.

A nurturing employee will quickly uncover the boss's favorite foods, family constellation, and health concerns. While Nurturers are diligent workers, these individuals always have time to talk—especially if someone needs their emotional support. They gladly provide a shoulder to cry on and a tissue to wipe away the tears.

When it comes to workload, Nurturers like to be needed. They are always willing to pitch in and help out. Nurturers aren't afraid of getting their hands dirty. They like to support causes and help out in any way they can.

SOUND FAMILIAR? RESPOND TO THESE QUESTIONS TO SEE IF YOU'RE A NURTURER.

- When you first meet a new boss, do you bring that person a plant, a coffee mug, or some other item to make him or her feel welcome? Yes ___ No ___
- Do you make sure the office is ready—clean and organized—for his or her arrival? Yes ___ No ___
- Do you make it your business to find out how your boss takes his or her coffee and what his or her favorite foods/drinks are? Yes ___ No ___
- Do you know the personal stories—marital status, medical conditions, financial woes—of everyone at your job? Yes ___ No ___
- Do your coworkers come to you for tissues, candy, or a quick cry? Yes ___ No ___
- Do you frequently volunteer to help out when others are drowning? Yes ___ No ___
- Do you keep the office birthday list on your computer? Yes ___ No ___
- Do you have a hard time telling your boss when you are overwhelmed with work? Yes ___ No ___
- If you are excluded from an important meeting, project, or initiative, do you worry that you aren't needed? Yes ___ No ___
- If you accidentally forget your boss's birthday, do you scold yourself for being cold and uncaring? Yes ___ No ___

Total Nurturer "Yes" responses _____

The Harmonizer

Friendly, warm, and caring, these are the people who discriminate the least and generally don't judge books (or people) by their covers. Harmonizers pride themselves on figuring out how to get along with anyone. They aim to be model team players.

Harmonizers need to be liked and go to great pains to find out who their boss is and what makes him or her tick. They gladly take on responsibilities that will relieve the boss or reduce stress for the staff. These are the people who naturally tune in to the boss's moods and pressures. They aim to alleviate tension and offer support.

Harmonizers fear encroaching on someone else's territory or ruffling anyone's feathers. They package and deliver information in a way that they think will create minimal emotional distress. They look for common goals and they strive for cooperation. They often serve as unofficial mediators at staff meetings.

ARE YOU A HARMONIZER? ANSWER THE FOLLOWING QUESTIONS TO FIND OUT.

- If you have a new boss, do you naturally greet him or her with a warm welcome? Yes ___ No ___
- Do you ask your boss questions to show that you care about his or her well-being? Yes ___ No ___
- Do you secretly hope that your boss feels comfortable and at ease in your company? Yes ___ No ___
- Do you gladly take on responsibility as long as it doesn't infringe on someone else's territory at work? Yes ___ No ___
- Do you pride yourself on being a team player? Yes ___ No ___
- Do you find it easy to have conversations with just about anybody? Yes ___ No ___
- Do you sometimes tell white lies to bring people together? Yes ___ No ___
- Do you have a hard time asking your boss for raises and promotions? Yes ___ No ___
- If you need to have a difficult conversation with your boss, do you carefully prepare what you're going to say? Yes ___ No ___
- Does the thought of making a mistake or causing a problem fill you with dread? Yes ___ No ___

Total Harmonizer "Yes" responses _____

CATEGORY 2: THE EXTROVERTS

These employees expect to be seen, heard, and respected at work.

The Star

Warm and engaging, Stars have a knack for connecting with people easily and quickly. They are natural people persons. Most Stars possess a good sense of humor. They are generous with their ideas and their knowledge.

Stars like to be visible, so they take on responsibilities where they are sure to be seen. (Stars do not hide out in the back room shredding documents.) They strive to grow professionally, and work hard to make their mark in the company.

Stars value constructive criticism. They also welcome opportunities for training and advancement. Ideally, they want to be trailblazers in their field.

Stars also enjoy lighting the trail for others. They don't mind working hard as long as they are recognized as *important* members of the team. They want ownership. Give them the job, and they will do it.

RESPOND TO THE FOLLOWING QUESTIONS TO ASSESS YOUR STAR QUALITIES.

- If you have a new boss, do you naturally seek that person out before everyone else and introduce yourself? Yes ___ No ___
- Do you feel an urgent need to convey your importance to him or her? Yes ___ No ___
- Do you secretly hope that someone has already told your boss how terrific you are? Yes ___ No ___
- Do you like tackling big projects where you are seen as the leader and trailblazer? Yes ___ No ___
- Do you welcome opportunities to speak publicly or present information to large groups of people? Yes ___ No ___
- Are you at ease with communicating your ideas to others, including people in positions of authority? Yes ___ No ___
- If your boss takes responsibility away from you, do you feel deflated and held back? Yes ___ No ___
- If your boss doesn't publicly acknowledge you or give you credit for your work, do you become unmotivated and resentful? Yes ___ No ___
- If you work for someone who repeatedly overrides your decisions, do you get furious and start looking for a new job? Yes ___ No ___

- If you're excluded from an important meeting, project, or initiative, do you think that it must be a mistake and insert yourself anyway? Yes ___ No ___

Total Star "Yes" responses _____

The Challenger

The slogan for Challengers is "Question authority." These innovative thinkers have a hard time trusting anyone who wields power over them. Their bosses must prove themselves worthy of respect.

Challengers want to be recognized for their fresh ideas and astute approach to tackling problems. They possess a competitive spirit and like to win. These are the employees who are willing to question the status quo. They make the uncomfortable-but-true statements at a staff meeting. Challengers can follow instructions, but only if they agree with the plan.

Challengers feel that they have to speak up, because if they don't, no one else will. They have an instinctive concern for fairness and will often champion causes for the disenfranchised or downtrodden. They are willing to tackle tough assignments as long as their efforts are recognized and their ideas respected.

RESPOND TO THESE QUESTIONS TO FIND YOUR CHALLENGER QUOTIENT.

- If you have a new boss, are you eager to introduce yourself and impress that person with your knowledge? Yes ___ No ___
- Do you get a kick out of saying something slightly provocative to people in positions of authority? Yes ___ No ___
- Do you secretly hope that your boss recognizes your ideas as more insightful and innovative than anyone else's? Yes ___ No ___
- Do you like to take on responsibility as long as you can do things your way? Yes ___ No ___
- Are you the one who others count on to challenge the status quo at a staff meeting? Yes ___ No ___
- Do you feel it's up to you to state the uncomfortable truth? Yes ___ No ___
- Are you a natural advocate for people who are underrepresented or downtrodden? Yes ___ No ___

- Are you frequently called into your boss's office and reprimanded for a lack of diplomacy? Yes ___ No ___
- Do you see yourself as someone who will always fight for what you believe in? Yes ___ No ___
- If your boss ignores or minimizes your input, do you find ways to speak up louder? Yes ___ No ___

Total Challenger "Yes" responses _____

CATEGORY 3: THE INTROVERTS

These employees don't seek high visibility and prefer minimal fanfare. They wish to be given a job and the freedom to execute it. Once finished, they'll welcome the boss's appreciation.

The Observer

Deep, quiet thinkers who watch to see who you are, these are the cool cats of the workplace. Observers are naturally skeptical of authority. You have to prove that you are worth their time and effort. This can be disconcerting to a boss.

Observers are excellent workers who need to take the situation in before they can take action. Once an authority figure wins their respect, Observers work diligently for that person. These are the employees who don't speak unless they have something to say. When they do speak, they expect you to listen.

Observers don't naturally lead meetings or discussions. They sit back and watch. These employees are more introverted by nature. They want to understand the people around them before revealing anything about themselves.

Observers are process-oriented. They need time to synthesize anything new, whether it's ideas, information, or people. They don't like surprises, and they don't like being pressured to do something before they are ready. They need time to prepare for meetings or presentations where they are expected to speak. The Observer's motto: "Never let them see you sweat."

RESPOND TO THE FOLLOWING QUESTIONS TO FIND OUT HOW MUCH OF AN OBSERVER YOU ARE.

- If you have a new boss, do you hang back and study his or her behavior? Yes ___ No ___
- Do you need to wait and see if you respect your boss before you can work hard on his or her behalf? Yes ___ No ___
- Do you secretly hope that the boss will grant you enough independence to accomplish your work without interference? Yes ___ No ___
- Are you someone who speaks up in large groups only when you have something to say? Yes ___ No ___
- Do you quietly lead your boss to give you more responsibility in the areas that are interesting to you? Yes ___ No ___
- Do you want your expertise to be rewarded without having your work style scrutinized? Yes ___ No ___
- Before speaking in public or running a meeting, do you need ample time to prepare your thoughts? Yes ___ No ___
- When given a new assignment, do you fear that you cannot deliver results fast enough for your boss? Yes ___ No ___
- Does a demanding boss trigger feelings of panic in you? Yes ___ No ___
- Do you fear being caught off guard or unprepared by your boss? Yes ___ No ___

Total Observer "Yes" responses _____

The Worker Bee

Smart, capable, diligent, these are the backstage workers who want to do their jobs, achieve positive results, and avoid all interpersonal conflict. Worker Bees like to take on big projects and dive into them. They are often the quiet experts in the workplace.

Unlike Stars, who need to be visible, Worker Bees prefer a quiet round of applause for their efforts. They want their work to speak for itself. These employees generally prefer to be left alone. Ideally, Worker Bees like to be given assignments and trusted to complete the work on their own.

These individuals are good listeners, but poor communicators when it comes to speaking up on their own behalf. Interestingly, many

Worker Bees gladly engage in conversations about their hobbies and interests. They like sharing information on topics that they value.

Difficulties arise for Worker Bees in the realm of interpersonal differences. They don't know how to effectively express contrary opinions and they don't know how to deal with conflict of any kind. Emotional outbursts scare them.

COULD YOU BE A WORKER BEE? RESPOND TO THE FOLLOWING QUESTIONS.

- If you have a new boss, do you naturally hang back, waiting for that person to approach you? Yes ___ No ___
- When meeting with this person, do you bring samples of your work, hoping it will speak for you? Yes ___ No ___
- Do you wish that your boss would give you interesting assignments and then leave you alone to complete them? Yes ___ No ___
- Do you like to be acknowledged for a job well done, even though you may feel embarrassed by the attention? Yes ___ No ___
- Do you avoid collaborating with others? Yes ___ No ___
- Do you steer clear of situations where you'd have to speak publicly or give a presentation to a large group of people? Yes ___ No ___
- Do you find it challenging to communicate effectively when you disagree with others? Yes ___ No ___
- When you need to ask for something from your boss (such as a raise or time off), do you get nervous and avoid doing it? Yes ___ No ___
- When your boss is in a bad mood, do you avoid contact by hiding behind your work? Yes ___ No ___
- In meetings, are you the quiet listener who secretly judges everyone? Yes ___ No ___

Total Worker Bee "Yes" responses _____

CATEGORY 4: THE WORDSMITHS

Gifted communicators, this group of employees relates through the spoken and written word.

The Storyteller

This is a friendly, outgoing, chatty person who shares personal stories in order to connect with others. A Storyteller is the opposite of an Observer. Whereas the Observer sizes people up and then speaks, the Storyteller speaks in order to size people up: Are you listening? Do you care? Can you relate to what I am telling you? These individuals bond through conversation. For Storytellers, your ability to listen shows that you are available to their ideas.

A storytelling employee will expect the boss to be interested in his or her narratives. This person tests authority figures by sharing a personal account of something and seeing if they tune in. Once a Storyteller feels heard, he or she will gladly take on responsibilities.

Because Storytellers want to do the job right, they desire clear, detailed instructions. This is especially true when they take on new projects. They also need access to decision makers so that they can ask questions and give progress reports.

Storytellers don't like to make mistakes. They are horrified when they discover a slipup of their own doing. They respond well to words of appreciation and acknowledgment.

DOES THIS TALE SOUND FAMILIAR? RESPOND TO THE
FOLLOWING QUESTIONS TO SEE HOW MUCH OF A
STORYTELLER YOU ARE.

- When you meet a new boss, do you try to connect by telling a personal story about yourself? Yes ___ No ___
- Do you watch for the boss's reaction to see if he or she is listening and receptive to you? Yes ___ No ___
- Do you secretly hope that your employer values your detailed accounting of events that occur both inside and outside of the office? Yes ___ No ___
- Are you happy to take on new responsibilities as long as you know exactly what is expected of you? Yes ___ No ___

- Are you good at mapping out projects and figuring out the details? Yes ___ No ___
- Do you perform best with a boss who is available to answer questions and willing to receive frequent progress reports? Yes ___ No ___
- If someone interrupts you while you're recounting an experience, do you feel an urgent need to return and complete the story? Yes ___ No ___
- Do you feel hurt or insulted when someone doesn't want to hear what you have to say or cuts you off? Yes ___ No ___
- Have you ever been reprimanded for talking too much? Yes ___ No ___
- Do you feel mortified when you make a mistake? Yes ___ No ___

Total Storyteller "Yes" responses _____

The Disarmer

Highly responsible, very independent, and very funny, these are the employees who are great at winning over the boss with their humor. Disarmers use words, gestures, and timing to make others laugh and to cut tension when it arises. They also have a knack for completing work assignments in an organized, efficient manner.

Disarmers are able to package and deliver information in a way that leads to minimal emotional distress. To temper their boss's response, they emphasize the positive side of any difficulty. Disarmers often bring harmony to the workplace by filtering the boss's bad moods.

These employees don't really see the hierarchy in a business setting. Everyone is equal in their eyes. As a result, they don't like condescension or being spoken down to. Disarmers require mutual respect.

READ AND RESPOND TO THE FOLLOWING QUESTIONS TO SEE HOW DISARMING YOU ARE.

- If you have a new boss, do you immediately check to see if he or she has a sense of humor? Yes ___ No ___
- Do you look for opportunities to disarm your boss with witty or funny remarks? Yes ___ No ___
- Do you work hard to create a positive, professional, can-do work environment? Yes ___ No ___

- Do you secretly try to maintain harmony by intercepting your boss's bad moods? Yes ___ No ___
- Are you frequently given additional responsibilities because of your efficient and organized work style? Yes ___ No ___
- Do you ever feel pressured to maintain an upbeat, entertaining veneer at work? Yes ___ No ___
- Do you consider yourself to be an independent thinker and operator? Yes ___ No ___
- Are you generally unaffected by a person's title or position in the company hierarchy? Yes ___ No ___
- If someone speaks to you in a condescending tone, do you see red? Yes ___ No ___
- Do you sometimes worry that you aren't being taken seriously enough? Yes ___ No ___

Total Disarmer "Yes" responses _____

CATEGORY 5: THE MELLOWS

These individuals have little interest in climbing the corporate ladder. They'd prefer to do their job and go home.

The Coaster

These are the people who show others at work how to relax. They try to take everything in stride and do not take work home with them. For these individuals a job is a job. It should pay the bills; it should not cause undue stress.

Coasting employees see the boss as someone to befriend and win over. They consider it their job to make people (including the boss) feel good. They also see themselves as the voice of reason that encourages others not to work too hard.

Coasters attend all company parties. They are willing to organize activities to lift morale, such as fantasy football, lottery ticket sales, and bake sales. For them, personal needs come first—they have no problem taking time off from work to attend to family, friends, or health matters.

RESPOND TO THE FOLLOWING QUESTIONS TO FIND HOW YOU
SCORE ON THE COASTER SCALE.

- If you have a new boss, do you try to impress this person with your relaxed, friendly attitude? Yes ___ No ___
- Do you work hard to charm your boss and win his or her friendship? Yes ___ No ___
- Do you secretly hope that your manager won't pressure you or criticize you? Yes ___ No ___
- Do you like to work on small projects where you can control the pace? Yes ___ No ___
- Do you avoid taking on any additional responsibilities that will cut into your personal life? Yes ___ No ___
- Do you encourage your overworked colleagues to do less and relax more? Yes ___ No ___
- Do you welcome non-work-related office activities such as birthday parties, sports events, and company contests? Yes ___ No ___
- Do people in positions of authority often tell you that you're not working to your full potential? Yes ___ No ___
- Do they ever ask you to take on more responsibilities and work harder? Yes ___ No ___
- Is that kind of feedback very stressful to you? Yes ___ No ___

Total Coaster "Yes" responses _____

The Low Beamer

This individual approaches authority in a cautious, risk-averse manner. He or she wants to stay off the radar and keep interactions friendly and neutral. These employees are usually intelligent, skilled, and capable, but something prevents them from giving 100 percent to their jobs.

Low Beamers need everything spelled out so that they do not have to risk making the wrong decision. They require explicit directions and want to know the correct protocol in any situation. They like to play by the rules.

Because they don't like making mistakes, Low Beamers often find themselves waiting to be instructed. While other members of a work team may seem busy and overwhelmed, a Low Beamer will put off tackling a project until he or she receives specific instructions. These employees perform best under attentive, detail-oriented managers.

HOW HIGH IS YOUR LOW BEAMER SCORE? RESPOND TO THESE QUESTIONS.

- If you have a new boss, do you naturally sit back and wait for that person to approach you? Yes _____ No _____
- Do you look to your boss to define your job and lay out explicit expectations of you? Yes _____ No _____
- Do you secretly hope that your boss will dole out work in small, simple assignments where there is little room for error? Yes _____ No _____
- Do you steer clear of projects that appear challenging and demanding of your time? Yes _____ No _____
- If you are asked to take on additional responsibilities at work, do you first consider whether it is an appropriate request considering your job description? Yes _____ No _____
- Do you pride yourself on living a balanced life and protecting your time outside of the workplace? Yes _____ No _____
- Do you often feel that you could produce more if you were given better direction from those who supervise you? Yes _____ No _____
- Do you keep track of your company's policies regarding work hours, attendance, benefits, vacation, because you want to protect your rights in these areas? Yes _____ No _____
- Have you ever been reprimanded for not giving 100 percent to your job? Yes _____ No _____
- Does the thought of making a mistake sometimes prevent you from taking action? Yes _____ No _____

Total Low Beamer "Yes" responses _____

TALLYING YOUR RESULTS

Congratulations! You've answered the yes/no questions for each of our ten authority profiles. It's time to tabulate your scores. Go back to the bottom of each description and transfer your score on that page to the score grid that follows, then fill out the list of your top three authority profiles.

SCORES

Nurturer _____

Harmonizer _____

Star _____

Challenger _____

Observer _____

Worker Bee _____

Storyteller _____

Disarmer _____

Coaster _____

Low Beamer _____

My top three authority orientations:

1. _____

2. _____

3. _____

Now that you know your top three orientations toward any authority figure, you can continue to develop your Boss Baggage Profile by taking the next step in the assessment.

The checklists that follow enumerate some of the expectations, needs, and fears that are typical for each of the ten profile types. Find the checklists for each of your top three profiles and check off the items you agree with.

If you scored high as a **Nurturer**, here's a list of some potential expectations, needs, and fears that you may bring to your relationships with authority. Please check the items that match your experience.

EXPECTATIONS

___ I expect the boss to trust and confide in me.

___ I expect to feel needed by my boss.

___ I expect to be appreciated for my caring and thoughtfulness.

___ I expect acts of kindness to be valued in the workplace.

NEEDS

___ I need to be needed.

___ I need to be useful and helpful.

___ I need to be appreciated for my acts of kindness.

___ I need to establish caring connections with my boss and other members of the staff.

FEARS

___ I fear being found lacking.

___ I fear appearing cold or uncaring.

___ I fear not carrying my weight.

___ I fear not holding it together.

If you scored high as a **Harmonizer**, here's a list of some potential expectations, needs, and fears that you may bring to your relationships with authority. Please check the items that match your experience.

EXPECTATIONS

___ I expect to get along with everyone.

___ I expect to be an important member of the boss's team.

___ I expect to be entrusted with responsibility.

___ I expect to be appreciated as a bridge-builder.

___ I expect to exert a positive influence on my colleagues.

NEEDS

___ I need to get along with everyone.

___ I need to be liked.

___ I need to be appreciated for my efforts.

___ I need to be given the benefit of the doubt when a mistake is made.

___ I need to help people feel good about themselves and get along.

FEARS

___ I fear constant discord or infighting among staff.

___ I fear confrontation.

___ I fear seeing anyone in emotional pain.

___ I fear being perceived as difficult.

___ I fear disappointing the boss or other members of my work team.

If you scored high on the **Star** profile, here's a list of some potential expectations, needs, and fears that you may bring to your relationships with authority. Please check the items that you agree with.

EXPECTATIONS

___ I expect to be given an audience with the boss.

___ I expect to receive opportunities to grow professionally.

___ I expect to receive constructive criticism and training.

___ I expect to be given clear direction.

___ I expect to work for someone who has a vision and communicates it.

NEEDS

___ I need to be able to shine.

___ I need to be given responsibility.

___ I need to be allowed to make decisions.

___ I need to feel important.

___ I need authority figures to value my skills, knowledge, and talent.

FEARS

___ I fear doing tasks that will never give me visibility.

___ I fear being held back.

___ I fear being micromanaged.

___ I fear being marginalized.

___ I fear not being respected.

If you scored high as a **Challenger**, here's a list of some potential expectations, needs, and fears that you may bring to your relationships with authority. Please check the items that you agree with.

EXPECTATIONS

___ I expect that my boss wants to hear what I have to say.

___ I expect my boss to appreciate honest opinions.

___ I expect that my ability to think outside of the box will be valued.

___ I expect my boss to prove him- or herself worthy of respect.

___ I expect that irreverence has a place in the workplace.

NEEDS

___ I need to be heard.

___ I need to be allowed to try new things.

___ I need to think outside of the box.

___ I need to be told "You were right" as often as possible.

FEARS

___ I fear not being heard.

___ I fear being marginalized.

___ I fear being taken lightly.

___ I fear being labeled a troublemaker.

If you scored high as an **Observer**, here's a list of some potential expectations, needs, and fears that you may bring to your relationships with authority. Please check the items that correspond with your experience.

EXPECTATIONS

___ I expect to be given time to process people, places, and information.

___ I expect my boss to prove him- or herself worthy of my respect.

___ I expect to be seen and appreciated for my efforts.

___ I expect to be heard when I have something to say.

___ I expect to be trusted to do a good job.

NEEDS

___ I need to be given time to assess a situation before taking action.

___ I need to be left alone until I'm ready to perform.

___ I need to be given time to prepare for any meeting or presentation.

___ I need to be judged on the final results of my efforts rather than the process by which I do things.

___ I need to have my opinions and experiences respected by others.

FEARS

___ I fear being pressured to perform before I am ready.

___ I fear being unfairly judged or criticized.

___ I fear being brushed aside or devalued.

___ I fear being overshadowed by flashy people who play politics.

___ I fear being caught off guard.

If you scored high as a **Worker Bee**, here's a list of some potential expectations, needs, and fears that you may bring to your relationships with authority. Please check the items that match your experience.

EXPECTATIONS

___ I expect to be given responsibility.

___ I expect to be trusted to do a good job without being micromanaged.

___ I expect to be respected and appreciated for my efforts.

___ I expect to do my job quietly and be left alone.

___ I expect to develop specific areas of expertise.

NEEDS

___ I need a certain level of independence on the job.

___ I need a certain amount of positive feedback.

___ I need to be given instructions and left to accomplish the tasks on my own.

___ I need to be trusted for my sound judgment.

___ I need to be appreciated for my knowledge and expertise, not second-guessed.

FEARS

___ I fear being ridiculed.

___ I fear being mistrusted.

___ I fear being rejected.

___ I fear having to defend myself.

___ I fear having to deal with anyone else's anger.

If you scored high as a **Storyteller**, here's a list of some potential expectations, needs, and fears that you may bring to your relationships with authority. Please check the items that correspond with your experience.

EXPECTATIONS

___ I expect that the boss wants to hear my personal account of events.

___ I expect that my attention to detail is important and will be appreciated.

___ I expect that my efforts will be noticed and acknowledged.

___ I expect that any new responsibility will come with instructions.

NEEDS

___ I need to be listened to.

___ I need to hold other people's attention.

___ I need to have my experiences acknowledged.

___ I need to be appreciated for my thoroughness.

FEARS

___ I fear being misunderstood.

___ I fear not being heard.

___ I fear being unfairly criticized.

___ I fear being ostracized.

___ I fear being perceived as incompetent.

If you scored high as a **Disarmer**, here's a list of some potential expectations, needs, and fears that you may bring to your relationships with authority. Please check the items that correspond with your experience.

EXPECTATIONS

___ I expect to win the boss over with humor.

___ I expect to be trusted to do my job well.

___ I expect to get along with my colleagues and be successful on the job.

___ I expect to be left alone to do my job.

NEEDS

___ I need to be treated with respect.

___ I need to have my sense of humor appreciated (my boss laughs at my jokes).

___ I need to be given clear directions and the authority to accomplish the task.

___ I need to be taken seriously when I have something important to say.

FEARS

___ I fear not being respected.

___ I fear being talked down to.

___ I fear not being taken seriously.

___ I fear not being heard.

___ I fear appearing foolish or incompetent.

If you scored high on the **Coaster** profile, here's a list of some potential expectations, needs, and fears that you may bring to your relationships with authority. Please check the items with which you agree.

EXPECTATIONS

___ I expect to charm my boss.

___ I expect to avoid stressful work assignments.

___ I expect to be valued for living a balanced life.

___ I expect work to be a necessary activity that shouldn't be taken too seriously.

NEEDS

___ I need to be liked.

___ I need to be praised and acknowledged.

___ I need to have low stress (a light workload).

___ I need to have low expectations placed on me.

FEARS

___ I fear failing in a high-pressure environment.

___ I fear looking foolish or stupid.

___ I fear high stress or pressure to perform.

___ I fear being ridiculed.

If you scored high on the **Low Beamer** profile, here's a list of some potential expectations, needs, and fears that you may bring to your relationships with authority. Please check the items that you identify with.

EXPECTATIONS

___ I expect to have a clearly defined job.

___ I expect the company to have well-defined policies and procedures.

___ I expect to be handed work assignments with explicit instructions.

___ I expect my boss to communicate clearly his or her expectations of me.

___ I expect to have a full life outside of work.

NEEDS

___ I need clear, detailed instructions from the people who supervise my work.

___ I need to minimize the chances of bringing negative attention to myself.

___ I need to avoid taking on responsibilities in areas with which I am not familiar.

___ I need to have a balanced life—no overtime or working extra hours at home.

FEARS

___ I fear making mistakes.

___ I fear making the wrong decision.

___ I fear being given assignments without clear directions.

___ I fear being asked to do things I don't know how to do.

PUTTING IT ALL TOGETHER

Now you can discover your full Boss Baggage Profile. First, list your top three profiles. (Remember, it's okay if you have a tie score among the profiles. Some people have more than three orientations toward authority. For example, you may score equally high as both Harmonizer and Storyteller. If that's the case, you can list the two on the same line.)

My top three authority orientations:

1._____

2._____

3._____

Next, go over the expectations that you identified in the checklists above and pull out the top five.

1. _____

2. _____

3. _____

4. _____

5. _____

Now, comb through the needs you checked off and list your top five.

1. _____

2. _____

3. _____

4. _____

5. _____

Finally, pull out the top five fears from among those you checked off.

1. _____

2. _____

3. _____

4. _____

5. _____

Your top three authority profiles, your top five expectations, your top five needs, and your top five fears make up your complete Boss Baggage Profile. Now that you know your BBP, we invite you to observe yourself as you interact with your boss, a favorite customer, an important board member, or any other person whose decisions influence your well-being at work. If the relationship is going well, then the authority figure is probably able to meet your needs and expectations to some extent, and your fears are minimal. If the relationship is challenging or difficult, your needs and expectations probably aren't being met, and your fears are activated.

What's next? In Chapter 6, we are going to show you specific strategies for depersonalizing each of the top twenty boss misbehaviors that we've covered in previous chapters.

WORK IT OUT
Depersonalize

IT'S NOT ABOUT YOU . . . OR IS IT?: ASSESSING YOUR BOSS BAGGAGE PROFILE

WHAT'S IN YOUR SUITCASE NOW (WITH YOUR CURRENT BOSS)?

_____

EXPECTATIONS THAT MY BOSS FAILS TO FULFILL

1 _____

2 _____

3 _____

NEEDS THAT MY BOSS CANNOT MEET

1 _____

2 _____

3 _____

FEARS THAT MY BOSS'S BEHAVIOR TRIGGERS

1 _____

2 _____

3 _____

CHAPTER 6

Depersonalizing Twenty Boss Behaviors: Taking Out the Emotional Sting

I N THE LAST chapter, you learned that when you depersonalize some-one else's behavior, you're able to see that you're not the first person who's experienced his or her poor conduct and you won't be the last. You now know it's not about you.

You then uncovered your own Boss Baggage. By taking the Boss Baggage Assessment, you determined whether you are a Nurturer, a Harmonizer, a Star, a Challenger, an Observer, a Worker Bee, a Story-teller, a Disarmer, a Coaster, or a Low Beamer. You also discovered the expectations, needs, and fears that you bring to any boss/employee relationship.

In this chapter, we'll show you how to apply that information to help you take specific boss behaviors less personally. For immediate as-sistance with your bothersome boss, read on.

HOW TO USE THIS CHAPTER

This chapter is organized around the twenty boss behaviors we introduced in Chapter 2. Go to the boss behavior that best describes your situation and see how someone with your authority profile can most effectively depersonalize the relationship with that kind of boss. For example, if you are a Disarmer, and you work for a Control Freak, go to page 160 and see how a disarming employee can successfully depersonalize a controlling boss's antics.

We realize that your boss may exhibit more than one difficult characteristic, and likewise you may have more than one orientation toward authority. Let's say you detect that your boss is not only Spineless but also an Underminer. Your Boss Baggage Assessment revealed that you approach authority as an Observer/Challenger. In that case, look up both boss behaviors (Spineless and Underminer) and see what it takes for both an Observer and a Challenger to depersonalize each of them.

For further entertainment, you can peruse the entire chapter and see how your colleagues, friends, or family members can best depersonalize from the annoying authority figures in their lives.

CATEGORY 1: HEAD GAMES

Depersonalizing from Chronic Critics

You can never fully please this kind of boss. The Chronic Critic boss must find the flaw, mistake, shortcoming, or imperfection in any situation.

UNIVERSAL LAW: THEIR NEED TO BE CRITICAL HAS NOTHING TO DO WITH YOU.

Nurturer Nurturers work hard to fulfill their boss's needs and dread falling short of expectations. The cutting remarks of a Chronic Critic are very hard for a nurturing employee to take. To depersonalize, get ready to have your boss tell you on a regular basis what is wrong with your performance. Understand and remind yourself that it's not because you are lacking. Everyone is lacking in this person's eyes.

Harmonizer Your first instinct is to take the boss's nonstop nitpicking as an indictment on your character. Instead of taking it personally, see your boss's criticism as his or her way of relating to you. You aren't a disappointment. The critic just doesn't know how to relate in any other way.

Star Initially, you may experience your boss's carping as a form of petty micromanagement. The Chronic Critic's corrections will roll off your back once you realize that this manager finds fault in everything everyone does.

Challenger While you're skilled at pointing out the misguided thinking of others, you may chafe under the constant negative scrutiny of a Chronic Critic. You can take your employer's caustic comments less personally if you view this person as a prisoner of his or her own perfectionism.

Observer Because you fear being unfairly criticized, this kind of boss can easily get under your skin. To depersonalize from this person you need to experience his or her negative commentary as opinion rather than fact. The fact that Chronic Critics are driven to find fault with others doesn't mean that the harsh judgments they deliver are true.

Worker Bee Everything about a Chronic Critic may rub you the wrong way. You will wish that this kind of boss would just buzz off and leave you alone. The best way to depersonalize is to tell yourself that your critical leader's compulsive faultfinding is not about you—it's an ingrained habit that he or she cannot break. On the outside, try buffering the boss's feedback with a response like, "Thank you. I'll think about that."

Storyteller Because you have a deep need to be recognized for your thoroughness and attention to detail, the sting of a highly critical boss can be hard to take. Your best strategy for depersonalizing is to see your boss as handicapped with the affliction of finding fault. You can then experience his or her complaints as a form of illness rather than deliberate meanness.

Disarmer Fortunately, you naturally see the humor in things and tend to use that to deflect criticism. Take this kind of boss less personally by drawing on your disarming qualities. See his or her negativity as a burden that he or she has to carry and try to lighten the load.

Coaster Chronic Critics usually don't respond well to your attempts at charming them. You'll feel pressured by their high standards and frustrated at your inability to meet them. The best approach with this kind of boss is to know that you will be the recipient of constant correction, but that you are not alone. Try not to feel singled out, and find supportive people to remind you of your value.

Low Beamer Chronic Critics usually spell out their expectations quite explicitly, and you like your job to be clearly defined, so you may initially appreciate this kind of boss. Problems arise when the same person zeroes in on your mistakes. Your boss's negative evaluation of the work will seem unfair and unjustified. To depersonalize, understand that your difficult leader has trashed the work of everyone before you. Instead of defending yourself, make the corrections as best you can and move on to the next project.

Depersonalizing from Rule Changers

Your boss is not consistent—this Rule Changer does not want to be pinned down, hemmed in, or held to any fixed commitments. The rules, plans, decisions, and policies under this person will always change.

UNIVERSAL LAW: THEY CANNOT FOLLOW DECISIONS, PROJECTS, OR SCHEDULES CONSISTENTLY.

Nurturer Most Nurturers have an innate ability to go with the flow and adjust to their boss's changing needs. They are happy to accommodate a Rule Changer's ever-fluctuating calendar. If you become overwhelmed by your leader's mercurial managerial style, however, you can take the behavior less personally by understanding that your boss doesn't mean to foil your best efforts. He or she is simply constitutionally incapable of staying the course.

Harmonizer Because you pride yourself on getting along and adapting to the needs of others, you may not struggle too much with this kind of boss behavior. Most Harmonizers naturally depersonalize by being proactive: once they understand that their boss habitually changes the rules, they adjust by constantly checking in with their leader to see what the most recent adjustments are in decisions, policies, and plans.

Star This kind of boss can be difficult for Star employees, who are action-oriented and like to take ideas and run with them. The Rule Changer's tendency to change course and alter decisions strikes the Star as wishy-washy and disrespectful. To depersonalize from a rule-changing boss, it's best to take a step back before charging forward. You'll need to temper your eagerness to accomplish tasks with a willingness to keep checking in with the boss to make sure that plans crafted yesterday are still his or her plans for today.

Challenger Challengers like to know what the rules are so that they can push against them. This kind of quixotic boss is very taxing for a Challenger because it's hard to buck the system when the system is always in flux. To manage a rule-changing boss, you'll need to remind yourself (perhaps daily) that this person's behavior is not personal. He or she is incapable of staying committed to a plan, and the ever-changing rules are not designed to irritate you. Do your best to go with the flow.

Observer Most Observers are planners. They do not respond well to sudden changes or altered plans. To take your waffling boss less personally, you'll have to practice the Zen of letting go. When your boss announces a plan, schedules an appointment, or endorses an idea, take it as a first draft or prototype only.

Worker Bee Worker Bees are, by nature, detached. Because they like to be given instructions, then left alone to accomplish the task, Worker Bees can work with rule-changing bosses without getting too hot under the collar. You don't lean heavily on the boss for direction, so you won't be disappointed when plans and policies change.

Storyteller Rule Changers are somewhat annoying to Storyteller employees, but not intolerable. You'll like your boss's willingness to share stories and discuss ideas. Your frustration level rises when you attempt to carefully execute your boss's plans, only to find out they've changed. Depersonalizing from this kind of boss requires a revised job description. Understand that one of your jobs is to confirm and reconfirm decisions, appointments, and logistics as you begin to carry them out.

Disarmer Once you discover that your boss is a Rule Changer, you can adapt your work style and sense of humor to accommodate that behavior. You'll be the one who can lightly inquire, "Are we still having that scheduled meeting today? If not, I'll need to let everyone down gently."

Coaster Most Coasters will pick up on this kind of boss quickly and adjust accordingly. You understand that changing plans can translate into less work for you. While you watch your coworkers rush forward and try to make things happen, you can sit back and ask, "What's the plan for today?" Your rule-changing boss may appreciate your relaxed attitude as he or she keeps changing course.

Low Beamer Your need for explicit directions and consistent expectations will make this kind of boss extremely distasteful. It will be very challenging to take the Rule Changer's behavior less personally, but to survive on the job, you must.

Depersonalizing from Yellers

Your boss has an anger problem that you didn't cause but that you also can't control. This Yeller will continue to erupt at both predictable and unpredictable moments.

UNIVERSAL LAW: THIS PERSON HAS UNRESOLVED RAGE THAT GETS TRIGGERED NO MATTER WHAT YOU DO.

Nurturer This loud leader is a real challenge for nurturing employees who work hard to make the boss and other people in the workplace feel cared for. Nurturers experience the Yeller's outbursts as unnecessary and unkind. The Nurturer's office becomes the emergency room where targeted employees come to cry, decompress, and receive emotional support. To depersonalize from a Yeller, you have to tell yourself and others that any explosive reaction your boss has is not about you and is not something you can change.

Harmonizer Because Harmonizers strive for peaceful work environments, this kind of boss is exhausting for them. Typically, a harmonizing employee will work double time to prevent the boss from erupting. These attempts ultimately fail, and the Harmonizer feels defeated and depressed. To take your yelling boss less personally, you need to focus on doing your job and refrain from working overtime at managing his or her temper. Your boss *will* explode. You don't cause these flare-ups and you can't control them.

Star Most Stars are strong personalities and stellar performers. Their confidence and competence make them less susceptible to the wrath of a yelling boss. Still, on occasion, even a Star employee may receive a blast of rage. You can depersonalize these verbal lashings by reminding yourself that this has nothing to do with your performance. Your boss has a problem that you didn't cause and you can't repair.

Challenger These employees do best in environments where their differing opinions can be heard and respected. A yelling boss may view your bold statements as subversive and disruptive. In some cases, you may become the office scapegoat for the Yeller's rage. Your natural desire will be to fight back, but your best defense is to watch your boss like you're watching a bad movie. If you zip your lip, the Yeller's erratic behavior will become transparent to you and anyone else in the room.

Observer Observers take their time in evaluating their bosses and don't like surprises. The first time a Yeller explodes, an Observer may quake, but over time, you won't respect a boss who can't control his or her temper. To depersonalize, practice your powers of objective viewing—tune the anger out and watch the show. Do your best to remember that, no matter what your boss says, it's not about you.

Worker Bee A manager who confronts or attacks employees in an angry manner is the Worker Bee's worst nightmare. Soft-spoken by nature, Worker Bees will want to run for cover when they sense that the boss is about to explode. Your biggest challenge is learning to take this person's vitriol less personally. Remember that what your boss spouts during a tirade is not the absolute truth about you. You're hearing a distorted story from a person who is out of control.

Storyteller When someone angrily accuses or attacks you, you naturally attempt to rectify the situation by explaining what really happened. This tactic only makes a yelling boss angrier—it's like dowsing an already raging fire with gasoline. To depersonalize your relationship with a Yeller, you want first to zip your lip. Don't engage with your hotheaded leader until he or she has cooled off. Whatever your boss says in the heat of the moment is an exaggerated accusation. Don't bite the bait.

Disarmer Disarmers have a knack for winning their bosses over and deflecting other people's bad moods. Still, Yellers throw temper tantrums regardless of who is in the room. If you get caught in the crossfire, it may be some time before you'll want to make that same person laugh. To depersonalize this kind of situation, remember that you're dealing with someone who is emotionally handicapped. Your boss will continue to appreciate your humor, but you cannot fix his or her bigger emotional issues.

Coaster Coasters have a low-key approach to work and desire minimal stress. Working for a yelling boss runs counter to their nature. At the same time, the Coaster's laid-back attitude can be interpreted by a high-strung, demanding boss as reason for attack. Your boss may want to unleash his or her anger and frustration on you, but you don't have to take it in. To depersonalize from a Yeller, try picturing a protective shield in front of you that absorbs the cutting words and negative energy.

Low Beamer Because Low Beamers try to stay out of the limelight, they may be able to go unnoticed most of the time with a yelling boss. Still, you may incur your boss's wrath if you fail to meet his or her expectations by playing it too safe. Perhaps you finished only part of a report, or maybe you failed to address a technical problem because it wasn't in your job description. Situations like these can set a Yeller off. Should your boss give you an unfair verbal lashing, you can depersonalize by not taking the words or accusations literally. Wait for the emotional storm to pass before attempting to rectify the situation.

Depersonalizing from Underminers

You are working for someone who will continue to give you responsibility and then take it away. Your boss is incapable of truly trusting others to effectively carry out his or her plans.

UNIVERSAL LAW: THIS KIND OF BOSS HAS TRUST AND CONTROL ISSUES WITH EVERYBODY.

Nurturer When your undermining boss first gives you an assignment, only to override your authority later, you may feel hurt and offended. Nurturers pride themselves on being trustworthy and taking care of the people they serve. To depersonalize the Underminer's controlling ways, remind yourself that you work for someone who is constitutionally incapable of trusting others. It's not about you. An undermining boss does this to everyone in his or her life.

Harmonizer Because Harmonizers expect to be entrusted with responsibility, the undermining boss's tendency to assign and reassign tasks can be disheartening at first. Over time, however, you can adjust your expectations and incorporate your boss's compulsive second-guessing and reshuffling of work assignments as part of his or her management style.

Star Initially, a Star employee may find this kind of boss's behavior insulting: "Why doesn't my boss give me full responsibility? I should be trusted to do the job." To depersonalize from an undermining boss, the confident Star can approach this leader and clarify the situation. A Star may say, for example, "You gave this assignment to two of us. I can handle it. Why don't you just give it to me?" Understand that you may have to win your boss over a number of times before your stellar performance eventually gains the Underminer's trust.

Challenger With your forceful personality and ability to challenge the status quo, you have the skills to handle an undermining boss's sketchy behavior fairly well. By the time you notice that your boss gave you responsibility and then tried to take it away in some fashion, you've already barreled through the project. Your competitive spirit allows you to override your wavering boss's mixed signals and forge ahead.

Observer Observers are naturally perceptive employees who quickly catch on to the Underminer's ways. You may have a tough time respecting this kind of boss. You definitely won't like being caught off guard or set up to fail. To depersonalize from your undercutting leader, you'll need to understand that he or she pulls the rug out from under everybody—not just you.

Worker Bee With your desire to be given assignments and then quietly left alone to accomplish them, this kind of boss can truly offend you. Worker Bees take pride in completing their work without fanfare. When you deliver a finished project only to realize someone else has replicated your efforts, you'll see red. To take your undermining boss less personally, remind yourself that this person's lack of trust is not directed at you. It's a one-size-fits-all practice that will be applied to you and everyone else in the workplace.

Storyteller Storytellers see themselves as thorough, steady workers who fare well when given clear, consistent directions. This kind of employee experiences distress as undermining bosses keep changing the plot line—whether it concerns who is responsible for a certain project or who is slated for a specific promotion. To depersonalize from your maneuvering manager, trust that the story will keep changing. Check with others to uncover your boss's latest edits to the workplace script.

Disarmer This is one boss who will not succumb to your winning ways. Even if you're able to keep your boss in stitches, an Underminer will still give and take responsibility away from you on a regular basis. To depersonalize, you have to remind yourself that your boss does not doubt your competence. He or she simply has control issues that result in an undercutting of your ability to be effective at work.

Coaster In an odd way, the shifting directives of your undermining boss could work to your advantage. Once you realize that you work for someone who habitually hands out the same assignment to more than one person, you can sit back, relax, and let others try to impress this authority figure.

Low Beamer If you are a Low Beamer, your greatest need is to receive clear, detailed instructions regarding work assignments. You want to do your job and go home. Undermining bosses tend to generate great distress in their Low Beamer employees. The minute you perceive that your boss's initial instructions no longer hold true, you become angry. To depersonalize from this kind of boss, try to remember that he or she has trust and control issues that manifest in the form of mixed messages. Check in frequently to see if the instructions have changed.

CATEGORY 2: BIG SHOTS AND MOTHER SUPERIORS

Depersonalizing from "I'm Always Right"

This person must believe that his or her ideas, opinions, decisions, and policies are always correct. Your boss will never admit to being wrong.

UNIVERSAL LAW: YOUR "I'M ALWAYS RIGHT" BOSS EQUATES BEING WRONG WITH BEING WEAK AND CANNOT TOLERATE APPEARING WEAK IN ANY SITUATION.

Nurturer Nurturers understand that every boss needs a certain amount of ego stroking. The Always Right boss is an extreme case of this, but you can depersonalize his or her over-the-top behavior by reminding yourself that making your boss right is how you get the most out of this person.

Harmonizer It takes practice for the harmonizing employee to wrangle the Always Right boss. Initially, you'll be tempted to try and show the boss alternative opinions and approaches to handling different business situations. When your headstrong boss refuses to consider your point of view, you quickly realize that it's best to back off and approach the issue at another time. To depersonalize, understand that your confident leader has an indisputable need to win every discussion. Agree first before offering alternative ideas, opinions, or suggestions.

Star Initially, the Star may be a bit put off by this boss's refusal to acknowledge any point of view beyond his or her own. Over time, however, Star employees can see the bigger picture and learn to use agreement as a tool to get what they want. Depersonalize by reminding yourself that the best way to shine is to always agree with and acknowledge your boss's perspective first before delivering your own ideas.

Challenger Because Challengers like to be recognized and respected for their clever ideas, the Always Right boss is extremely difficult for them to manage. Conversations between the two sides in this boss/employee combination usually devolve into a power struggle. The problem is that your boss has the upper hand. To depersonalize from this kind of boss, you have to put your need to be heard on hold. You can put your ideas and opinions in writing, but wait for the appropriate opportunity to share them. Most of the time, you'll have to zip your lip.

Observer Observers wait for their bosses to prove themselves worthy of respect. If you're an Observer, an Always Right boss may strike you as pompous and arrogant. To depersonalize from this kind of authority figure, try to see his or her need to be right as a mental disability that you did not cause and cannot cure. Do your best to look beyond it.

Worker Bee Always Right bosses do not bother Worker Bees as much as they bother other employees. Your overly confident employer may allow you to work independently—which you like. The challenge comes when the boss starts to correct your assignments and diminish your accomplishments. At those times, you can take his or her critical comments less personally by recognizing that this individual corrects and admonishes all employees in order to feel superior.

Storyteller Generally speaking, Always Right bosses are not good listeners. This inability to hear the full story will rub a storytelling employee the wrong way. To depersonalize this situation, find other people who want to hear your anecdotes and ideas. Realize that your leader can tolerate only short, concise comments. Even these statements must be offered after the boss has asserted his or her views. Aim for brief sound bites rather than full disclosure.

Disarmer Disarmers see the writing on the wall quickly when it comes to an "I'm Always Right" boss. Once you've discovered that your manager must be correct on every issue, you can depersonalize by using humor to deflect any negative reactions to your ideas.

Coaster Coasters don't seek recognition or responsibility in most work situations. They're rarely bothered by bosses who believe that only their ideas and opinions matter. If you need to depersonalize from an Always Right boss, use your friendly personality to affirm and acknowledge your boss on a regular basis.

Low Beamer Low Beamer employees generally appreciate this employer's ability to spell out the correct way of doing things. They also welcome solid leadership, which Always Right bosses provide. The most challenging moment may be when your boss corrects or criticizes your work because it does not reflect his or her views. To depersonalize from these moments, refrain from arguing over who is correct. Take notes, make the adjustments, and understand that everyone, not just you, is adhering to your Always Right boss's rules.

Depersonalizing from "You Threaten Me"

You can never outshine the "You Threaten Me" boss. Should you attract too much positive attention to yourself, your boss will take actions to hold you back.

UNIVERSAL LAW: YOUR BOSS HAS TROUBLE WITH OTHER PEOPLE'S SUCCESS.

Nurturer Nurturers work hard to support their bosses. They are not that concerned about receiving accolades for their accomplishments. For this reason, "You Threaten Me" bosses aren't threatened by them.

Harmonizer In general, a harmonizing employee will downplay his or her workplace successes so as not to threaten anyone. If, however, you sense that a colleague's success could threaten the boss, you may help that person depersonalize by suggesting ways to defuse your boss's envy. Helping others helps you.

Star The first time this kind of boss says or does something to diminish your success, you won't like it. Instead of challenging his or her attempts to shoot you down, you can depersonalize. Until you are ready to move on, focus on doing your usual excellent work and let the criticism roll off your back.

Challenger It's important to remember that a "You Threaten Me" boss can listen to your ideas if you don't question his or her authority. You will have to deliver your ideas and express your opinions in a friendly, measured fashion. Depersonalize by understanding that your employer must have top billing. You can win some points, but you must support his or her overall success.

Observer Observers generally aren't bothered by this brand of behavior. As long as the boss allows you to work at your own pace, and respects the results you produce, you won't have many problems. Should you be disturbed by "You Threaten Me"'s envy of other people's success, you can depersonalize by seeing your boss's insecurity with compassion rather than disdain.

Worker Bee Worker Bees generally don't require attention, but they do seek recognition for their performance. If, by chance, you receive special recognition for your work from a client, association, or high-ranking executive, be prepared for a negative reaction from your easily threatened boss. To depersonalize, remember that you deserve the praise, even if your boss tries to convince you otherwise.

Storyteller The Storyteller's greatest need is to be heard and to have his or her experiences acknowledged. While a "You Threaten Me" boss may be competitive regarding success, he or she is often willing to listen to employees in exchange for their loyalty and support.

Disarmer As long as you do not attempt to outshine your boss, your ability to infuse humor into the workplace will be appreciated by your easily threatened, insecure leader. Should you receive too much positive attention—in the form of either general popularity or appreciation from high-level executives—you may have to depersonalize your manager's sudden cutting comments. To do this, remember that you didn't do anything wrong. It's just that your boss can't tolerate being outshined in any way.

Coaster Because Coasters aren't competing to be recognized for their excellent work, you pose no threat to a "You Threaten Me" boss. This kind of leader should be no problem for you.

Low Beamer Like the Coaster, you aren't trying to gain visibility in the workplace. Your low-risk approach to work virtually guarantees smooth sailing with a "You Threaten Me" boss.

Depersonalizing from Grandiose

Part of your job is reinforcing your boss's ego with compliments, acknowledgment, and respectful treatment. Your Grandiose boss must be recognized as the best in any situation.

UNIVERSAL LAW: YOUR BOSS SPENDS A GREAT DEAL OF ENERGY REINFORCING HIS OR HER SELF-IMAGE. UNDERNEATH THE BLUSTER IS A FEAR OF BEING FOUND LACKING.

Nurturer Nurturers tend to see through the Grandiose boss's blustery ways and focus on supporting their emotionally needy leader without judgment. You may not need help depersonalizing from your boss, but make sure to restore your energy on a daily basis (see Chapter 3).

Harmonizer Harmonizers are able to tune in to a Grandiose boss's need to be center stage and don't mind listening to the war stories for short periods of time. To depersonalize your relationship with this overbearing manager, keep the amount of time you spend in his or her company to a minimum. Working around a Grandiose boss usually yields the best results.

Star Star employees find the Grandiose boss's shameless self-promotion entertaining. You'll quickly learn that this loud leader attributes any success you have on the job to his or her brilliance: "I made you who you are today!" To depersonalize, learn to let your boss have the credit while you move forward with your career. Trust that both colleagues and contemporaries know the truth about your accomplishments, despite your manager's grand claims.

Challenger This kind of boss is very difficult for a Challenger because your ideas, opinions, and outlook fall on deaf ears. If the Grandiose boss senses that you don't respect his or her authority, you'll receive verbal lashings and public putdowns. To depersonalize from your big-ego boss, remember that his or her inability to acknowledge your point of view is not about you. Save your ideas for more receptive audiences and vent your frustration outside of work.

Observer Observers aren't easily swayed by authority figures. The sweeping statements and flashy gestures of a Grandiose boss probably won't impress an observing employee. To depersonalize from this brand of leader, try limiting your contact—if possible. When you do have to listen, try to respond to your boss's self-aggrandizing statements with a glimmer of respect.

Worker Bee Because Worker Bees fear being ridiculed or having to deal with another person's anger, the blustery Grandiose boss can be intimidating and overpowering. To depersonalize from your Grandiose manager, don't take his or her dramatic delivery of criticism or anger to heart. Instead, try giving your boss the praise, recognition, and acknowledgment that he or she desires.

Storyteller Anyone who works for a Grandiose boss quickly learns that this person has very little interest in listening. He or she wants only to be heard. A storytelling employee will find this characteristic extremely frustrating. Unfortunately, your need to hold your boss's attention as you carefully recount your own experiences will never be fulfilled. To depersonalize, you'll have to incorporate your boss's constant tale-telling as one of the realities of your job. Look for friends and colleagues who can hear your personal and professional stories.

Disarmer Generally speaking, disarming employees can handle Grandiose bosses quite well. You'll learn how to make this attention-seeking supervisor laugh. You'll also be able to follow the showy leader's explicit instructions regarding how to perform each aspect of your job. You know not to take the boss's bluster and bragging personally.

Coaster Initially, a coasting employee can charm the boss by listening intently to his or her war stories. Over time, however, your employer may be disappointed by your lack of initiative and drive. Grandiose bosses hold high standards for everyone around them and tend to ride those who don't measure up. To depersonalize, learn to hear your blustery boss's claims about your incompetence as part of his or her superiority song.

Low Beamer This could be a good boss/employee match. Grandiose bosses like to teach. This kind of manager will be happy to give explicit instructions to a low-beaming employee. He or she will also answer any questions that come up as you attempt to accomplish your assigned tasks. Your biggest challenge with a Grandiose leader involves the energy-zapping effect of tending to your boss's outsized ego. To depersonalize, add "listen to my boss talk" to your job description and take frequent breaks to reenergize.

Depersonalizing from Control Freaks

Your Control Freak boss has a very hard time trusting anyone to carry out his or her directives properly. No decisions can be made without the boss's direct approval.

UNIVERSAL LAW: PLAGUED BY PERFECTIONISM, THIS PERSON IS TERRIFIED OF LOSING CONTROL.

Nurturer This kind of boss can be very challenging for a nurturing employee who is accustomed to winning the boss's trust immediately. You may find your controlling boss's rigid rules confining and, frankly, somewhat insulting. To depersonalize, understand that the Control Freak's need to scrutinize everything you do is not a reflection of your value or competence. You can earn this leader's trust if you hang in there and do exactly what he or she asks.

Harmonizer Initially, a harmonizing employee may find the Control Freak's tight grip irritating. Harmonizers like to be entrusted with responsibility and don't appreciate waiting around for approval. With time, however, you can depersonalize by understanding that your boss needs to carefully oversee all functions before he or she can loosen the reigns.

Star Stars do not fare well under micromanagers. The Control Freak's need to weigh in on every decision and review every action slows the Star down. It also triggers the Star's fear of being held back. To depersonalize from your boss's constricting behavior, realize that this person's inability to let you charge ahead is not about you. Slow down, follow the rules, and wait for opportunities to shine.

Challenger This brand of boss is particularly difficult for Challengers. Your manager will thwart your attempts to shake things up until he or she believes you are a trustworthy member of the team. If you can slow down and play by your boss's rules, you may be able to win his or her trust.

Observer On the one hand, Observers appreciate the consistency and predictability that a Control Freak boss has to offer. On the other hand, they don't like to be scrutinized and they resent anyone telling them how to perform their job. To depersonalize, your best bet is to prove that you don't require constant surveillance by following your boss's explicit instructions for a period of time.

Worker Bee Worker Bees may find this boss's need to hone in on their work and dictate the exact way of doing things unnerving. Because Control Freaks need full disclosure, you'll have to defend and explain each action you take. This will feel confrontational. To depersonalize from a Control Freak boss, understand that this person needs time and experience to ease up on the oversight.

Storyteller This employee/boss combination is a mixed bag. Most Control Freak bosses will appreciate the Storyteller's thoroughness and attention to detail. Troubles arise when the Storyteller experiences the boss's heavy-handed management style as a message of incompetence. To depersonalize, try to develop a thicker skin when your controlling leader starts to correct you. Remember that this individual needs to micromanage everyone, not just you.

Disarmer Disarmers usually have a special gift for reading their bosses' moods and deciphering their needs. Control Freaks will appreciate the Disarmer's ability to lessen their anxiety with humor. They will also like the Disarmer's inclination to produce work that meets their detailed requirements. To depersonalize, remember that there will be times when you miss the mark. Your boss can't resist finding the one detail that you overlooked. It doesn't mean you're incompetent.

Coaster Coasters do not respond well to pressure and may find this boss's constant requests for status reports stressful and annoying. To depersonalize from your vigilant manager, realize that your boss isn't questioning your competence. Controlling bosses drill their employees with questions to reduce their own anxiety. Try to play along.

Low Beamer For Low Beamers, this brand of boss could be a perfect fit. A Control Freak boss gives low-beaming employees clear instruction, detailed assignments, and constant oversight. Your boss won't ask you to do anything without showing you how to do it.

CATEGORY 3: LINE CROSSERS

Depersonalizing from Love-Struck

You cannot control your boss's feelings of affection for you. You will eventually have to set a limit.

UNIVERSAL LAW: YOUR LOVE-STRUCK BOSS IS EMOTIONALLY
HUNGRY AND PROFESSIONALLY DANGEROUS.

Nurturer Nurturers who sense that the boss is Love-Struck are in a
double bind. First, they worry that their acts of kindness and concern
toward the boss may have triggered his or her amorous feelings. Second,
they fear being perceived as cold and uncaring if they reject the boss's
affections. To depersonalize, realize that you didn't cause this to happen,
and your boss will survive no matter what you do.

Harmonizer Harmonizers feel extremely uncomfortable in any situation
where they think someone will get emotionally hurt. If Harmonizers
notice that their boss is Love-Struck, they will feel nervous and worried
about the consequences of rejecting his or her affections. To depersonalize, understand that your boss will survive any verdict you arrive at.

Star Stars enjoy attention and admiration. A Love-Struck boss may be
enjoyable at first. At the same time, your clearheaded ambition will help
you draw the line and turn your Love-Struck boss's admiration into professional support. To depersonalize, see that your boss's feelings are his
or hers to manage. Enjoy the special attention, but don't return it in kind.

Challenger It can be exciting for Challengers when the person who holds
power over them also finds them irresistible. For once, your boss sees you
and appreciates your work. You aren't the office scapegoat. If you've got
a Love-Struck boss, enjoy the ride, but be careful when playing with this
workplace fire. Depersonalize by remembering that one of you may get
hurt in the end. Proceed carefully.

Observer Observers can tolerate a wide variety of behaviors. An observing employee will notice the Love-Struck boss's flirtatious behavior and
be amused by it at first. Over time, however, you may feel increasingly
uncomfortable. To depersonalize, use your cautious behavior to deliver a
consistently cool message. Know that your smitten leader will eventually
move on to a more receptive audience.

Worker Bee Because Worker Bees fear making other people angry, a
Love-Struck boss can be very intimidating. To depersonalize from a boss
who has amorous feelings for you, understand that you don't have to do
anything to address the situation directly. Your boss's feelings are not
your responsibility.

Storyteller Storytellers are often so busy communicating that they don't notice when the boss develops a crush on them. If your boss is Love-Struck, he or she may find everything you have to say fascinating—an experience you will relish. To depersonalize from a Love-Struck boss, keep in mind that you don't have to explain or defend your reasons for keeping the relationship professional.

Disarmer Disarmers are generally attractive people who are used to both colleagues and authority figures adoring them. Should your boss's admiration cross the line, you can use humor and compassion. Depersonalize by keeping the focus on doing your job. Your boss will still like you even if you don't reciprocate his or her amorous feelings.

Coaster Because Coasters are charming, they can handle a Love-Struck boss with minimal distress. A coasting employee will enjoy the attention and be able to manage the relationship without getting entangled. To depersonalize, help your boss steer the relationship into safer waters.

Low Beamer Low Beamers desire clearly defined roles and rules at work. A Love-Struck boss can feel very threatening. If you're already in a solid relationship, the overtures of a smitten manager will make you nervous and uneasy. If you're looking for love, your boss's open arms could be very tempting. To depersonalize, remind yourself that you are not responsible for your boss's feelings. You don't have to do anything to fulfill his or her romantic desires. Cross this line cautiously.

Depersonalizing from Calculating Confidants

These bosses will use your personal information for their own professional gain. Your Calculating Confidant boss does not truly care about your personal problems.

UNIVERSAL LAW: THIS PERSON WILL TRY TO GET CLOSE TO YOU TO GET THE UPPER HAND.

Nurturer Nurturers naturally want to be needed by and useful to their bosses. They approach leadership eager to help out. You may discover that your boss is calculating long after you've confided personal secrets about yourself and your colleagues. To depersonalize from this kind of boss, understand that not everyone who appears nurturing actually is. Learn to keep confidential information to yourself.

Harmonizer Because Harmonizers are natural bridge-builders, they become uncomfortable in situations where gossip or personal information is used in the workplace. To depersonalize from this kind of leader, trust your instincts when you sense that your boss's need for the intimate details about your life outside of work may have ulterior motives. Don't be seduced.

Star Stars like to be seen and appreciated and will initially enjoy the attention that a Calculating Confidant offers. This kind of boss will want to know *all* about you. You may divulge a good deal about yourself both personally and professionally before you catch on to the game. To depersonalize, understand that you are not alone. You're working for someone who embodies the fact that not all attention is positive. Be cautious when your boss seems overly eager to know the intimate details of your life, and share less.

Challenger Challengers approach any relationship with authority from a slightly skeptical perspective. This serves them well when faced with a Calculating Confidant boss. Chances are you'll be hesitant to share too much personal information with this person. Trust your gut and keep your invasive boss at arm's length.

Observer Most Observers have built-in poser radar—they can spot a bogus boss from miles away. To depersonalize from a Calculating Confidant, trust your internal signals and keep your private information under wraps.

Worker Bee Quiet and unassuming, Worker Bees may have mixed reactions to this kind of employer. On the one hand, you may enjoy the attention. On the other hand, you aren't someone who naturally offers personal information to anyone. And you aren't interested in hearing about the dirty laundry of your colleagues. For these reasons, you won't have to work at taking a Calculating Confidant less personally. It's your instinctive inclination.

Storyteller While Storytellers like to share numerous anecdotes about themselves and the people they know, their material is generally not very intimate. Calculating Confidants are usually looking for more incriminating evidence than a storytelling employee will deliver. This brand of boss may grow impatient with you and become critical of your performance— in part because you aren't playing his or her game. To depersonalize, try not to take this authority figure's dismissive attitude toward you to heart. This is one inner circle that you don't want to belong to.

Disarmer To the Calculating Confidant's dismay, disarming employees are actually quite private about their lives outside of work and quite adept at keeping other people's secrets. If your boss tries to dig for confidential information, your tendency will be to brush off the inquiry with a joke. To depersonalize, understand that your boss has a bad habit of uncovering other people's secrets only to misuse them. Don't add any fuel to the fire.

Coaster Unfortunately, Coasters can easily succumb to the Calculating Confidant's ways. Your ability to be insightful about others will appeal to this kind of manager, who will encourage you to supply news, gossip, or juicy details about your colleagues. To depersonalize, keep in mind that your willingness to offer information about others could backfire. Should your boss be taken to task for unfairly bad-mouthing someone at work, he or she may point the finger back at you.

Low Beamer True low-beaming employees do not wish to mix business with pleasure. They also want to minimize the chances of bringing negative attention to themselves. A Calculating Confidant will quickly learn that you are not interested in divulging much of anything except your time sheets and workplace requirements.

Depersonalizing from Tell-Alls

Your boss is self-centered and obsessed with his or her own problems. Sharing stories about personal dramas is the Tell-All's way of seducing you into taking care of him or her.

UNIVERSAL LAW: THIS PERSON CONFIDES IN OTHERS TO ELICIT SYMPATHY AND PROTECTION.

Nurturer Nurturers live to take care of others. At first, a Tell-All boss will seem like the answer to your caregiving dreams. Problems arise when you find yourself doing two jobs—yours and your employer's. To depersonalize, recognize that your boss is using you (and others). Consider whether propping this person up is helping or hurting you.

Harmonizer When a harmonizing employee encounters a Tell-All boss, the initial impulse will be to try to solve this leader's problems. With time, however, you'll notice that your best advice goes unheeded, and there's no end to the Tell-All's woes. To depersonalize, remind yourself that the person you work for doesn't really want to get better. You aren't the first person who failed to rescue your boss, and you won't be the last.

Star Tell-Alls can be very alluring to Star employees. After confessing their problems, these bosses then draw on the Star's strength, drive, and competence. Your emotionally manipulative boss reels you in by telling you how wonderful you are and how much he or she relies on your assistance. Over time, you end up taking on all of this leader's responsibilities. The burden never ends; it escalates. To depersonalize, realize that you aren't responsible for solving your boss's problems. Tell-Alls can always find someone else to lean on.

Challenger This boss/employee combination tends to be problematic. Tell-Alls don't like to be challenged. They want their employees to listen, feel sorry for them, and do their work. Challengers don't believe in emotional hand-holding. They'll either give advice or take action to tackle the problem. Tell-Alls experience Challengers as abrasive and bossy. To depersonalize from this helpless manager, understand that some people have no interest in changing, getting better, or resolving their personal problems.

Observer Because Observers approach their managers from a more detached perspective, they aren't as easily sucked into solving the Tell-All's many problems. At the same time, observing employees like to take on important projects and may need to guard against overcompensating for this kind of boss. To depersonalize, check in regularly to make sure your in-box isn't overloaded with your manager's responsibilities. Remember that Tell-Alls tend to take advantage of those who are willing to carry a heavy load.

Worker Bee A Tell-All boss can be both entertaining and overwhelming for a Worker Bee employee. You may find this employer's colorful tales and personal dramas both fascinating and amusing. You may also want to do what you can quietly to lighten your beleaguered manager's emotional burdens. To depersonalize, realize that your boss's dramas and difficulties will never end. Avoid becoming emotionally and professionally drained.

Storyteller Because Tell-Alls require a constant audience from their employees, this kind of boss is tough for a Storyteller, who needs to be heard in order to feel understood. A Tell-All boss won't want to listen to your anecdotes or explanations. In fact, your manager may push you aside if it appears that you'd rather talk than listen. To depersonalize, understand that your boss is incapable of hearing anyone's story but his or her own.

Disarmer Tell-Alls like comic relief and appreciate having funny people around them. The Disarmer's capable attitude is also a source of comfort for this kind of boss. Using your humor and charm, you'll naturally know how to dodge the emotional neediness of a Tell-All manager. To depersonalize, trust your instincts and set limits.

Coaster When the Tell-All boss encounters a coasting employee, both parties feel at ease. Coasters have no problem listening to their boss's many personal travails. A Coaster sees these confessional sessions as a good excuse for not working too hard. When the Tell-All shares a personal tragedy, you're all ears. You may have to draw the line, however, if your manager pressures you to take on his or her responsibilities. To depersonalize, don't take to heart the pressure the Tell-All puts on you.

Low Beamer Most low-beaming employees see a job as a job and resent situations where they are asked to shoulder additional responsibilities. This is especially true with Tell-All bosses, who lean on others emotionally, imploring them to have pity and take on a heavier workload. This kind of boss will pressure you to perform beyond your comfort zone. To depersonalize, realize that you didn't do anything to warrant this pressure. Tell-Alls can't help enlisting everyone around them to feel responsible for their happiness.

Depersonalizing from Liar, Liars

You work for someone who feels comfortable altering the truth. Your Liar, Liar boss is not trustworthy.

UNIVERSAL LAW: YOUR BOSS BENDS THE TRUTH TO SUIT HIS OR HER PURPOSES.

Nurturer While it may not be pleasant to work for someone who lies, Nurturers can handle this kind of leader better than most. You're able to see the boss's habit of stretching, bending, or altering the truth through somewhat compassionate eyes. You know that he or she has a deep-rooted problem, and it's not going to go away. To depersonalize, continue to regard your manager's lying as a problem that you didn't cause.

Harmonizer Harmonizers have a very hard time with Liar, Liar bosses because they see and feel the fallout when this kind of leader deceives or misleads others. To depersonalize, realize that you are not responsible for the falsehoods that your boss fabricates. The next time this person overpromises or misrepresents the truth, resist the urge to rush in and cover for him or her. Let the boss's lies be exposed.

Star Star employees like to hear the truth, but they also appreciate how a slight exaggeration can enhance one's professional standing. Exaggeration is one thing. Telling a blatant lie is another. Stars don't like being lied to. To depersonalize from this kind of leader, know that you work for someone who is incapable of being honest. Carefully decipher what's truly going on—regardless of what your lying boss says.

Challenger Every Challenger has a strong orientation toward fairness. When a Challenger senses that the boss is lying and manipulating the truth, internal alarms go off. To depersonalize from a Liar, Liar boss, you have to realize that you didn't cause this person's condition and you aren't going to change it. If you need a fair boss, look elsewhere.

Observer Liar, Liar bosses play into observing employees' worst fears. Observers cannot stand disingenuous behavior. They also feel diminished and marginalized by this kind of leader's flagrant disregard for the truth. To depersonalize, understand that your boss lies to everyone—not just you.

Worker Bee Worker Bees tend to give the people they work for the benefit of the doubt. It may take a Worker Bee longer than it takes other coworkers to discern the boss's propensity for stretching or ignoring the truth. Once your manager's mendacious ways become obvious to you, however, it is a great disappointment. To depersonalize, understand that your boss operates from a unique moral code. These individuals lie because they believe it's the only way to accomplish their goals.

Storyteller Because Storytellers like details and facts, they don't appreciate anyone tampering with these things. Storytelling employees work hard to earn people's trust and do not respond well to someone breaking theirs. To depersonalize from a Liar, Liar boss, you'll have to realize that you work for someone whose words and actions don't always match. It's not about you. This person is constitutionally incapable of consistently telling the truth.

Disarmer When disarming employees perceive that the boss may be a Liar, Liar, they immediately work on damage control. Disarmers have a gift for gently cornering this kind of boss, offering evidence of whatever lie has been told. While you may be able to uncover certain falsehoods, you'll still need to depersonalize by understanding that your boss will continue to lie.

Coaster Unlike other employees, Coasters can tolerate Liar, Liar bosses as long as the truth-stretching doesn't threaten their own reputation or increase their workload. Coasters don't mind exaggeration, overpromising, or false advertising unless it adds pressure to their jobs. To depersonalize, realize that, if caught in a lie, this kind of boss will probably try to lay the blame on you. This unfair finger-pointing is not about you, although it may feel very personal.

Low Beamer Because Low Beamers need to know exactly what's expected of them and like clear-cut rules and policies, a Liar, Liar boss is their worst nightmare. You may have a hard time deciphering the truth of any situation, and your boss will not help you. To depersonalize from this kind of leader, you'll have to understand that you're working for someone who doesn't value the truth the way you do. Stop expecting your boss to live up to your standards.

CATEGORY 4: AMBIVALENT LEADERS

Depersonalizing from Sacred Cows

Your boss may not be competent, but this Sacred Cow isn't going anywhere. If you challenge your boss's authority, you will lose.

UNIVERSAL LAW: THIS PERSON IS RISK-AVERSE AND INVESTED IN MAINTAINING THE STATUS QUO. HE OR SHE IS A PROTECTED LEADER.

Nurturer Sacred Cow bosses sense that nurturing employees care about them and appreciate their acts of kindness. You're able to see your guarded leader's need for constant reassurance and inclusion in any project. On those occasions when the Sacred Cow thwarts your attempts at trying anything new or innovative, you can depersonalize by remembering to give your boss credit for any positive results. The more secure and praised your Sacred Cow boss feels, the more likely he or she is to see things your way.

Harmonizer Initially, a harmonizing employee may butt heads with a Sacred Cow boss. Harmonizers are accustomed to gaining their boss's trust and approval. They have a hard time with anyone who would systematically block their best efforts. To depersonalize, realize that you are working for someone whose greatest fear is looking foolish. You can win your boss over by taking a friendly stance and sharing credit for any achievements that you or your colleagues produce.

Star Sacred Cow bosses tend to trigger Star employees' worst fears. As your fearful boss continually puts the brakes on any project you'd like to push forward, you start to feel dismissed, marginalized, and held back. To depersonalize, use your strong people skills to work around the problem. Understand that the first line of business is to make your ideas seem as if they are also the property of your boss. You have to slow down enough to share the credit and make the boss feel as if he or she plays an integral part in the planning process. You do the work; you and your Sacred Cow boss share the glory.

Challenger For the freethinking Challenger, a Sacred Cow boss is the absolute nemesis. Every idea, opinion, position, or plan you offer will quickly be shot down. You'll feel as if you're locked inside a bureaucratic prison. To depersonalize, you'll need to constantly remind yourself that your infuriating manager is probably threatened by your innovative approach to problem solving. This person isn't going anywhere, so your best bet is to back off and look for ways to build trust. Instead of condemning and confronting your boss, take on the challenge of working with your polar opposite.

Observer Because you are able to take a broader view of your manager, this kind of authority figure should be manageable for you. On the one hand, you'll like the fact that your Sacred Cow boss doesn't pressure you to perform. On the other hand, you may find it difficult to respect someone whose only concern is maintaining the status quo. To depersonalize, use your perceptive abilities to determine when your boss is open to taking action and when the door is closed. It's a lot of work, but you can keep a careful watch on this leader's mind-set and push your ideas when the perfect opportunity arises.

Worker Bee Ever-resourceful Worker Bees are masters of the workaround and do not find the Sacred Cow's static ways too cumbersome. If, at times, you are frustrated by the lack of progress that your department or division seems to make, you can depersonalize by realizing that this leader isn't going anywhere. You need to continue to work around the boss and share the credit for your achievements.

Storyteller Generally speaking, Sacred Cow bosses can relate well to storytelling employees. A friendly Sacred Cow will gladly share anecdotes, seeing the tale-telling as a valuable workplace activity. Your ability to give detailed accounts of workplace events and personal adventures will provide this leader with hours of entertainment. Your boss will feel informed and safe in your company. Should you work for a dour Sacred Cow, he or she may be less appreciative of your conversational skills. You can depersonalize from a brusque boss by understanding that this brand of bovine is not open to anyone's stories. Stick to doing your job, and share your narratives somewhere else.

Disarmer Disarmers like a certain amount of independence on the job and pride themselves on being productive. A Sacred Cow boss could be quite frustrating. You'll know how to humor this kind of leader, but your best jokes won't move the boss to relinquish control. To depersonalize, remember that this individual is extremely risk-averse and fears doing anything beyond the status quo. Use humor and warmth to build trust.

Coaster A coasting employee and a Sacred Cow boss make the perfect match. You'll appreciate the fact that your employer isn't overly concerned with producing results. Your boss will like your relaxed attitude on the job and your desire to balance work and home life.

Low Beamer This kind of manager fulfills many of the low-beaming employee's needs. Sacred Cow bosses will ask you to do your job by the book. Because they don't like to make mistakes, change policies, or look bad, Sacred Cows will instruct you to do your work carefully, exactly as it has been done in the past.

Depersonalizing from Checked Out Bosses

This leader is preoccupied with non-work-related personal matters. Your Checked Out boss is not capable of managing you or anyone else effectively.

UNIVERSAL LAW: YOUR BOSS IS EMOTIONALLY AND
MENTALLY CHECKED OUT FROM THE WORK ENVIRONMENT
AND UNABLE TO LEAD.

Nurturer Nurturers like to be needed. When you first discover that your boss is Checked Out, you'll probably work hard to cover for him or her. After a while, however, you'll start to crave some direction, and your absentee leader won't be able to give it to you. Because you're shouldering too much responsibility, you'll feel stressed out and overwhelmed. To depersonalize, understand that you're in a temporary situation. Try delegating some of the responsibilities you're shouldering to colleagues who can help carry the weight.

Harmonizer When harmonizing employees detect that the boss is Checked Out, the first impulse is to try to make their wounded leader feel emotionally supported and understood. Once it becomes evident that the boss cannot meet the demands of his or her post, Harmonizers then look to galvanize the troops. To depersonalize from a Checked Out boss, realize that you cannot cure your employer's personal malaise. Focus instead on building cooperation among your colleagues and distributing the work.

Star Star employees quickly identify situations where the leader is not taking charge. Initially, Stars will approach a Checked Out boss and offer to step into the leadership role. The boss may thank them for the offer but insist on keeping the reigns of control. To depersonalize, focus on the boss's actions and the fact that he or she is not capable of steering the company ship. You can then step into a leadership position, keep the boss informed of your actions, and wait for your manager's safe return.

Challenger This may be hard to believe, but Challengers actually like having someone to push against or challenge. If the boss is Checked Out, Challengers find the lack of leadership frustrating and a little disorienting. You may misinterpret your boss's preoccupation with personal concerns as a message that he or she doesn't care about you or the company. This can lead to rebellious acts on your behalf (designed to catch your employer's attention). It's important to depersonalize by realizing that your boss's behavior has nothing to do with you and that acting out is not likely to help the situation. This individual needs your cooperation to weather this difficult period of time.

Observer Observing employees may not be disturbed by a Checked Out boss. As long as you know what your job is, you'll carry on until someone tells you to do otherwise. Keep cool, continue to do your work, and know that the boss will eventually return.

Worker Bee Worker Bees prefer to be left alone to do their jobs, so this kind of boss may not be troublesome for them. You may be concerned for your boss's well-being, but you won't mind the distant look in his or her eyes. Depersonalizing this person's mental and emotional absence will come naturally to you.

Storyteller When a boss is unable to listen or give you the attention you seek, you may interpret that behavior as a rebuke or rejection of some kind. To depersonalize, understand that the boss's disinterest is not an indictment of you. The person you used to work for has temporarily been replaced by a hologram. Your real boss will return once his or her personal crisis has subsided.

Disarmer Because you are accustomed to your boss's being an apprecia-tive audience, it may be challenging when this person checks out and pulls away. You may feel hurt and a bit disrespected. To depersonalize, realize that your employer is on a temporary hiatus. He or she will return and be willing to laugh again soon.

Coaster Coasters don't like pressure and are good at keeping relation-ships light. For these reasons, a Checked Out boss may not cause any kind of distress. You can maintain your usual relaxed, friendly stance and wait for the old boss to come back.

Low Beamer This is not an easy boss/employee combination. Low Beamers like explicit directions and want someone at the helm who will always clarify where the department or company is headed. You may feel abandoned and set up to fail. To depersonalize from a Checked Out boss, focus on doing your job to the best of your ability. Understand that this leader is not out to foil you. See if anyone else in the office can take the lead while you wait for your troubled employer to check back in.

Depersonalizing from Spineless Bosses

Your Spineless boss is not capable of defending anyone—including him- or herself. This person will never enforce a rule or policy that may incur someone else's wrath.

UNIVERSAL LAW: THIS INDIVIDUAL CANNOT TAKE A STAND.

> **Nurturer** Nurturers are generally very valuable employees for this kind of boss, who appreciates the caring and protection that they naturally offer. The only time you'll have to depersonalize is when the boss fails to stand up for you when it's time for a promotion, a raise, or some other form of recognition. To take this leader's wishy-washy behavior less personally, consider mounting a "soft" campaign for any results that you want to create. You'll need to consistently remind your boss of the raise, promotion, award, or policy change that you're seeking. Be willing to hold your boss's hand through the slow process of making something happen.
>
> **Harmonizer** While you may not mind the fact that your boss cannot stand up on your behalf, you'll find it very disheartening when this manager's lack of a backbone causes distress to other members of the staff. To depersonalize, you'll need to step back and see that this person is constitutionally incapable of making strong decisions or coming to someone's aid. Use your bridge-building skills to help staff members figure out how to get what they need without calling on their employer's protection.
>
> **Star** Stars want and appreciate strong leadership. This kind of boss quickly loses the Star employee's respect because he or she isn't doing a fundamental part of the job—making tough decisions and taking a stand when conflicts arise. To depersonalize, use your leadership skills to fill in the gap. You can step in, take charge, and act as the office, department, or company leader.
>
> **Challenger** Because Challengers have a natural orientation toward fairness and desire justice, a Spineless boss presents serious problems. You'll want your nonconfrontational leader to change—grow a spine, stand up, and take charge. Very quickly, you'll learn that this person is incapable of such a transformation, and you'll be sorely disappointed. To depersonalize, do your best not to hold your boss in contempt. Stick to your job and zip your lip.

Observer Using their keen powers of perception, observing employees promptly detect when they're working for a Spineless employer. You can depersonalize by scanning your work environment and determining who the real decision makers are. Get your workplace needs met through the help of colleagues and coworkers other than the boss.

Worker Bee Once you identify that your boss is incapable of being decisive or engaging in protective or confrontational behavior on your behalf, your sense of safety at work will rapidly decrease. Worker Bees fear incurring the wrath of others and will have a hard time if their supervisor does not defend them against irate customers, angry coworkers, or abusive vendors. To depersonalize, you'll have to let go of any hope that your boss can advocate for you. Instead, look for people within the company who can come to your aid when the going gets tough.

Storyteller Spineless leadership is frustrating for storytelling employees because while the boss may listen to their ideas and nod in agreement, he or she never takes action. You can offer your boss explicit descriptions and details of improvements that you think would smooth out operations, but you aren't likely to see any results. To depersonalize, don't waste your words on someone who can only nod in agreement. Instead, look for those people who actually accomplish things and can help you get what you need.

Disarmer Even though your Spineless boss may laugh at your jokes and enjoy your sense of humor, you'll be annoyed by his or her refusal to take decisive action. Depersonalize by learning how best to work around your employer. You may find that you need to make decisions and take a stand on behalf of your boss.

Coaster Generally speaking, this kind of ambivalent boss is not terribly difficult for you. The only time you may have trouble with a Spineless employer is when someone—a customer, a colleague, or a coworker—targets you and the boss doesn't come to your aid. To depersonalize, understand that this individual is incapable of protecting anyone at work. See if someone else can come to your assistance.

Low Beamer Spineless bosses are usually capable in their areas of expertise. This kind of manager knows what needs to get done and, if you ask for instructions, will take hours explaining the specifics of performing certain on-the-job tasks. As long as you know what's expected of you, you may not be concerned with whether this authority figure defends your work. To depersonalize, you may have to forgive your boss for failing to come to your aid when someone attacks your performance. Learn to seek guidance and protection elsewhere.

Depersonalizing from Artful Dodgers

Your boss will always avoid delivering any kind of information that may tarnish his or her image. Underneath the friendly exterior lies a calculating and manipulative person.

UNIVERSAL LAW: THIS ARTFUL DODGER IS INCAPABLE OF BEING TRULY HONEST WITH ANYONE.

Nurturer Your greatest desire is to support the boss. With this kind of leader, "support" often means delivering bad news to coworkers or colleagues. After your boss has a pleasant meeting with an employee, you may be instructed to tell that same person that his or her work is substandard. You'll dread playing the role of bad cop on an ongoing basis. To depersonalize, understand that you work for someone who is incapable of giving negative feedback to anyone. Acting as this leader's bearer of bad news is part of the job.

Harmonizer Initially, a harmonizing employee will try to carry out the Artful Dodger's biddings. After receiving a few negative messages from the Harmonizer, however, members of the staff may turn against the messenger, creating a truly intolerable situation for this peace-seeking person. To depersonalize, realize that being the bad cop is a primary function of your job. Taking the flack for your boss is what anyone in this position must do.

Star Artful Dodgers are very good at building people up by showering them with compliments. Star employees enjoy being noticed and appreciated. The Star will happily take on any request that this flattering leader makes. It's not until your coworkers start to view you as the boss's hit man that you become aware of your tarnished reputation. To depersonalize, realize that your boss is using you to do his or her dirty work. Try becoming a bit less available as the negative mouthpiece.

Challenger You view yourself as a truth-teller and require the same from others. Challengers are quick to detect the disingenuous behavior of an Artful Dodger boss. You'll have trouble respecting this person or working hard on his or her behalf. To depersonalize, do your best to zip your lip. You'll want to expose the boss's two-faced ways, but that won't help anyone—especially you.

Observer Observers can smell a phony from a mile away. You'll be suspicious of this person's polished veneer and seductive use of flattery. Chances are that this kind of boss will also sense your skepticism. To depersonalize, keep a safe distance from your manager by artfully avoiding too much contact. Focus on doing your job with minimal fanfare.

Worker Bee A Worker Bee may like the Artful Dodger's polished presentation. In addition, Worker Bees enjoy receiving the accolades that this kind of boss dishes out. Problems arise when your employer asks you to confront a coworker, colleague, or vendor with some piece of bad news that he or she is unwilling to communicate directly. Your fear of incurring someone's anger will be in direct competition with your fear of disappointing the boss. To depersonalize, understand that your seemingly kind, appreciative boss is actually afraid of soiling his or her perfect image. Use your diplomatic side to communicate the boss's criticism.

Storyteller While other employees may have trouble with the Artful Dodger's methods, storytelling employees are equipped to handle this authority figure's management style. You'll be able to convey your boss's criticisms and concerns to others in a diplomatic way. Your boss will appreciate your willingness to deliver any message—no matter what the content.

Disarmer Disarmers like taking on responsibility and are able to deliver tough news with a light touch. An Artful Dodger boss will pick up on this ability and ask these capable employees to inform other members of the staff when their performance is not satisfactory. To depersonalize, consider this an exercise in using your humor to deliver negative feedback in a way that the staff can hear without being offended.

Coaster Because Coasters generally avoid positions that involve a great deal of responsibility, they don't have to worry about being asked to act as a mouthpiece for an Artful Dodger boss. A coasting employee may feel the sting, however, of being praised by this ingratiating employer, only to later receive scathing criticism via a third party. To depersonalize in these situations, notice that this two-faced approach to relating applies to everyone in the Artful Dodger's life. You are not alone.

Low Beamer The Artful Dodger boss is very confusing for a low-beaming employee who takes direction and feedback at face value. The first time you discover that your boss is incapable of giving you honest feedback, you'll lose all respect for this person. To depersonalize, console yourself with the fact that everyone receives the same treatment. Your leader's primary concern is looking good at all costs.

CATEGORY 5: DELICATE CIRCUMSTANCES

Depersonalizing from Junior Bosses

Although your boss is young and inexperienced, he or she has valuable skills that you don't possess. Your Junior boss may not appreciate the value of your experience.

UNIVERSAL LAW: LIKE IT OR NOT, THIS PERSON REPRESENTS THE FUTURE.

Nurturer When faced with a boss who is half your age, your nurturing instincts are likely to kick in. You may go overboard with attempts to make your manager feel at home. A Junior boss may push back—refusing the snacks you offer, politely closing the door instead of inviting you in to chat. To depersonalize, you'll need to step back and see that you're working for someone who requires a different kind of support than you're accustomed to offering. Relax and let the boss show you what kind of support he or she values most. You may have to trade in your tissues and candy for instant messages and a BlackBerry.

Harmonizer A harmonizing employee will approach a Junior boss with an air of curiosity—what makes this person tick, and how can I bridge the gap? It may be challenging when the Junior manager discounts your experience or treats older colleagues with disdain. To depersonalize, realize that your boss is inexperienced and could use interpersonal support. Find subtle ways to build bridges with the more senior members of the staff.

Star Normally, Star employees welcome the change and innovation that a Junior boss brings. You are likely to embrace your youthful leader as long as he or she recognizes your value. If the boss fails to respect your drive or recognize your talents, you can depersonalize by stepping back to discover what your new boss needs from you. Make it your business to help your newly instated Junior boss shine.

Challenger Because Challengers view themselves as mavericks in the workplace, they usually see the opportunity in having a Junior boss. They assume that a younger manager will embrace their fresh ideas and novel problem-solving techniques. Your job is to refrain from overwhelming this talented but inexperienced boss, who needs time to acclimate before adopting your plan. To depersonalize, do your best to back off until this leader comes to you.

Observer Observers naturally sit back and assess a new authority figure. A Junior boss won't feel threatened by you and may appreciate your cool approach to getting acquainted. If you feel pressured to adopt your youthful manager's high-tech ways, you can depersonalize by understanding that the stress you feel today will yield a stronger skill set for tomorrow.

Worker Bee Some Junior bosses come on strong with their ideas about how procedures need to be changed and what kinds of technology must be introduced. Worker Bees take a while to adjust to changes that are imposed on them from the outside and may find a Junior boss's schemes threatening. To depersonalize, try to view your newbie leader's plans and suggestions as opportunities to stay current.

Storyteller Storytelling employees are eager to please and may greet a Junior boss with open arms. They're willing to take on new methods of conducting business as long as they believe that the boss wants to hear about their experience and knowledge from the past. If you happen to have a youthful employer with little interest in history, you can depersonalize by finding someone else in the company with a sympathetic ear. Let this person act as a sounding board who can respect your experience and let you vent.

Disarmer A Junior boss is least difficult for the Disarmer to handle. You'll quickly try to make this inexperienced leader feel at ease. You'll jump on the change bandwagon and learn whatever skills are necessary to do the job. If your boss says or does things that leave you feeling incompetent, depersonalize by chalking his or her behavior up to technological arrogance. Take the new technical skills and run.

Coaster Junior bosses usually come into a department or division to usher in change. For a coasting employee, this is not a welcome development. You may fear the pressure of having to learn new skills or perform at a higher level. To depersonalize, know that whatever the change is, it's happening to everyone around you. Try to go with the program.

Low Beamer Low Beamers basically like to do their jobs and go home. The concept of having to learn new skills or approach work in a fresh way is stressful. A low-beaming employee won't necessarily be receptive to the Junior boss's plans to update and improve the current workplace. To depersonalize, try to see this youthful leader as a necessary teacher. The stress of learning new skills is temporary.

Depersonalizing from Former Colleagues

Your former relationship with this person will never return. Your colleague's new position requires that he or she hold you accountable.

UNIVERSAL LAW: YOUR FRIEND'S PROMOTION HAS PERMANENTLY CHANGED THE BALANCE OF POWER BETWEEN YOU.

Nurturer Because Nurturers form close bonds with their friends and colleagues, the distance that's created when a former colleague becomes the boss can be very painful. You'll enthusiastically congratulate your friend, but you'll miss the close contact, shared secrets, and mutual support. To depersonalize, give your ex-buddy boss time to adjust to the new position. Allow this individual to establish and communicate his or her new workplace boundaries. In time, you can find other ways to be close.

Harmonizer Initially, a harmonizing employee may have difficulty adjusting when a workplace friend becomes an authority figure. Harmonizers pride themselves on their relationships and see themselves as valuable assets to their peers. The important role that you played in your former colleague's work life may suddenly be diminished. To depersonalize, focus on discovering new ways that you can support and assist this friend who happens to be the boss.

Star Star employees may grapple with feelings of jealousy when they see a friend get promoted above them. Why him (or her) and not me? You may find your lower status in the new relationship very humbling. Rather than focus on the unfairness of the situation, depersonalize by examining what your former colleague did right to move ahead. Use your competitive spirit to learn from his or her success.

Challenger Challengers will experience a wide range of emotions over this hierarchical change. Initially, you may assume that your newly promoted colleague is going to be your greatest ally. You envision this person facing down the establishment; enacting all of the changes that you've been advocating for years. Once you realize that your workplace buddy has a new set of requirements to fulfill (none of which involve your agenda), you may feel quite deflated. To depersonalize, give your former colleague time and space to learn the ropes of the new job. Stay in touch, but try to keep your demands in check.

Observer Observers are naturally skeptical of authority, so when a friend gets promoted to management or supervisory status, it's not a welcome change. While you may wish your friend well in his or her new position, you'll also keep a careful eye to see how power changes (and corrupts) this former colleague. To depersonalize, try tempering your judgment by becoming knowledgeable about your former colleague's current responsibilities. Don't assume that he or she has gone over to the dark side.

Worker Bee Worker Bees are usually shy and very selective about their friendships at work. When a colleague gets promoted, the Worker Bee may quietly covet the recognition, but won't envy the added visibility or pressure. Your ability to keep a cool emotional distance allows you to incorporate the change without feeling slighted.

Storyteller When a good workplace friend gets promoted above them, Storytellers experience a significant sense of loss. Gone are the days of long, caring conversations. You'll yearn for both the camaraderie and the commiserating. To depersonalize, understand that the diminished time and attention you're receiving are not meant as a personal affront. Try to back off and schedule chatting time outside of the workplace.

Disarmer While you may not show it, you may feel some envy when a good friend moves above you on the corporate ladder. Taking orders from that person may also be a bit challenging. To depersonalize, realize that your former colleague is simply doing his or her new job. Use your competitive spirit to move your own career forward.

Coaster Generally speaking, Coasters don't mind watching their colleagues move ahead. They can be happy for an ambitious friend's success. Still, you may not be as joyful when your former colleague asks you to perform at a higher level. To depersonalize, understand that holding you accountable is part of your former colleague's new job description. Take it in stride.

Low Beamer Because Low Beamers don't compete for advancement in the workplace, they can tolerate a friend's promotion without feeling threatened. You may regret the loss of a friendship, but as long as your former colleague effectively manages you, you can adjust to the change in his or her status. If you have trouble with the shift in power, depersonalize by understanding that your colleague's management status requires a more formal way of interacting with you.

Depersonalizing from Unconscious Discriminators

Your boss is unintentionally treating you unfairly. This Unconscious Discriminator is uncomfortable with the differences between the two of you.

UNIVERSAL LAW: THIS PERSON IS UNAWARE OF THE WAYS IN WHICH HE OR SHE DISCRIMINATES.

Nurturer When this kind of boss says or does something that is discriminating to a nurturing employee, the first reaction is to feel hurt and embarrassed. Nurturers see themselves as strong and supportive; they don't like to admit it when the boss's behavior hurts their feelings. To depersonalize from an Unconscious Discriminator, try to hear and see the biased behavior as an indication that your unaware leader lacks information. Focus your efforts on educating this person.

Harmonizer The first time a Harmonizer experiences prejudicial treatment from an Unconscious Discriminator, it may cause embarrassment and distress. Harmonizers hate being misunderstood. In response to the jab, you may want to pull away from your manager for fear of being further misinterpreted. To depersonalize, realize that whatever the boss is saying or doing, it comes from a place of misinformation, not malice. Try to gently dispel your leader's distorted perceptions.

Star When Star employees detect discrimination from the boss, they immediately become alarmed. They fear that the boss's bias will hold them back. Once you have a moment to calm down, however, you can see the situation in a different light. To depersonalize, let your natural teaching ability come to your aid. Focus on imparting your wisdom to the uneducated. The Unconscious Discriminator will be grateful for the enlightenment.

Challenger Faced with discriminatory treatment from the boss, Challengers become completely incensed. They feel attacked by this careless chief—unfairly judged and misperceived. A Challenger's natural tendency under such conditions is to launch a counterattack, which only makes matters worse. To depersonalize, try to see your uninformed leader as innocent instead of guilty. If you give this person the benefit of the doubt, you can diplomatically communicate your concerns.

Observer When Observers realize that their employer has an unconscious prejudice against them, the first reaction is to lose all respect for that person. The next step may be to label your boss as a loser, a jerk, an idiot, or a moron.While it may be gratifying to fight fire with fire, try to depersonalize. You can do this by assuming that your leader might benefit from a carefully crafted correction of his or her bias.

Worker Bee Worker Bees don't like being attacked or having to defend themselves. If you notice that your boss unconsciously discriminates in some way, you're likely to assume that you just have to take it. To depersonalize, draw upon your ability to let hurtful words roll off your back. Understand that whatever the boss says or does is a reflection of him or her, not you.

Storyteller Storytellers have less trouble depersonalizing from this kind of situation than do other employees. As skilled communicators, they will tackle the discriminatory behavior head on, in a kind but thorough manner.

Disarmer Disarmers use humor and charm to control the outcome of their relationships. When a boss inadvertently says or does something that reveals a prejudice against some aspect of a Disarmer's appearance, intelligence, or ethnicity, the cut runs very deep. To depersonalize, realize that your leader's bumbling ways are not meant to harm you. When you're ready, it may be worthwhile to let the boss know the impact of his or her behavior.

Coaster Most Coasters won't admit when they sense that their employer is treating them unfairly due to unconscious prejudice. Instead, a coasting employee lets the insensitive remarks of a clueless manager slide. To depersonalize, do your best to see the boss as oblivious, not spiteful. His or her injurious words or behavior have nothing to do with your character. Let them go.

Low Beamer When an Unconscious Discriminator delivers an insensitive remark to a low-beaming employee, it's immediately experienced as a personal affront. You'll be tempted to go directly to HR and report the behavioral misdemeanor to the office "police." To depersonalize, see if you can give the boss an opportunity to amend his or her egregious conduct before reporting it to the authorities.

Depersonalizing from Persecutors

For reasons you may not understand, your boss has decided to target you as a recipient of negative feedback. There is very little you can do to change your Persecutor boss's mind.

UNIVERSAL LAW: THIS INDIVIDUAL SINGLES OUT AND PERSECUTES EMPLOYEES ON A REGULAR BASIS.

Nurturer This kind of boss isn't easy for anyone, but it's extremely uncomfortable for Nurturer employees who are used to having close associations with the boss and being appreciated for their emotional support. If you are the target of a persecuting manager, depersonalize by seeing your boss as emotionally handicapped. Continue to express your concern, but keep your distance.

Harmonizer Harmonizers pride themselves on forging excellent relationships and winning the boss's trust. A persecuting boss is the Harmonizer's worst nightmare. You'll spend hours trying to figure out what you did or said that caused your boss to become displeased with your performance. To depersonalize, realize that your boss is unhappy with you because he or she is unhappy. Stop trying to win the boss over and stick to doing your job.

Star Accustomed to impressing the boss and rising up in the ranks, Star employees recoil in the presence of a persecuting manager. You're likely to read the writing on this abusive boss's wall quickly and immediately look for an exit. To depersonalize, know that there is a way out, and your employer cannot hold you back for long.

Challenger When a Challenger becomes a persecuting boss's latest victim, every workplace fear gets triggered. Your boss will dismiss you, marginalize your contributions, and label you a troublemaker. These negative experiences activate feelings of anger, hurt, and despair. You may be tempted to strike out against your boss's unreasonable accusations, but this will only worsen your situation. To depersonalize, you have to practice extreme self-restraint. Understand that there is nothing you can do to change the boss's mind. Lie low, do your job without fanfare, and plan your exit.

Observer Observers generally have a sixth sense about when to approach the boss and when to leave him or her alone. This ability serves them well when dealing with a Persecutor. You may be able to dodge this employer's accusatory bullets, but you'll still suffer from seeing your vengeful boss take your colleagues down. To depersonalize, see your boss's destructive behavior as a sign to start looking for a more sane work environment for the long run.

Worker Bee Because Worker Bees work hard to stay out of the limelight, they can usually avoid becoming this boss's target for a while. Still, should the Persecutor zero in on your performance, you'll have to brace yourself for a very bumpy ride. Your boss's attacks, admonishments, and devaluing remarks will be extremely difficult for you to stomach. To depersonalize, trust that your colleagues and coworkers know your value. They also know that the Persecutor is off base. Reach out to the people who know you for support and a reality check.

Storyteller Persecuting bosses don't usually care much for stories of any kind. They like to keep conversation to a minimum, unless it's focused on them. To avoid this leader's ire, you want to minimize the amount of talking you do while at work. If you do become the object of your boss's disdain, depersonalize by leaning on your colleagues for support. You can help each other plan a mass evacuation.

Disarmer A disarming employee may be able to make this brand of boss laugh on occasion, but won't be immune to the Persecutor's ways. Once your manager turns on you, you'll find it difficult to show up for work on a daily basis. To depersonalize, know that you aren't the first target and you won't be the last. Try not to take anything this person says or does to heart as you polish up your résumé.

Coaster Because Coasters expect to charm and befriend the people they work for, a persecuting boss presents special challenges. Once this authority figure singles you out, you'll feel as if you can't win on any workplace front. To depersonalize, trust that your colleagues see what's happening. Turn to them for support as you make alternative plans.

Low Beamer Low Beamers cannot understand why someone would single them out and treat them badly for no reason. The emotional stress of this kind of situation will wreak havoc on a Low Beamer's carefully balanced personal life. To depersonalize, you'll have to do your best to leave the boss's negativity at the office—until you can secure a position elsewhere.

SECTION IV

Reader's Alert: Read all of chapter 7 and then check out chapters 8 through 12 to find concrete solutions to your exact boss/employee combination. Use your Boss Baggage Profile to guide you.

If you are . . .

CHAPTER 7

Your Pain Ends Here

Y OU'VE FINALLY ARRIVED at the fourth D—*Deal.* At this point, you've acquired a lot of tools and information. You know how to *Detect* a difficult boss/employee relationship and determine what phase you're in. You've learned how to *Detach* from your enervating manager by accepting certain facts about this person and taking steps to reclaim your personal power. You've become skilled at *Depersonalizing*— taking your challenging chief's words and actions less personally. All of this information can now be used to *Deal*—devise a plan of protection for managing your boss.

When we say *deal,* we mean the internal and external actions you can take to prevent your boss from having a negative impact on your self-image and your career. You've already learned a lot about yourself. Now, we want to take that information and create a customized plan so that, when your boss acts out, you can defend yourself.

At first glance, you might assume that this plan addresses only the boss's behavior. That's partially true. However, a good plan of protection can also help you manage your internal reactions when the boss fails to meet your needs and expectations. Ideally, it gives you concrete tools to alleviate your fears and take a more objective, constructive approach to your job and your career.

Dealing should shield you from the boss's behavior. It should also give you a plan for adjusting your expectations, addressing your unmet needs, and alleviating any fears that are triggered by your interactions with the boss.

To get a sense of what dealing might look like, let's visit a frustrated employee named Dan.

Dan recently changed jobs to become a senior software designer for a medical software company. His new boss, Al, manages the company's product-development department. Al hired Dan to bring fresh, cutting-edge ideas to the team. Dan comes from a competing company, where he was highly regarded, but severely underpaid. He's excited at the prospect of bringing his expertise to Al's team in exchange for better pay and a better title.

Dan begins his new job on a high note. Everything starts out fine, until he suggests a new product idea at a staff meeting. Al says, "Why don't you just write that up and submit it to me." Dan writes and submits a pitch explaining his product idea that same day. After e-mailing his proposal to Al, he waits for a response.

A few days pass, and Dan hears nothing. One week goes by; still no word. Dan decides to check on the status of the e-mail he sent and discovers that it's never been opened. He resends it, marking it urgent. The next day, Dan runs into his new boss and pops the question. "What did you think of my proposal?" Al's reply is gruff and defensive. "I haven't gotten to it yet," he barks. "By the way, don't send me an e-mail twice." Dan feels an internal alarm going off. His initially welcoming boss just turned sour.

The following week, Dan shoots an e-mail asking Al whether he's ready to move forward on his proposed initiative. Al shoots a one-liner back: "Not ready to move on this yet."

Dan goes in to talk to him about it. "I really think we need to act fast on this product idea or the competition will beat us to it. What's preventing us from taking action?"

Al's response is short and unapologetic. "We're not going to move on it until I say we are."

Over the course of the next six months, Dan offers several more "fresh" ideas, and each one is shelved in the same manner. Dan becomes angry, disappointed, and depressed. He blames himself for taking this dead-end job. Because he's being held back, he loses confidence and becomes full of self-doubt. He wonders why he left his previous position. He starts to act out by coming to work late and stewing in silence during meetings.

After work, Dan spends the bulk of his time obsessing and complaining about Al. His girlfriend laments, "You seem so unhappy. Where's the fun guy I first went out with?" She starts pulling away from him. Dan realizes that he needs to do something. Working for Al is not working for Dan, but he can't let it ruin the rest of his life.

In an attempt to take control of the situation, Dan can apply the Four D's to his relationship with Al.

Detect Dan detects that he's in phase five of a distressing boss/employee relationship—Rehearsing and Rehashing. His coping behaviors include obsession, acting out, bad-mouthing, and avoidance. Mary, a fellow software designer, also explains that Al is a Sacred Cow. (The fact that he's married to the company founder's sister guarantees his position.)

Detach Now that Dan understands his circumstances, he starts to accept the fact that Al may not be competent, but he isn't going anywhere. Dan also accepts that his Sacred Cow boss will block any initiatives that he attempts to push forward. To take back his personal power, Dan returns to playing basketball with his buddies. In addition, he teams up with his colleague Mary to craft a strategy for working around Al. Finally, Dan joins a local software developers' group so that he can stay informed and build his credibility outside of the company.

Depersonalize With Mary's help, Dan is able to take the emotional sting out of Al's obnoxious behavior. He sees that Al (aka Dr. No) says no to every employee and every new idea. This bullish behavior is not directed solely at Dan; Al simply fears making a mistake and looking bad. Dan also completes the Boss Baggage Assessment and discovers that he scores highest as a Star. Al is exactly the kind of boss that does not work for him. Not only is this lackluster leader unable to meet any of his needs or expectations, but Al also exacerbates Dan's worst fear—being held back.

Dan is ready for the final step . . . **Deal.**

DEAL: THE THREE A'S

Dealing requires *adjusting* your unmet expectations, *addressing* your unfulfilled needs, and *alleviating* your fears. It takes the information you gleaned from your Boss Baggage Assessment and puts it to good use. After taking the assessment, you've clarified the expectations, needs, and fears that you bring to any relationship with authority. And it's probably painfully obvious how your current boss is falling short. Using the Three A's, you can deal with the harsh reality of your boss's shortcomings and still find ways to do your job while you move your career forward. Here's how it works.

Adjusting Expectations of Authority

It's normal to come to any boss/employee relationship with certain expectations. An expectation is a confident belief or a strong hope that a particular event will happen. Expectations aren't bad. It's fine to hope for a certain kind of leadership from your employer. But when faced with the reality of a boss who fails to meet your expectations, you have two choices: resist reality and insist that the boss change, or adjust to reality and find other venues for fulfillment.

Expectations cause trouble when you insist that they be fulfilled by a boss who cannot deliver. For example, Dan expects to work for someone who has vision and communicates it. Yet his boss, Al, is incapable of doing that. If Dan continues to think that Al should fulfill that expectation, he'll remain stuck in anger, frustration, and depression. If however, Dan accepts that the only vision Al has is of his own paycheck, then he can stop going to Al for vision and look for inspiration and forward thinking from other sources.

Remember Joyce from Chapter 3? She expects her boss to show appreciation for a job well done. Yet her manager, Rhonda Steeleman, is incapable of doing that. Rhonda doles out compliments only to high-profile clients and press contacts—people who can enhance her public image. Joyce will continue to be disappointed if she holds on to any hope of receiving praise from her boss. Instead, Joyce can look to her coworkers, colleagues, and industry relationships for the appreciation that she desires.

If you expect a workaholic boss to be considerate of your home life, then you're setting yourself up for constant disappointment. Rather than wait for this obsessed overachiever to declare that you deserve to go home at a decent hour, try enlisting the support of sympathetic coworkers who can help lighten your workload and limit your work hours.

You may think that lowering your expectations is equivalent to lowering your standards. You may refuse to make excuses for your boss. You may not want to let your employer off the hook. We suggest you approach this issue of workplace expectations from a different angle.

Consider *adjusting your expectations* as a form of protection. To adjust is to adapt to the reality of your environment or workplace. Once you realize who your boss is and what he or she is capable of offering, you can minimize this authority figure's ability to disappoint, hurt, anger, or otherwise make you miserable.

To manage his unmet expectations, Dan returns to his Boss Baggage Profile and pulls out his top three orientations to authority:

- I expect to receive opportunities to grow professionally.
- I expect to be given clear direction.
- I expect to work for someone who has a vision and communicates it.

Clearly, Al is incapable of fulfilling any of these requirements. Once Dan lowers his expectations of Al, he can construct a plan (based in reality) for getting his workplace needs and expectations fulfilled.

Addressing Unmet Needs

A workplace need is something that you want or require from work. Needs differ from expectations because, if they are not addressed in some way, you always feel unfulfilled. Once you've identified your workplace needs, and assessed your boss's ability to meet them, it's your job to find alternative ways to get the unmet needs met.

It's rare that any single authority figure can fulfill anyone's needs completely. A charismatic leader may fulfill your need to be inspired, but if you also need to be appreciated and liked by the boss, that individual may be lacking. A kind boss may give you the care and encouragement you crave, but when it comes to fighting on your behalf for a promotion or a raise, this humanitarian may waiver. A technical expert may meet your need to gain knowledge on the job, but should you need to be given more responsibility, that same specialist may resist sharing his or her turf.

It's a setup to assume that any boss will fulfill all of our needs. But here is the good news: Now that you've completed the Boss Baggage Profile and determined your workplace needs, you can take steps to find other people and situations to fill the bill. And this is where *addressing your unmet needs* becomes the second A of dealing.

Refer back to the list of needs in your Boss Baggage Profile. Now that you recognize your boss's limitations, get to work on filling the gap. Identify the workplace needs that really matter to you and come up with creative ways of fulfilling them.

Begin by thinking about the resources available. Are there co-workers who can support you? Is there an association that could benefit from your skills and talents? What events, projects, task forces, or committees can give you the positive feedback and professional inspiration that you desire? Perhaps there's a church, synagogue, club, parent association, volunteer group, or civic cause outside of work that will satisfy a need.

Dan takes his top three unmet needs and devises a plan for addressing them:

1. He needs to be able to shine. Plan: Participate in his professional association (the software development group) so that he can showcase his skills, knowledge, and talents.
2. He needs to be given responsibilities. Plan: Form a task force within the group to research and discuss the latest trends in medical software.
3. He needs to be heard. Plan: Dan joins forces with Mary. They launch a campaign to keep Al informed regarding trends in medical software development as well as products launched by competing companies. Both Dan and Mary understand that they won't get immediate results from their discussions with Al. Their goal is to familiarize Al regarding innovative software ideas so that he can feel more at ease with the subject.

Alleviating Your Fears

The most challenging aspect of any distressing boss/employee relationship is alleviating the fears that come up. Fear is an unpleasant feeling of apprehension or distress caused by the presence or the anticipation

of danger. If you've completed the Boss Baggage Profile, you've identified your five greatest fears as they relate to authority.

Congratulations. Awareness is power. At the same time, simply
knowing your fears is not enough. You need to actively alleviate those
fears so that you don't act them out.

This may seem like a daunting task in the workplace. At work, you
can't show your fears openly because it's a sign of weakness. And yet,
anyone who holds a job secretly harbors certain fears: Am I competent?
Will my work be noticed and appreciated? Can I get along with others?
Is there room for me to shine? Can I perform to my boss's satisfaction?
Am I smart enough? Is my boss willing to hear my opinion?

Typically, when we're fearful of something, we automatically act (or
react) in a defensive manner to protect ourselves and to prevent anyone from seeing our vulnerabilities. For example, if you fear not being
heard, you may state your opinions repeatedly, in an aggressive manner.
This defensive behavior eventually leads to the very result you were trying to avoid—the boss stops listening. If you fear being controlled or
held back, you may assert yourself and challenge the boss so that he or
she knows you're in charge. The boss, in turn, may try to tone your behavior down. You'll feel reigned in instead of recognized.

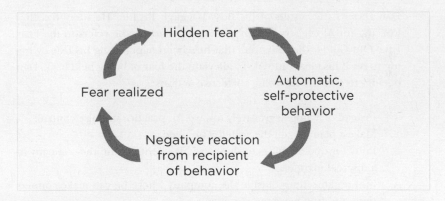

As you look at this diagram, you may think, "How do I break out of
this cycle?" Have no fear. There is a way out. Instead of unconsciously, automatically acting your fears out, you can take steps to alleviate them.

How? By examining your fears and discovering exactly what self-
sabotaging behaviors they trigger in you. If you can clearly identify what
you do to exacerbate your worst fears, you can take corrective actions

to lessen their impact. Over time, as you take positive actions that challenge your fears, they will have less and less power over you.

How to Alleviate a Fear

We're going to introduce a final process that can lessen the impact of any fear that your boss's behavior triggers in you. We call it Pick Your Pain. The idea is to pick the biggest fear that your employer's conduct activates in you and apply specific corrective actions to reduce its effect. You don't have to erase the fear from your mind, you don't have to cover it up or push it down. You just have to take concrete steps to counteract it. As you alleviate one fear, the others are likely to lessen as well. To pick your pain, follow these instructions:

1. Review your fears from Chapter 5's Boss Baggage Profile.
2. Identify the fear that is causing you the most distress at work today.
3. Refer to the Fear Fake-Out Guide below. Once you find your fear, follow the directions for correcting it.

Let's see how Dan does this process:

Dan reviews the results of his Boss Baggage Profile. He identifies that working for Al triggers his *fear of being held back*. As he refers to the Fear Fake-Out Guide, Dan discovers that he's been aggravating his fear by trying to push his ideas onto Al. To alleviate the fear of being held back, Dan decides to take the following corrective actions:

1. Instead of acting aggressively toward Al, practice impulse control.
2. Make a plan to gain the visibility he needs.
3. Look for opportunities to showcase his talents within the company in a discreet manner.
4. Join organizations outside the company where he can make connections and find new opportunities.

As he looks at the corrective action list, Dan can already give himself credit for joining the software developers' group and for collaborating with Mary. Together, they can introduce ideas to Al in a less threatening, more gradual way. Dan continues with these steps and looks for additional opportunities for discreetly showcasing his talents within the company.

Now it's your turn. Pick your pain. Go to the Fear Fake-Out Guide, find your fear, and see what you can do to decrease the power that it holds over you at work.

FEAR FAKE-OUT GUIDE

The following guide lists twenty boss-related fears and provides specific actions to counteract each one. Look for your top fear and see if you can take the corrective actions to alleviate it at work.

Fear of Appearing Cold or Uncaring

SIMILAR FEAR: FEAR OF BEING PERCEIVED AS "DIFFICULT" OR DEMANDING

This fear makes it extremely difficult to set boundaries with the boss. You can't say no. Because you know too much about your manager's personal business, you constantly make excuses and cover for this individual. When and if you finally try to set a limit with the boss, you come off as cold and uncaring.

> **Actions that aggravate the fear:** Servicing the boss's needs at your own expense: you constantly work overtime or on weekends to "help out." You get caught in long conversations and unproductive meetings. You become too involved and too knowledgeable regarding your boss's personal issues.

> **Corrective actions:** Practice staying out of the boss's private affairs. See if you can focus only on work-related issues and steer clear of personal concerns. If the conversation steers toward private matters, calmly listen and say, "I wish I could help, but that's not my area" or "Hmmm. Sounds like a tough situation." Bottom line is . . . work to keep a healthy distance between you and the boss.

Fear of Appearing Foolish or Incompetent

SIMILAR FEARS: FEAR OF NOT HOLDING IT TOGETHER, FEAR OF
LOOKING FOOLISH OR STUPID

If you have this fear, you feel ashamed and embarrassed whenever you're caught off guard in a situation. To avoid looking foolish, you cover up whenever the boss asks a question that you don't have the answer to. You say things like, "I'm on it" or "I'm working on it." If and when the boss discovers your cover-up, you appear dishonest and unintelligent in his or her eyes.

> **Actions that aggravate the fear:** Refusing to admit what you don't know. Lying to avoid looking bad.

> **Corrective actions:** Admit up front when you haven't finished something, don't know something, or can't find something. Instead of covering up, try telling the truth in a way that the boss can hear. When your boss asks for the report that you promised (but forgot to complete), try saying, "Thanks for following up with me. I'll have something to you by the end of the day."

Fear of Asking Questions

This fear usually stems from an internal assumption that you should have all the answers. When you come across a situation that you don't fully understand, instead of asking for clarification, you forge ahead in what you hope is the right way. Your lack of knowledge becomes apparent to the boss because the work you produce is faulty. You end up looking uninformed and foolish.

> **Actions that aggravate the fear:** Failing to ask questions when given assignments or presented with something you don't fully understand. Making assumptions instead of clarifying what the boss wants.

> **Corrective actions:** The remedy to this fear is to practice asking questions even when you think you have the answer. Say, "I think I understand, but I just want to get this right. Do you want . . . ?" Assume that questions clarify, even if you have the answers.

Fear of Being Criticized

SIMILAR FEAR: FEAR OF BEING JUDGED

Out of the fear of being criticized, you may omit, cover up, or otherwise hide mistakes you make and problems that arise. This tactic backfires when the truth inevitably comes out in a way that surprises and infuriates the boss. In addition to receiving the very criticism you were trying to avert, you also break the boss's trust.

> **Actions that aggravate the fear:** Hiding or omitting information. Spotting a problem and hoping no one will notice. Waiting until it's too late to address a mistake or problem. Not addressing problems in a timely manner.

> **Corrective actions:** Practice delivering bad news up front, at the time that it happens. Don't ignore or sit on pressing issues that need to be addressed. If you identify a mistake, go to the boss immediately and say, "I want to alert you to a possible problem" or "We have a problem here."

Fear of Being Devalued

If you're afraid of being devalued, you don't ever want to put yourself in a position where someone could put you down or say that you aren't good enough. People who have this fear have a very difficult time standing up and asking for what they want from the boss—whether it concerns money, promotions, assistance, vacation, or feedback. As a result, their needs and accomplishments often go unrecognized. They feel undervalued and misunderstood.

> **Actions that aggravate the fear:** Instead of mentioning your accomplishments to the boss, you stand by passively, hoping that he or she will notice how hard you work and how much you contribute. Wishing that the boss would recognize when you deserve a raise, promotion, or other kind of reward without your having to ask for it. Quietly resenting the more aggressive employees who blow their own horns.

> **Corrective actions:** The next time the boss overlooks your accomplishments, use the anger you feel to propel you: prepare and rehearse asking for what you want. Practice reporting your accomplishments whether or not you think anyone wants to hear them.

Fear of Being Dismissed

SIMILAR FEAR: FEAR OF BEING MARGINALIZED

This fear causes individuals to introduce their ideas, opinions, and suggestions to authority figures in a very strong and forceful manner. You want bosses to know that you are strong, smart, and valuable—that they can rely on you. The force of your presentation can feel overpowering to the boss, causing him or her to push you away.

> **Actions that aggravate the fear:** Inserting your ideas and opinions forcefully, early in the relationship, rather than letting the boss discover your abilities. Appearing overly confident. Being defensive about your opinions and what you know.

> **Corrective actions:** Addressing this fear starts with trusting that people will see your value without your forcing them to recognize it. Try pacing yourself—attend meetings and take notes. Offer your opinion after two or three people have already spoken. When you speak up, begin with phrases like, "I have a suggestion . . ." or "Here's one approach to this problem. . . ." Try to refrain from assuming that you have the only answer.

Fear of Being Found Lacking

SIMILAR FEARS: FEAR OF NOT DOING ENOUGH, FEAR OF NOT CARRYING MY WEIGHT

Out of the fear that you aren't doing enough comes the tendency to do too much. You compensate for this fear by taking on any project just so that you can prove your value.

> **Actions that aggravate the fear:** Saying yes when you should be saying no. Taking on more work than you can humanly accomplish. Becoming overwhelmed from trying to meet the boss's needs. You overpromise and underdeliver.

> **Corrective actions:** Focus on completing your responsibilities instead of volunteering to do more work. Practice impulse control. When you feel the impulse to help out, count to ten before you say anything. When the boss tries to add another project to your plate, state the following: "I will need more help to do that." "I can't get that done in the time frame

you've given me." "I'd like to pass this on to someone who's less busy than I am."

Fear of Being Held Back

SIMILAR FEARS: FEAR OF DOING TASKS THAT WON'T GIVE ME VISIBILITY, FEAR OF BEING UNDERUTILIZED

This fear comes up when you have a boss who squashes your ideas or shows a lack of interest in your initiative. His or her inability to utilize your talent leaves you feeling trapped. In reaction to your boss's indifference, you feel undervalued. You assume the boss underestimates your abilities. You aggressively attempt to gain visibility. The boss then tries to censor you further.

Actions that aggravate the fear: Making statements like, "You're missing a great opportunity by not utilizing me." Trying to go over the boss's head to get your ideas heard and seen. Openly selling yourself to people outside of your department with the threat that if the boss won't recognize your capabilities, you'll go elsewhere.

Corrective actions: Try replacing this fear with patience. Instead of acting out your dissatisfaction in an aggressive manner, practice impulse control. Carefully examine your situation. Make a plan to gain the visibility you need. Look for opportunities within the company to showcase your talents in a discreet manner. Join organizations outside the company where you can make connections and find new opportunities.

Fear of Being Labeled a Troublemaker

Individuals who have this fear usually see themselves as original thinkers who solve problems in a creative way. Rather than join the crowd, they want the crowd to join them. As a result, these nonconformists insist on doing things their way. The refusal to follow the rules leads to being labeled a troublemaker.

Actions that aggravate the fear: Questioning and challenging rules. Refusing to follow instructions. Revising and redesigning every plan.

Corrective actions: If you want to keep your job, find ways to play by the rules. Practice following plans, instructions, and directives without inserting your revised version of what you (and everyone else) should be doing. If you have a great idea or an important suggestion to offer the boss, write it down and run it by a trustworthy friend or colleague. Solicit help in communicating your opinions without appearing too insistent.

Fear of Being Misunderstood

If you have this fear, you are very concerned about the boss seeing you in a fair light and appreciating your efforts. Out of the desire to be understood, you tend to overinform those who supervise you—describing your actions in any work situation in great detail. These in-depth explanations flood the listener with too much information. Your boss ends up feeling overwhelmed and confused.

> **Actions that aggravate the fear:** Saying too much; giving long-winded explanations with too much detail so that the important points get lost; spending too much time defending your actions (in story form) rather than finding out what information your manager actually needs.
>
> **Corrective actions:** This is a case where less is more. If you're worried about the boss misinterpreting your actions, focus on the facts. Write the facts of what happened in a list form. Deliver your message with minimal descriptive details. Look for signs of disinterest, boredom, or frustration from the listener. If you see signs of restlessness, stop and ask, "Is this the information you're looking for?"

Fear of Being Pressured to Perform

SIMILAR FEARS: FEAR OF BEING CAUGHT OFF GUARD, FEAR OF FAILING IN A HIGH-PRESSURE ENVIRONMENT

Employees who have this fear have a very hard time taking on responsibility beyond their comfort zone. If the boss asks them to make a presentation or take on a challenging project, these employees say yes, but internally they're afraid that they can't deliver. They usually end up taking a few initial steps, then dropping the ball as soon as an obstacle arises. Because they don't complete the task, they never feel relief.

Actions that aggravate the fear: Saying yes to the boss, then avoiding the work you have to do. Not speaking up when you need help. Procrastinating when it comes to any task or action that you find difficult.

Corrective actions: Take baby steps toward achieving any challenging assignments. If you are asked to give a presentation, ask the boss for any examples (presentations given previously) that are similar to what he or she wants. Enlist the assistance of someone who has already made a presentation. Let others show you how to break down daunting projects into manageable steps. As you break down big projects into smaller pieces, the pressure you feel will lessen.

Fear of Being Rejected

This fear can immobilize you when it comes to dealing with the boss. Out of the fear of being rejected, you reject first. If there's a promotion available, you convince yourself that you don't want it. If there's a project you'd like to take on and someone else expresses interest, you assume the other person is more qualified.

Actions that aggravate the fear: Instead of trying new things, asking for advancement or taking on a leadership role, you keep yourself small to avoid rejection.

Corrective actions: Seek to build rejection resilience. Be aware when you prematurely disqualify yourself from any work opportunity. The next time you are up for a promotion, for example, tell yourself, "It's worth the effort to see this through."

Fear of Being Ridiculed

SIMILAR FEAR: FEAR OF BEING OSTRACIZED

If you have this fear, you probably fly under the radar to avoid any chance of being ostracized. You may refrain from asking questions, remain silent during meetings, and generally stay out of the way. As a result, others may fail to include you in decision making or to keep you updated regarding changes in policy. You feel left out and marginalized—in short, ridiculed.

Actions that aggravate the fear: Working quietly out of sight. Keeping your ideas and opinions to yourself. Not participating fully in meetings, team projects, or other company initiatives.

Corrective actions: Get on the radar. Participation is the key. Make it your goal to raise your hand and speak up in meetings. If you have an idea or opinion that you want to communicate, ask your boss for suggestions regarding the best way to present your thoughts. Be willing to be seen in small ways so that you don't fade into the woodwork.

Fear of Confrontation

SIMILAR FEARS: FEAR OF DEALING WITH SOMEONE ELSE'S ANGER, FEAR OF BEING YELLED AT

People who harbor this fear tend to let problems come to a boil before they're willing to address them. Because they avoid or try to ignore the problem, it eventually blows up. Avoidance results in angry confrontation.

Actions that aggravate the fear: Sensing the boss is unhappy with something, but avoiding or ignoring it. Hoping that difficult situations will blow over or go away. Procrastinating when it comes to asking for raises, promotions, or help because you fear a negative reaction.

Corrective actions: Be willing to address difficult situations directly before they come to a boiling point. If you sense a problem brewing, alert the boss. Say, "I want to let you know that there is a problem in this area." If you need to ask for a raise or a promotion, you should arrange a meeting, prepare your notes, and rehearse what you're going to say with a friend or family member.

Fear of Disappointing

If you have this fear, the very thought of disappointing someone makes you cringe inside. Because you're terrified of letting the boss down, you can't say no. Unfortunately, this approach forces you to overwork, overextend, and overexert, which leads to your dropping the ball in some area—thus disappointing the boss.

Actions that aggravate the fear: Because the need to please is so great, you overestimate what you can actually accomplish. You end up taking on an overwhelming amount of work. Once overloaded, you fail to prioritize or delegate. You don't say no for fear of making the boss unhappy.

Corrective actions: This is a no-action remedy. The most important thing you can do is to zip your lip. Do not offer or volunteer your services when the need for help arises. Practice letting other people jump in and do the job. Notice how much work you can actually accomplish in a workday. Aim to underpromise and overdeliver rather than overpromise and underdeliver.

Fear of Having to Defend Myself

Anyone who holds this fear hates having his or her faults or mistakes pointed out. To avoid unpleasant confrontations, this person covers up, ignores, or withholds information. This is a put-your-head-in-the-sand approach to solving problems. When the boss discovers whatever you've ignored, covered up, or withheld, he or she insists that you defend your actions.

Actions that aggravate the fear: Ignoring potential mistakes or problems as they arise. Instead of bringing a difficult situation to your boss's attention, you work quietly, hoping it will go unnoticed. When confronted with a mistake, you have a hard time admitting your fault in the matter.

Corrective actions: Speak up now so that you won't have to defend yourself later. Become an overcommunicator when it comes to anticipating problems that may arise. Practice saying, "I just want to alert you about this." "Let's take care of this before it becomes a problem."

Fear of Making Mistakes

SIMILAR FEARS: FEAR OF RECEIVING ASSIGNMENTS WITHOUT CLEAR DIRECTIONS, FEAR OF BEING ASKED TO DO THINGS I DON'T KNOW HOW TO DO

Individuals who harbor this fear are usually perfectionists. The fear of making a mistake prevents them from taking action. This rigid approach yields little output and a tendency to wait for explicit instructions from the boss. The boss gets frustrated and becomes critical of their low performance.

Actions that aggravate the fear: Needing and wanting explicit instructions regarding any work assignment or project. Waiting to be told what to do rather than taking action of your own accord. Taking a long time to complete assignments for fear of "not doing it right."

Corrective actions: Reframe what a mistake is. Consider mistakes evidence that you are participating in life rather than proof that you are a faulty human being. Practice taking on projects that involve a little risk. Try writing that proposal and asking for correction. Offer up your creative ideas in the form of "first drafts" or "rough outlines."

Fear of Making the Wrong Decision

This fear causes individuals to deliberate and procrastinate on making any kind of decision. The failure to take action leads to decisions being made for you—the flight you wanted to book is full, you can't submit the proposal because you missed the deadline, the program can't get printed without paying a rush fee. The boss gets frustrated with you and ultimately accuses you of poor judgment.

Actions that aggravate the fear: Procrastinating on every decision you need to make. Asking numerous people for their opinions before you can make a decision. Spending hours and hours researching without being able to come to a conclusion regarding purchases, policies, or projects.

Corrective actions: Instead of looking outside for the "right" answer, try developing your "gut" or internal decision maker. Practice making small decisions and living with them. If a large decision looms, enroll the assistance of a trusted (decisive) coworker.

Fear of Not Being Heard

People who harbor this fear have a strong desire to have their ideas, opinions, and experiences heard. When they think the boss is not listening to or valuing what they have to say, they tend to turn up the volume. They may repeat or restate the same idea several times. In return, the boss tunes them out.

Actions that aggravate the fear: Assuming that the boss is not listening to you. Interpreting the boss's lukewarm response as a signal that he or she doesn't want to hear what you have to say. Stating and restating your message.

Corrective actions: This is a case where less is more. If you really want to be heard, you need to package your information in such a way that the listener can receive it without feeling bombarded. Once you've stated your idea or opinion, back down and cool off. If you wonder whether the boss actually listened to what you said, go back and ask. "I just wanted to confirm that I told you _____."

Fear of Not Being Respected

SIMILAR FEARS: FEAR OF BEING TALKED DOWN TO, FEAR OF NOT BEING TAKEN SERIOUSLY

This is a fear that can be set off quickly. If you fear being disrespected, it's easy to hear and interpret the boss's words and actions as dismissive or rude. Feeling disrespected then leads to anger, withdrawal, hostility, and shutting the boss out. In return, the boss resents and judges your behavior.

Actions that aggravate the fear: Sulking, brooding, withholding information, bad-mouthing the boss, refusing to follow instructions, making hostile remarks, shutting down.

Corrective actions: Give the person or situation in question the benefit of the doubt. Anytime you believe that your supervisor said or did something disrespectful, go back and calmly ask for clarification. "I don't want to misinterpret what you said/did. Can you clarify what you meant for me?" Even if you are being treated in a disrespectful manner, ask for clarification.

WORK IT OUT
Deal
Your Pain Ends Here

HOW WILL YOU ADJUST YOUR UNMET EXPECTATIONS?

Unmet expectation #1: _____

Actions I will take: _____

_____

_____

Unmet expectation #2: _____

Actions I will take: _____

_____

_____

Unmet expectation #3: _____

Actions I will take: _____

_____

_____

HOW WILL YOU ADDRESS YOUR UNMET NEEDS?

Unmet need #1: _____

Actions I will take: _____

_____

_____

_____

Unmet need #2: _____

Actions I will take: _____

_____

_____

_____

Unmet need #3: _____

Actions I will take: _____

_____

_____

_____

HOW WILL YOU ALLEVIATE YOUR BIGGEST FEAR?

Name the fear: _____

What am I doing to aggravate the fear? _____

_____

_____

Corrective actions I will take to combat the fear:_____

_____

_____

_____

_____

CHAPTER 8

First Aid for Caregivers: Dealing with Twenty Boss Behaviors

NURTURERS AND HARMONIZERS foster safety, courtesy, coopera- tion, and comfort in the workplace. Their warm personalities make newcomers feel welcome and old-timers feel appreci- ated. They are the unpaid social workers, counselors, mediators, and diplomats of the office.

In exchange for their warmth and caring, these individuals require a certain degree of appreciation, trust, and confidence. If you are a Nur- turer or Harmonizer working for a boss who doesn't appreciate your giving, trustworthy nature, *dealing* will involve going beyond the boss to colleagues, other departments, and industry associations for the recog- nition and emotional safety you deserve.

To alleviate your fear of being found lacking or of disappointing others, *deal* by practicing impulse control: refrain from taking on too many responsibilities at work and set limits in terms of shouldering other people's personal problems.

In the pages that follow, you'll find concrete suggestions for deal- ing with each of the twenty difficult boss behaviors that we've covered throughout the book. Each Deal remedy includes:

1. An overarching approach—a quality or attitude that you should em- body when interacting with this individual.

2. A tactic for handling the boss's behavior "in the moment" (as your boss criticizes you, or undermines you, or begins to yell).
3. A strategy for managing the situation "behind the scenes" (actions that will lead to a better outcome in the long run).

Go to your profile category—whether you are a Nurturer (page 118) or a Harmonizer (page 119). Find the boss behaviors that drive you bonkers at work. Read the Deal remedies below and practice applying them to your circumstances.

DEALING FOR NURTURERS

Deal with a Chronic Critic

Overarching approach: Resilience

In the moment: Now that you understand your boss must always find fault, don't try to defend yourself against the Chronic Critic's corrections. Smile, take notes, and walk away without taking the negative feedback to heart.

Behind the scenes: Instead of working overtime to avoid making mistakes, be prepared to receive ongoing criticism. Look for your boss's positive attributes and chalk up the rest to insecurity.

Deal with a Rule Changer

Overarching approach: Flexibility

In the moment: When your boss cancels a plan, reverses a decision, or contradicts a previous statement, remind yourself that, with this person, change is the rule, not the exception.

Behind the scenes: Make it your business to check in regularly with a Rule Changer (more often than you think you should). Daily updates may help you stay abreast of the always-changing plans.

Deal with a Yeller

Overarching approach: Shield

In the moment: When the Yeller lets loose, tell yourself, "I am not this person's problem." Picture your boss as a two-year-old having a temper tantrum. Do not absorb his or her pain.

Behind the scenes: Try to get transferred or find another job ASAP.

Deal with an Underminer

Overarching approach: Meet head-on

In the moment: When your boss once again gives you responsibility then hands the authority over to someone else, take a deep breath and tell yourself, "This is not about my competence, it's about my boss's inability to delegate properly."

Behind the scenes: Confront the boss in private and see if he or she is willing to own up to the event. The next time your undermining boss offers you an assignment, look for discrepancies—see whom else your boss may be entrusting with similar or conflicting responsibilities.

Deal with "I'm Always Right"

Overarching approach: Tolerance

In the moment: No matter how tempting it may be to introduce another way of seeing an issue with this boss, stick to quiet agreement or "I see what you mean."

Behind the scenes: If there's a cause you care about or a decision you'd like the boss to make, approach him or her with a statement like, "I think this might fit with your priorities."

Deal with "You Threaten Me"

Overarching approach: Compassion

In the moment: Do what comes naturally to you—play down your successes and ascribe credit to the boss.

Behind the scenes: Coach your colleagues regarding the boss's insecurity in the area of public recognition and help them minimize friction over their accomplishments.

Deal with Grandiose

Overarching approach: Patience

In the moment: You're very good at giving this kind of boss the audience that he or she needs. Sit back and watch the show.

Behind the scenes: Schedule and take regular vacations. Find ways to restore your energy through exercise, sleep, and a healthy diet.

Deal with a Control Freak

Overarching approach: Appeasement

In the moment: Do your best to follow your boss's explicit instructions. If he or she wants a specific kind of report, chart, or agenda, serve it up.

Behind the scenes: Understand that earning your boss's trust will happen faster if you're able to fulfill your actual job requirements. Focus on delivering what the boss wants.

Deal with Love-Struck

Overarching approach: Restraint

In the moment: When you feel your boss's amorous feelings intensifying, stay neutral. Respond to any compliment with a cool thank-you and move on to the business at hand.

Behind the scenes: This may be tough for you, but your best strategy is to pull back from your usual nurturing role. That means you will refrain from bringing food, candy, or other comforting items to the boss. Do not linger to hear about your manager's personal experiences. Stick to the tasks of your actual job.

Deal with a Calculating Confidant

Overarching approach: Caution

In the moment: Anytime your boss attempts to glean personal information about you or a colleague, do not bite the bait. Respond to friendly inquiries with short responses like, "We'll see." "Same as usual." "I'm out of the loop."

Behind the scenes: Keep your distance from this kind of leader. When you do have to meet, keep all aspects of your personal life private.

Deal with a Tell-All

Overarching approach: Setting limits

In the moment: As the Tell-All dumps more and more of his or her personal problems in your lap, try not to assume the job of solving them. Instead, practice the Zen of not solving anything. Say, "I see." "That's rough." "I'm overloaded, but let me find someone else to help you out."

Behind the scenes: Practice setting limits with the boss. Whenever your manager starts confessing and confiding in you, try cutting the "meeting" short. Prepare to be called cold and uncaring. That means you're on the right track.

Deal with a Liar, Liar

Overarching approach: Discernment

In the moment: Whenever you sense that your boss may be bending the truth to suit his or her needs, take the statement or promise with a grain of salt.

Behind the scenes: Decide if you can live with the particular form of deception that your boss practices. If not, find greener pastures.

Deal with a Sacred Cow

Overarching approach: Allegiance

In the moment: If you sense that your risk-averse boss is unwilling to move forward on a business initiative or decision, back off.

Behind the scenes: Package your ideas so that they either support one of your Sacred Cow boss's cherished goals or they enhance his or her reputation.

Deal with Checked Out

Overarching approach: Fairness

In the moment: If a problem falls on your desk that the boss should be attending to, document the facts of the situation and record the amount of time it takes for you to address this issue.

Behind the scenes: Keep a careful record of the fallout that you're carrying because of your boss's absentee behavior. Meet with your manager, show him or her the facts, and ask how this situation will be remedied.

Deal with Spineless

Overarching approach: Take the lead

In the moment: When it's time for your manager to request your raise, offer any documentation (significant results, notable accomplishments, or added responsibilities) that will make it easier.

Behind the scenes: Build relationships with key players in the company so that you can get things done without having to solicit your reluctant leader's support.

Deal with an Artful Dodger

Overarching approach: Diplomacy

In the moment: The next time your boss sends you off to deliver a tough message to a colleague or coworker, reach outside of the workplace to a friend or associate who can help you script the message in a diplomatic way.

Behind the scenes: Should the cumulative effect of bearing bad news cause you ongoing distress, search for a new boss.

Deal with Junior

Overarching approach: Adaptability

In the moment Whenever you feel slightly shunned by your Junior boss, step back and follow his or her cues.

Behind the scenes: Carefully study your youthful leader to see what his or her priorities are and how you can be of greatest service.

Deal with a Former Colleague

Overarching approach: Patience

In the moment: In those moments when your former colleague suddenly pulls rank, it may hurt your feelings, but do your best just to follow orders.

Behind the scenes: The loss you feel is real. Over time, the two of you can redefine the friendship beyond the office. For the short term, focus your efforts on expanding your social network and reviving other friendships until the dust settles from this promotion.

Deal with an Unconscious Discriminator

Overarching approach: Benefit of the doubt

In the moment: If your boss unintentionally says or does something that reveals a clear prejudice, it will hurt; do your best not to react.

Behind the scenes: After you've cooled down, make sure to approach your manager privately to clear up the situation. Start the conversation with, "I know it wasn't your intention, but when you said _____[fill in the blank], it hurt my feelings."

Deal with a Persecutor

Overarching approach: Damage control

In the moment: Should this brand of boss target you with unfair accusations, snap judgments, or an air of disdain, do your best to view him or her as an emotionally handicapped person.

Behind the scenes: Once you've become the target, get out of this job as soon as possible.

DEALING FOR HARMONIZERS

Deal with a Chronic Critic

Overarching approach: Endurance

In the moment: The next time your boss begins to correct or complain about your work, instead of trying to defend yourself, respond with, "Thank you for letting me know."

Behind the scenes: Take concrete steps to find a better work environment: use your relationship skills to forge professional alliances that can lead to a new job with a less critical leader.

Deal with a Rule Changer

Overarching approach: Finesse

In the moment: Whenever your boss lays out a plan or schedules a meeting, know that it is tentative. Don't invest too much hope in any one outcome.

Behind the scenes: Work with your colleagues to keep projects moving forward and to coordinate schedules.

Deal with a Yeller

Overarching approach: Resilience

In the moment: The next time your boss erupts, watch it from a fresh perspective. Focus in on the physical effects of the anger—notice the red face, popping veins, and shaking body. Keep breathing deeply and gently, and do not defend yourself. Let the storm pass. When the Yeller is finished, simply say, "I heard you."

Behind the scenes: Do whatever it takes to purge your boss's toxic energy from your system. Update your résumé and start networking.

Deal with an Underminer

Overarching approach: Empowerment

In the moment: As you discover that your boss has once again overridden a decision that he or she asked you to make, try saying, "Well, I'm disappointed, but I can work with that."

Behind the scenes: Take action to forge relationships beyond your boss's reach, where you'll feel more respected and be given more responsibility. In the long run, you may want to get out.

Deal with "I'm Always Right"

Overarching approach: Strategic maneuvering

In the moment: The next time you're tempted to set the boss straight, take a deep breath, calm down, and back off. As you take notes regarding what your boss is saying, tell yourself that you can revisit this topic at another time.

Behind the scenes: See your boss as a puzzle. Focus on discerning the right moments to go to this manager and offer your point of view.

Deal with "You Threaten Me"

Overarching approach: Modesty

In the moment: Should you win an industry award or receive recognition from a high-level executive within the company, address your boss's jealous pride by saying something like, "I couldn't have done this without your support."

Behind the scenes: Assist any colleagues who become the object of "You Threaten Me"'s envy by showing them how to acknowledge this boss in a way that alleviates his or her fears.

Deal with Grandiose

Overarching approach: Avoidance

In the moment: As you listen to your boss tell the same success story for the tenth time, extract yourself by drawing on any workplace urgencies that you can think of. Try saying, "I've got to return an important call." "I'll be right back; there's a client matter I need to attend to." "I need to get that package out." Trust us. Your Grandiose boss will be okay.

Behind the scenes: Do whatever it takes to keep meetings, phone calls, and other interactions with this boss at a minimum. To keep him or her informed, send regular updates via e-mail.

Deal with a Control Freak

Overarching approach: Compliance

In the moment: When your boss zeros in and insists that you follow his or her exact instructions, fight the urge to resist. Instead, even though the direction may feel patronizing, try to listen intently, take copious notes, and thank your boss for the input.

Behind the scenes: Make it your mission to win this person's trust.

Deal with Love-Struck

Overarching approach: Straight talk

In the moment: If the tension of feeling your employer's amorous intentions becomes too great, try saying, "I value our work relationship too much to jeopardize it." Your boss may be cool for a while, but eventually he or she will recover.

Behind the scenes: Be willing to let the boss be disappointed while you focus on carrying out the responsibilities of your job.

Deal with a Calculating Confidant

Overarching approach: Discretion

In the moment: Notice when your meetings with the boss turn into chatting sessions. As the Calculating Confidant digs for dirt, say things like, "I wouldn't know about that" or "There's not much to tell." Take any personal information your boss reveals about others with a pound (not a grain) of salt.

Behind the scenes: Carefully start looking for other opportunities with more forthright and honest bosses. Even if it's a lateral move, you'll like the working conditions better.

Deal with a Tell-All

Overarching approach: Let go and let others help

In the moment: When your boss confesses a personal secret, then asks you to cover for him or her at work, don't rush to rescue him or her. Instead, say, "I feel terrible about your situation, but I can't take on any more." If the Tell-All then pleads with you, take the task and look for someone else to help you complete it.

Behind the scenes: Begin to explore other employment options where the person in charge does not require emotional babysitting.

Deal with a Liar, Liar

Overarching approach: Resignation or flight

In the moment: If you catch your boss making an empty promise, deceiving a colleague, or falsifying documents, stay cool in the moment—despite the fact that you may want to confront.

Behind the scenes: You'll have to decide whether you can live with the deception and disruption that the Liar, Liar causes. If not, plan your exit strategy.

Deal with a Sacred Cow

Overarching approach: Slow and steady

In the moment: The next time your Sacred Cow boss blocks one of your best ideas, don't get frustrated or indignant. Say, "I appreciate your feedback. Let me rethink this."

Behind the scenes: Break your idea or project into small baby steps that you can introduce to your risk-averse leader slowly, over time. Focus on showing this employer how your project can enhance his or her reputation.

Deal with Checked Out

Overarching approach: Take control

In the moment: When you realize that your boss is not emotionally or functionally present, take that as your cue to take charge.

Behind the scenes: Organize the people within your department. Create a workplace team so that you can make decisions and get the work done.

Deal with Spineless

Overarching approach: Work around the problem

In the moment: The next time you see your boss waffle, back down, or fail to stand up for a member of the staff, take it as a signal that this person cannot go to bat on anyone's behalf.

Behind the scenes: Advocate for yourself and others by building connections with people in higher, more influential positions.

Deal with an Artful Dodger

Overarching approach: Push back

In the moment: If your boss assigns you the task of delivering harsh feedback because he or she doesn't want to be perceived as the bad guy, try saying, "I think this message should come from you."

Behind the scenes: the wear and tear of acting as this employer's bad cop is too much for you to handle. Spend your time out of the office looking for a better work opportunity with a more forthright boss.

Deal with Junior

Overarching approach: Adaptability

In the moment: At those moments when this boss discounts your experience, it may sting a bit, but you can probably see his or her point of view.

Behind the scenes: Help yourself and others get up to speed in terms of learning the technology and adapting to your Junior boss's way of doing business.

Deal with a Former Colleague

Overarching approach: Understanding

In the moment: Should your former colleague exclude you from an important meeting or load you down with additional assignments, you may feel slighted. Try to put yourself in your friend's shoes. Understand that this person is making decisions based on a different set of responsibilities and information.

Behind the scenes: Maintain the relationship outside of work. Find out what your former colleague's new reality is and how you can be supportive.

Deal with an Unconscious Discriminator

Overarching approach: Thoughtful instruction

In the moment: If you catch your boss saying or doing something that clearly indicates a bias against your gender, race, appearance, or religious practices, you can register the information and tell yourself that you'll find a way to educate your boss on this issue.

Behind the scenes: Gather your thoughts and collect any data you need so that you can sit down with your boss, explain the inadvertent mistake that he or she made, and dispel the myth.

Deal with a Persecutor

Overarching approach: Escape

In the moment: As your boss attacks or disparages your behavior, do not attempt to defend yourself. Listen carefully, repeat the boss's complaints so that he or she knows you're paying attention, and respond with, "You may be right."

Behind the scenes: Work as fast as possible to find a better job with a civil boss.

CHAPTER 9

Escape Routes for Extroverts: Dealing with Twenty Boss Behaviors

S TAR AND CHALLENGER employees are the dynamic, ambitious, and forthright natural leaders of the workplace. They seek recognition and attention for their achievements. They expect the boss to appreciate their ideas and provide opportunities for them to shine.

Should you work for a boss who refuses to listen to your initiatives or entrust you with responsibility, you won't be happy. *Dealing* will require going beyond your employer's reach to shine. If you are a Star or a Challenger, you'll want to look for events, committees, projects, and professional venues to have your voice heard and your ideas executed.

To alleviate your fear of being held back or marginalized, deal by practicing patience and pacing. Avoid pushing or foisting your ideas upon the boss. At the same time, create a long-term strategy for showcasing your talents and getting the visibility that you need.

In the pages that follow, you'll find concrete suggestions for dealing with each of the twenty difficult boss behaviors that we've covered throughout the book. Each Deal remedy includes:

1. An overarching approach—a quality or attitude that you should embody when interacting with this individual.

2. A tactic for handling the boss's behavior "in the moment" (as your boss criticizes you, or undermines you, or begins to yell).
3. A strategy for managing the situation "behind the scenes" (actions that will lead to a better outcome in the long run).

Go to your profile category—whether you are a Star (page 121) or a Challenger (page 122). Find the boss behaviors that drive you bonkers at work. Read the Deal remedies below and practice applying them to your circumstances.

DEALING FOR STARS

Deal with a Chronic Critic

Overarching approach: Learning opportunity

In the moment: Whenever this brand of boss corners you to tell you what you've done wrong, simply say, "Thank you very much. I really appreciate knowing how I can be better."

Behind the scenes: Once you understand that this person can see only the details—not the bigger picture—start looking for your next career move.

Deal with a Rule Changer

Overarching approach: Move on

In the moment: The next time your boss changes course on a plan of action that you've been working toward, take a deep breath. Assess what change has just taken place so that you can figure out your role in the new direction.

Behind the scenes: Expand your professional network and look for a leader who is more decisive and growth-oriented.

Deal with a Yeller

Overarching approach: Cool objectivity

In the moment: At the moment that your boss starts yelling, listen very carefully to what he or she is saying and respond with, "I understand. I understand."

Behind the scenes: Repair the problem that triggered your short-fused boss's tirade. At the same time, put out feelers for a manager who is less volatile and more respectful.

Deal with an Underminer

Overarching approach: Direct communication

In the moment: As soon as you discover that your manager has overridden a decision that he or she asked you to make, confront this individual immediately. "I'm confused. You gave me the authority to make a decision, then you overruled it. Which way would you like to go? Are you making this decision or am I?"

Behind the scenes: Spend time proving your trustworthiness. Build trust by showing this leader your plans and the thinking behind your decision making.

Deal with "I'm Always Right"

Overarching approach: Agreement

In the moment: If you're caught in a situation where your boss insists that you're wrong and he or she is right, it's best to say, "You're right."

Behind the scenes: Observe the coworkers who are able to agree with the boss and still push their ideas, viewpoints, and projects forward. Follow their lead.

Deal with "You Threaten Me"

Overarching approach: Tactful exit

In the moment: It is not going to feel good when you experience this envious leader diminishing your success. Your best protection is to register the jealousy, but don't react.

Behind the scenes: Now that you know your boss is competing with you for the limelight, get busy networking for your next position.

Deal with Grandiose

Overarching approach: Entertainment

In the moment: As you sit in a meeting where the Grandiose boss chews your ear off, enjoy the show.

Behind the scenes: As long as your boss allows you to learn and grow on the job, you're okay. Once you hit a ceiling in terms of opportunities for advancement, move on.

Deal with a Control Freak

Overarching approach: Gradual success

In the moment: If you find yourself bristling as you wait for your boss's approval on every action, slow down and do it the boss's way.

Behind the scenes: Study your leader's detail-oriented style of completing tasks and mirror it. Focus on winning this person's trust by being an A+ student.

Deal with Love-Struck

Overarching approach: Professionalism

In the moment: If your employer suggests that the two of you could have a meaningful connection, say, "I have a policy not to mix business with pleasure."

Behind the scenes: Avoid your boss's advances by keeping your social calendar full.

Deal with a Calculating Confidant

Overarching approach: Censorship

In the moment: If your boss seems extremely interested in the intimate, personal details of your life, be suspicious. Do your best to limit the amount of personal information that you share with this individual.

Behind the scenes: Don't get seduced into going to this boss's house for dinner or getting into any situation where you might talk too much about coworkers or yourself. Talk to friends and family, not the boss.

Deal with a Tell-All

Overarching approach: Don't rescue

In the moment: The next time you're tempted to rescue this boss by doing portions of his or her job, stop. Instead of taking it on, suggest other people who can shoulder the added responsibility.

Behind the scenes: This kind of boss is likely to dump all of his or her responsibility on your trusty shoulders. As long as this association serves your career goals, stick with it. But the minute you start to feel like an underpaid servant, move on.

Deal with a Liar, Liar

Overarching approach: Eyes wide open

In the moment: When you catch your boss lying, confront in a humorous way. You might say, "Okay, that's one version of what happened. What's the real story? What else do I need to know?" Keep pressing until you feel as if you've uncovered 80 percent of the truth.

Behind the scenes: As long as you feel that your career is moving forward, you can work under this deceptive leader's rule. For the long run, however, decide whether being associated with this person really enhances your professional reputation.

Deal with a Sacred Cow

Overarching approach: Build alliances

In the moment: The next time this person rejects one of your best business ideas without even considering it, resist the urge to strangle him or her. Instead, say, "I understand." Then retreat.

Behind the scenes: Quietly build alliances with the people who can actually help you realize your ideas. At the same time, keep going to the boss, give this chief credit for any headway you make, and watch for opportunities to push your agenda gently forward.

Deal with Checked Out

Overarching approach: Conscious leadership

In the moment: If your boss seems unresponsive or absent for important decisions, step in and take the reins. Keep your Checked Out manager informed regarding any actions you take.

Behind the scenes: Rally your coworkers to act as a team while your leader is temporarily preoccupied. Delegate responsibilities and meet regularly to make sure that each person is carrying his or her weight.

Deal with Spineless

Overarching approach: Intervention

In the moment: If you need your boss to make a decision, settle a dispute, or reinforce a company policy, but you fear that he or she can't do it, offer your help. Say, "Would you like me to handle that for you?" Then step up and handle it.

Behind the scenes: Once you realize that acting as your boss's spine puts you in a precarious position with your peers (they resent you), it's best to move on.

Deal with an Artful Dodger

Overarching approach: Awareness of manipulation

In the moment: When your Artful Dodger boss comes to you (once again) to deliver a negative message to an employee, a vendor, or a customer, try saying, "They need to hear this message from you." Even if your Teflon leader insists that you act as the messenger, he or she will know that you're on to the game.

Behind the scenes: As a Star, you're more interested in creating results than acting as a manager's hit man. Start looking for your next (positive) career move.

Deal with Junior

Overarching approach: Stay current

In the moment: Should your significantly younger boss introduce technology or business processes that are beyond your comprehension, tell the truth about your experience. You might say something like, "It may be my age, but I don't see how to work this."

Behind the scenes: Take classes, hire a consultant, or find a willing colleague who'll help you get up to speed.

Deal with a Former Colleague

Overarching approach: Wait and see

In the moment: The first time your colleague-turned-boss addresses you in an authoritative manner, it may be very uncomfortable for you. Be professional in the moment by carrying out your new leader's orders without complaint.

Behind the scenes: Give yourself time to process the disappointment and envy you feel in response to this change in the balance of power. Figure out a way to retain the friendship while you decide whether you want to stay in this job.

Deal with an Unconscious Discriminator

Overarching approach: Patience

In the moment: If your boss says something that is tasteless and reveals a prejudice against your gender, race, ethnicity, appearance, or religious orientation, you may be tempted to speak up. Take a more professional tack by addressing the incident at another time in a more private setting.

Behind the scenes: Decide whether it's worth saying anything to your Unconscious Discriminator. Would this authority figure be receptive to the feedback? If so, begin the conversation with an "I" statement: "I felt hurt by your comment" or "I was embarrassed when you asked if I'd put on a few pounds." It's important not to blame.

Deal with a Persecutor

Overarching approach: Quick departure

In the moment: When the Persecutor is attacking your work or your behavior, resist the urge to attack back. Instead, respond to the assaults with, "I hear you," and wait for the conversation to end.

Behind the scenes: Put all your energy into networking and finding another job.

DEALING FOR CHALLENGERS

Deal with a Chronic Critic

Overarching approach: Let go

In the moment: When this boss starts to criticize your work, you'll instinctively want to defend yourself. Don't do it. Zip your lip, listen, and say, "Okay."

Behind the scenes: Practice letting go. Write down your boss's complaints and review them when you are in a relaxed state. If his or her comments are legitimate, see how you can incorporate them. Let the rest go.

Deal with a Rule Changer

Overarching approach: Adaptability

In the moment: As your manager informs you that yesterday's plans have been changed (again), use your creativity to adjust to the new reality and move forward.

Behind the scenes: Although you may find this kind of boss annoying, you can relate to the resistance to being tied down. Make it a point to stay in close contact with him or her. Check in regularly so that you can stay abreast of the latest developments.

Deal with a Yeller

Overarching approach: Caution

In the moment: If your boss starts yelling over something you've done, refrain from defending yourself—it will only fuel the fire.

Behind the scenes: After you've been lambasted, assess your situation. If you've become the office scapegoat, plan your exit strategy. If you work for an Equal Opportunity Yeller, stay as long as the work is appealing to you.

Deal with an Underminer

Overarching approach: Keep moving forward

In the moment: Should your boss assign the same project to you and a coworker or otherwise undermine your authority, don't let the news deter you. Instead, use your competitive spirit to barrel through.

Behind the scenes: Keep showing this uncertain leader that you can deliver on any assignment he or she dishes out. At the same time, be aware that your boss can't resist interfering after he or she gives anyone a new responsibility.

Deal with "I'm Always Right"

Overarching approach: Surrender

In the moment: As your boss asserts that his or her ideas, opinions, and perspective are correct, you'll want to challenge that information on the spot. Fight the urge to enter verbal combat with your boss and wait for the meeting to end.

Behind the scenes: If you can withstand a situation where you must agree with your boss before you can introduce any alternative information, you may be able to tolerate this position. Otherwise, read the writing on the wall and get out.

Deal with "You Threaten Me"

Overarching approach: Share credit

In the moment: Should you be recognized by a high-ranking executive or a professional association for your work, go directly to your boss and say, "This recognition is yours as much as it is mine."

Behind the scenes: Keep building goodwill with your easily threatened boss by drawing positive attention to his or her initiatives and successes.

Deal with Grandiose

Overarching approach: Vacate

In the moment: You'll be tempted to challenge this leader at every turn. Best not to question the accuracy of a Grandiose boss's statements or smirk as this big personality brags about past accomplishments.

Behind the scenes: Why would you stay in this kind of situation? Circulate your résumé.

Deal with a Control Freak

Overarching approach: Compliance

In the moment: If your boss hovers over you, refusing to let you make decisions, pull back, take a breath, and follow instructions.

Behind the scenes: Like it or not, your only job is to play by your boss's rules. As you build trust, this tightly wound leader may be able to loosen the reins of control.

Deal with Love-Struck

Overarching approach: Caution

In the moment: While it may feel great to be your boss's object of affection, tread carefully in this situation. Enjoy the attention, but avoid making an irreversible decision.

Behind the scenes: Weigh the consequences of engaging in a workplace romance. If you can handle any outcome—including getting fired—proceed with caution.

Deal with a Calculating Confidant

Overarching approach: Prevention

In the moment: Even though you usually have a reliable radar for phony friendliness, a truly skilled Calculating Confidant might fool you. If your boss shows an intense curiosity about your personal life or that of your colleagues, be cautious. Keep your answers as vague and as friendly as you can.

Behind the scenes: Stay on your boss's good side by doing your job without generating drama or conflict. You don't need to give this authority figure any material to hang you with.

Deal with a Tell-All

Overarching approach: Restraint

In the moment: Resist the urge to offer your boss solutions or remedies to his or her multitude of personal problems. Listen and say, "Uh-huh." Then go about doing your job.

Behind the scenes: Realize that your boss is not going to change and won't be open to your solutions. Start putting out feelers for future employment. See if you can find a boss who is open to your creative ways.

Deal with a Liar, Liar

Overarching approach: Personal integrity

In the moment: When you realize that your boss just lied to you, your first impulse will be to challenge this person. As difficult as it may be, resist the urge to go to combat over the transgression.

Behind the scenes: Consider whether you're willing to work with someone who habitually changes and reframes the truth to suit his or her needs. Decide how offensive your boss's deceptive ways are to you. If you can't live with them, search for a more forthright employer.

Deal with a Sacred Cow

Overarching approach: Self-control

In the moment: The next time your stubborn supervisor rejects one of your ideas or proposals, resist the urge to retaliate. You'll lose. Return to your desk and regroup.

Behind the scenes: Either decide how you can work around this person without soliciting his or her wrath or get out.

Deal with Checked Out

Overarching approach: Embrace leadership

In the moment: When you realize that your boss is missing from an important meeting, decision, or event, resist acting out. Instead, try taking on a leadership position where you coordinate efforts with your colleagues to get things done.

Behind the scenes: Understand that your boss will come back. Taking care of business while your employer is Checked Out will enhance your résumé and career.

Deal with Spineless

Overarching approach: Resignation

In the moment: When your boss refuses to resolve a conflict that you're having with a coworker or customer, zip your lip. Instead of lashing out, back off and let the moment pass.

Behind the scenes: If you cannot tolerate working for a leader who is incapable of confrontation or taking a stand, start circulating your résumé.

Deal with an Artful Dodger

Overarching approach: Endurance

In the moment: The minute this boss asks you to do some version of his or her dirty work, you'll want to rebel against it. If you want to keep your job, refrain from challenging your manager's orders.

Behind the scenes: Understand that acting as your boss's bad cop is part of your job. Decide whether you're willing to do it.

Deal with Junior

Overarching approach: Pace yourself

In the moment: As you meet with your new boss, do your best not to overwhelm this youthful leader with your ideas, opinions, and plans. Instead, focus on listening to and implementing Junior's goals and priorities.

Behind the scenes: You may be eager to introduce your manager to your innovative solutions to many workplace problems. Leave your boss wanting more by offering your ideas one suggestion at a time.

Deal with a Former Colleague

Overarching approach: Temperance

In the moment: The first time your fomer colleague attempts to manage you, you may be tempted to laugh it off. Instead, do your best to listen carefully and follow this person's lead.

Behind the scenes: Take some time to adjust to the new balance of power. If you can, approach your friend with a sincere interest in finding out about his or her new responsibilities. Ask how you can help.

Deal with an Unconscious Discriminator

Overarching approach: Tolerance

In the moment: The minute you detect that your manager unconsciously discriminates against some aspect of your identity, take a deep breath. Relax. Resist the temptation to strangle this person.

Behind the scenes: Go to a trusted colleague or friend and run the scenario by him or her. See how the listener interprets what happened and what suggestions he or she may have for addressing the boss.

Deal with a Persecutor

Overarching approach: Immediate exit

In the moment: As your boss attacks or disparages you in some way, don't even listen to his or her comments. Try to watch this person as if he or she is a horror-film monster. Do your best not to absorb the venom.

Behind the scenes: Get out. This is not a safe workplace for you.

CHAPTER 10

Intervention for Introverts: Dealing with Twenty Boss Behaviors

OBSERVERS AND WORKER BEES are quiet, productive, thoughtful, understated members of the workforce. They prefer to do their jobs with minimum fanfare and maximum freedom. They are solid, trustworthy employees who need to work at their own pace. Every team benefits from their quiet expertise and consistent input.

If you work for a boss who micromanages you, yells at you, or pressures you to perform under strict deadlines, you won't be happy. To *deal* with these circumstances, you will have to learn a different way of responding to stress. Draw on the expertise and advice of friends, colleagues, and professionals. Let these allies show you how to speak up, be prepared for scrutiny, and push back at authority when necessary.

To alleviate your fears of being ridiculed, judged, or criticized, practice going outside of your comfort zone and speak up sooner rather than later. Whenever you discover a problem, a mistake, or a discrepancy between what the boss wants and what you can deliver, do what doesn't come naturally—alert him or her before it's too late.

In the pages that follow, you'll find concrete suggestions for dealing with each of the twenty difficult boss behaviors that we've covered throughout the book. Each Deal remedy includes:

1. An overarching approach—a quality or attitude that you should embody when interacting with this individual.
2. A tactic for handling the boss's behavior "in the moment" (as your boss criticizes you, undermines you, or begins to yell).
3. A strategy for managing the situation "behind the scenes" (actions that will lead to a better outcome in the long run).

Go to your profile category—whether you are an Observer (page 123) or a Worker Bee (page 124). Find the boss behaviors that drive you bonkers at work. Read the Deal remedies below and practice applying them to your circumstances.

DEALING FOR OBSERVERS

Deal with a Chronic Critic

Overarching approach: Evaluate

In the moment: Although you may not like the sting of this authority figure's constant critiquing, do your best to take each comment with a grain of salt.

Behind the scenes: Document the criticisms you've received and decide which corrections are worth incorporating and which are meaningless opinions.

Deal with a Rule Changer

Overarching approach: Go with the flow

In the moment: When your boss alters the plans, you won't like it. Instead of fighting the change, let go and go with the flow.

Behind the scenes: This particular brand of boss is maddening to you. Circulate your résumé and find a better, more consistent leader.

Deal with a Yeller

Overarching approach: Self-protection

In the moment: If you find yourself the target of this person's angry outburst, try not to show your disdain. Do your best to keep breathing and shield yourself from the toxic energy.

Behind the scenes: While you may be able to tolerate this kind of treatment on occasion, it's not a good situation for the long run. Polish up your résumé and start networking.

Deal with an Underminer

Overarching approach: Wait and see

In the moment: When you discover that your boss has given the same assignment to you and another colleague, you may tactfully go to your coworker and sort out who is doing what.

Behind the scenes: Your boss's conflicting commands and mixed signals may cause you to sit back, watch what's happening, and decide where you want to put your energy.

Deal with "I'm Always Right"

Overarching approach: Courtesy

In the moment: If you sit in a meeting where your boss insists that only his or her perspective is the right one, resist rolling your eyes, looking at your nails, or yawning. Act as if you care by taking notes.

Behind the scenes: Do your best to stay out of the line of fire and do your job.

Deal with "You Threaten Me"

Overarching approach: Give praise

In the moment: Should you detect an air of envy from your boss when you're recognized for excellence by an outside source, you'll know to play it down and attribute your success to his or her support.

Behind the scenes: Because you work for someone who is easily threatened, remember to keep giving your needy leader credit for your successes.

Deal with Grandiose

Overarching approach: Graceful distancing

In the moment: As your boss holds court, bragging about his or her past successes, try "suddenly remembering" the phone call you have to make or the e-mail you have to send. Instead of sitting with a resentful look on your face, find a polite way to exit the scene.

Behind the scenes: Do your job. Look very busy so that you can avoid long meetings or lectures from the boss.

Deal with a Control Freak

Overarching approach: Patience

In the moment: If you start to feel oppressed because your employer is micromanaging you, try not to pout, roll your eyes, or get hot under the collar. Instead, take a deep breath and focus on delivering the work in the exact form that your boss is requesting.

Behind the scenes: Remember that you are on a trust-building mission with your Control Freak boss. Once you prove your capabilities, this leader will loosen the reins.

Deal with Love-Struck

Overarching approach: Subtle avoidance

In the moment: If your Love-Struck boss hints that he or she would like to take the relationship to a more intimate place, use your cool veneer to brush off the words and gestures; stick to the work at hand.

Behind the scenes: Make it your business to avoid being put in any compromising situations with this person. If your boss invites you to any events outside of work, show that you have no plans of spending "alone time." Say, "I'm busy," or bring a friend.

Deal with a Calculating Confidant

Overarching approach: Sidestep

In the moment: As you notice your boss digging for personal information, or egging you on to gossip about your coworkers, do what you do best: *observe* this individual's manipulative ways and say things like, "Oh, I didn't know that." "I don't know."

Behind the scenes: Stay on cordial but cool terms with your boss.

Deal with a Tell-All

Overarching approach: Limited servitude

In the moment: When your boss is confessing yet another personal problem to you during work hours, listen and say, "That's too bad." As this manager dumps his or her responsibilities in your lap, do what you can, but don't take on work assignments that are out of your comfort zone.

Behind the scenes: With your keen perceptive powers, you can see that this person is emotionally crippled in some way. If you get tired of buoying up your boss's fragile ego, you may want to begin networking outside of your company so that you can move beyond servicing this leader's needs.

Deal with a Liar, Liar

Overarching approach: Be alert

In the moment: When you catch your boss in a lie, try to conceal your disappointment. Register the information and proceed with caution.

Behind the scenes: Now that you've lost respect for your boss and you know that he or she is not trustworthy, it's best to plan an exit strategy. Look for a lateral move within your company or begin reaching out to your professional associates.

Deal with a Sacred Cow

Overarching approach: Persistence

In the moment: You may feel frustrated when the Sacred Cow says no to yet another idea that you'd like to push forward. Accept the no, for now. Reassess your plan and figure out a new approach.

Behind the scenes: Use your patience and resourcefulness to keep re-packaging your ideas until you're able to win the boss's support.

Deal with Checked Out

Overarching approach: Consistency

In the moment: When you realize that your boss is incapable of providing leadership or guidance because he or she is preoccupied, stay focused on performing your job in the steady, consistent manner that you always do.

Behind the scenes: Stay the course. Your boss will return when the personal crisis passes.

Deal with Spineless

Overarching approach: Circumvent

In the moment: If you notice that your boss hedges each time you bring up the topic of a raise or promotion, say, "Thanks for considering this," and walk away.

Behind the scenes: Identify who, within the company, can actually advocate for you in this regard. Start cultivating a positive work relationship with that person.

Deal with an Artful Dodger

Overarching approach: Dodge the Dodger

In the moment: The second time that your crafty boss asks you to act as his or her bad-news emissary to a member of the staff, pause and say, "That's beyond my capabilities. Someone else should deliver that message." The Artful Dodger will find another messenger.

Behind the scenes: If you're not willing to act as your boss's bad cop, you'll need to keep a cool distance. Should this limit your ability to excel in your career, you may eventually want to move on.

Deal with Junior

Overarching approach: Educate, don't isolate.

In the moment: As your Junior boss introduces a new system that affects how you perform your job, you may feel very pressured to adapt quickly. To avoid a stress meltdown, pace yourself. Trust that you will learn the new methodologies in a timely manner.

Behind the scenes: Get help. Take a class, hire a tutor, find a colleague to assist you. Reach out for the support you need to retool.

Deal with a Former Colleague

Overarching approach: Forgiveness

In the moment: When your fomer colleague calls you in and starts delegating projects to you, keep your feelings of resentment in check. Quietly take this new leader's directives and carry them out.

Behind the scenes: It may seem as if your colleague got promoted because he or she played the political game. Instead of jumping to that conclusion, try to keep the friendship intact. Uncover your friend's new responsibilities and see how you can help.

Deal with an Unconscious Discriminator

Overarching approach: Let it go.

In the moment: As soon as you experience some form of unconscious discrimination from your boss, you'll feel very hurt. You'll be tempted to lash back in your mind by labeling your employer a clueless idiot.

Behind the scenes: Trust that the better your boss gets to know you, the less his or her prejudice will influence your relationship. Instead of stewing in resentment, try letting the infraction go.

Deal with a Persecutor

Overarching approach: Protection

In the moment: If your persecuting boss attempts to make you the target of his or her negative treatment, tell yourself that you're dealing with a crazy person.

Behind the scenes: Take swift actions to find a better situation. Circulate your résumé and get out.

DEALING FOR WORKER BEES

Deal with a Chronic Critic

Overarching approach: Realistic assessment

In the moment: Every time your boss starts harping about some detail you missed or an error you made, you'll want to escape physically and emotionally. Instead, do your best to stay present and listen to the feedback. If it helps, write down your employer's comments so that you can refer to them (or burn them) later.

Behind the scenes: If you can't tolerate this individual's need to critique and find fault with everything you do, you may have to look for a less disparaging manager.

Deal with a Rule Changer

Overarching approach: Proactive communication

In the moment: When your boss decides that the report he or she requested should be totally revamped, draw on your patient nature to make the adjustments.

Behind the scenes: Instead of waiting for the next round of changes after you've spent hours on a work assignment, try checking in regularly for status updates from your manager. It might reduce your wasted efforts.

Deal with a Yeller

Overarching approach: Self-protection

In the moment: If your boss starts yelling at you, resist the temptation to disappear. Do your best to make eye contact and let him or her know you are listening by saying, "I hear you," clearly and audibly.

Behind the scenes: You'll have to take restorative actions to recover from these brutal incidents. Protect yourself in the long run by building your professional connections and getting out.

Deal with an Underminer

Overarching approach: Check in, don't check out

In the moment: Should you discover that your undermining boss has given the same assignment to two people, approach this leader and ask, "How can we avoid this next time?"

Behind the scenes: Learn to check in with your boss and colleagues regularly before investing a great deal of time or effort on any project.

Deal with "I'm Always Right"

Overarching approach: Tactful diplomacy

In the moment: The next time you offer an idea that your boss doesn't agree with, use your natural ability to back off to your advantage.

Behind the scenes: While you continue to agree with your boss in public, keep looking for opportunities to reintroduce your point of view.

Deal with "You Threaten Me"

Overarching approach: Share the credit

In the moment: Should you receive an industry award or some other form of public recognition, don't be shocked if your boss says something devaluing. Brush off his or her jealous comments and play down your notoriety.

Behind the scenes: The next time the possibility of public recognition arises, be sure to give your boss credit by saying, "This couldn't have happened without you."

Deal with Grandiose

Overarching approach: Surrender

In the moment: Should you become the target of your Grandiose boss's criticism, it's best to respond without defense. After this blustery boss tells you how you failed to live up to his or her very high standards, say, "You're right. Thank you. I'll make the necessary corrections."

Behind the scenes: When you tire of this very needy, egotistical employer, start a new job search.

Deal with a Control Freak

Overarching approach: Be prepared

In the moment: When a Control Freak asks you to explain and defend every action that you take on the job, you'll want to cut and run. Instead, bite the bullet and answer the inquiries as clearly as you can.

Behind the scenes: You'll have to decide whether you can endure the constant scrutiny of this micromanager. If so, learn to prepare yourself for these inquisitions. Bring whatever documentation or information you think the boss will need in order to trust that you're following his or her directives.

Deal with Love-Struck

Overarching approach: Professional demeanor

In the moment: If you feel the boss's loving (or lustful) gaze, stick to the work at hand and act as if it's not happening. Give no indication that you have any interest or that you reciprocate the feelings.

Behind the scenes: Draw on your ability to keep a cool distance from this dewy-eyed authority figure.

Deal with a Calculating Confidant

Overarching approach: Steer clear

In the moment: If your curious boss keeps trying to create a chummy connection, be yourself and give courteous but ambiguous answers.

Behind the scenes: You'll instinctively know to dodge this brand of leader and keep personal conversations to a minimum.

Deal with a Tell-All

Overarching approach: No reply necessary

In the moment: As your boss begins to confess another personal difficulty, listen and notice when you start to feel overwhelmed. You can nod your head and say, "Uh-huh." A detached response is your greatest weapon. It will send your Tell-All boss looking for a more receptive audience.

Behind the scenes: Be professional and maintain a cool distance.

Deal with a Liar, Liar

Overarching approach: Gradual extraction

In the moment: When you catch your boss in a lie, you'll do a better job than most at concealing your surprise. The important thing here is to make a mental note and realize that you are working for a dishonest person.

Behind the scenes: Once you acknowledge that you work for a Liar, Liar, you'll naturally keep him or her at arm's length. In the meantime, put out feelers for healthier work environments and know that your best career move is out of this relationship.

Deal with a Sacred Cow

Overarching approach: Endurance

In the moment: When your progress-blocking boss tells you to rewrite or revamp a proposal for the fifth time, focusing on the minute details that you left out, be grateful that you can handle this kind of treatment graciously.

Behind the scenes: Your willingness to follow the bureaucratic maze this kind of leader constructs will help you get things done. As long as you can follow instructions and give your boss credit for positive results, you'll do well.

Deal with Checked Out

Overarching approach: Stay in touch

In the moment: In the face of a leader who seems preoccupied and unavailable, you should be okay. Worker Bees can quietly tend to their responsibilities with minimal oversight or direction.

Behind the scenes: Get into the habit of keeping your absentee manager informed—even though he or she is not asking for it. Providing this brand of leader with regular updates will help both of you stay current. It will also prevent you from drifting too far away.

Deal with Spineless

Overarching approach: Self-preservation

In the moment: Should there come a time when you're being attacked by a colleague or customer and your boss doesn't come to your aid, you'll probably feel enraged. Tell yourself that you'll find protection from someone else within or outside of the company.

Behind the scenes: Seek out the true advocates in your workplace. If there are no potential protectors, you may have to look for a better work situation.

Deal with an Artful Dodger

Overarching approach: Learning opportunity

In the moment: When an Artful Dodger enrolls you as his or her bad cop who must deliver a tough message to some member of the staff, you'll probably feel sick inside. Know that you can find the words to communicate on behalf of your boss in a diplomatic way.

Behind the scenes: Think of the people you know who are great communicators. Approach one of them for assistance in crafting your message. Use your uncomfortable situation as an opportunity to learn the invaluable skill of delivering tough information to an unsuspecting audience.

Deal with Junior

Overarching approach: Don't hesitate to educate

In the moment: If you feel pressured as your Junior boss introduces a new office procedure, launches a software program, or rolls out a business development campaign, try not to check out. Instead, takes notes and trust that you can find the assistance you need to adapt.

Behind the scenes: Enlist the help you need to incorporate the change. Find a tutor, sign up for a class, or work with your more adept colleagues to master the new skills required for work.

Deal with a Former Colleague

Overarching approach: Wait and see

In the moment: When you find yourself in a meeting and your former colleague starts to give you orders, you may feel a twinge of resentment. Fortunately, you'll be able to push past it and fulfill your new boss's requests.

Behind the scenes: Remain cordial with this person until he or she lets you know how to proceed in this new version of your old relationship.

Deal with an Unconscious Discriminator

Overarching approach: Careful assessment

In the moment: Should an Unconscious Discriminator inadvertently say or do something that reveals a bias against some aspect of your gender, age, ethnicity, sexual orientation, or religion, draw on your inner reserve and let it roll off your back.

Behind the scenes: Decide whether the form and degree of discrimination is something you can live with. If you fear that your boss's bias prevents you from moving your career forward, you'll have to assess whether it's time to leave.

Deal with a Persecutor

Overarching approach: Don't look back

In the moment: To weather a Persecutor's verbal admonishments, listen, nod, and say, "You may be right."

Behind the scenes: Pack your bags and start looking for another position.

CHAPTER 11

New Podiums for Wordsmiths: Dealing with Twenty Boss Behaviors

S TORYTELLERS AND DISARMERS are the workplace communicators. Whether sharing a personal anecdote or announcing a policy change, these individuals thrive when they can craft a message and be heard. Wordsmith employees add color, humor, and animation to the day-to-day operations of any company. They delight in entertaining their colleagues. They also work hard to follow instructions and produce results that they can be proud of.

If you are a Storyteller or a Disarmer, you run into trouble when you work for people who aren't willing to listen. If your boss cuts you off, puts you down, shuts you out, or constantly criticizes you, you'll be very unhappy. To *deal* with any of these circumstances, seek a safer audience through colleagues, special events outside of work, or professional affiliations.

To alleviate your fears of being misunderstood or disrespected, practice pulling back and giving your boss the benefit of the doubt. Instead of assuming the worst and stewing in anger, take a new approach—go back to your employer and ask for clarification.

In the pages that follow, you'll find concrete suggestions for dealing with each of the twenty difficult boss behaviors that we've covered throughout the book. Each Deal remedy includes:

1. An overarching approach—a quality or attitude that you should embody when interacting with this individual.
2. A tactic for handling the boss's behavior "in the moment" (as your boss criticizes you, undermines you, or begins to yell).
3. A strategy for managing the situation "behind the scenes" (actions that will lead to a better outcome in the long run).

Go to your profile category—whether you are a Storyteller (page 126) or a Disarmer (page 127). Find the boss behaviors that drive you bonkers at work. Read the Deal remedies below and practice applying them to your circumstances.

DEALING FOR STORYTELLERS

Dealing with a Chronic Critic

Overarching approach: Less is more

In the moment: When your boss starts to nitpick or complain about some aspect of your work, resist defending yourself or explaining your point of view. Instead, take a deep breath and say, "Thank you. I'll take care of that."

Behind the scenes: If you need to complain about your boss's complaining, find a safe person, either in the office or outside of work, who can hear your story.

Dealing with a Rule Changer

Overarching approach: Flexibility

In the moment: Because Storytellers understand things by talking them through, you may need an explanation when the boss suddenly changes plans. You can go to the boss and say (or e-mail), "I understand we've adjusted course. How would you like me to proceed?"

Behind the scenes: Keep a finger on the pulse of your Rule Changer's shifting priorities by checking in frequently. When you write down a plan, use pencil.

Deal with a Yeller

Overarching approach: Self-control

In the moment: Self-control is the key component here. It won't feel good when this kind of boss starts yelling and making unfair accusations. Your best bet is to zip your lip. Listen, nod, and say, "Okay."

Behind the scenes: This is a bad situation for storytelling employees. Use your gift of gab to connect with others outside of the workplace. Put your efforts into finding your next job with a less volatile boss.

Deal with an Underminer

Overarching approach: Clarification

In the moment: You won't like it when you discover that your boss has given you an assignment, only to hand the same responsibility over to somebody else. Do approach the boss to explain the situation. Don't barrage your boss with your version of the story. Instead, make a brief statement such as, "I just found out that two of us are working on the same project. Could you clarify this situation?"

Behind the scenes: Learn to do some behind-the-scenes investigating whenever you're handed a new project or asked to take on more responsibility.

Deal with "I'm Always Right"

Overarching approach: Yield

In the moment: When your boss starts insisting that he or she is right about something, you may feel your blood boil. Instead of interrupting to prove this person wrong, take a deep breath and zip your lip. It doesn't matter. Let your boss be right.

Behind the scenes: If there are other people in the company or department to talk to and you can work around this person, aim to keep your distance and do your job. If, however, it's just you and this boss, you'll probably need to devise a strategy for getting out.

Deal with "You Threaten Me"

Overarching approach: Give credit where it's (not) due.

In the moment: If you receive notoriety for excellent performance from a high-level executive within the company or a professional association outside of the company, go directly to the boss and thank him or her for making it possible (even if your chief had nothing to do with it).

Behind the scenes: Continue to show loyalty to this leader and share the credit for any successes you have on the job.

Deal with Grandiose

Overarching approach: Temporary tolerance

In the moment: While your Grandiose boss holds court, making it impossible for anyone to get a word in, keep breathing.

Behind the scenes: This kind of boss is probably intolerable for a Storyteller. Your best bet is to start looking for another job with a more down-to-earth boss.

Deal with a Control Freak

Overarching approach: Building trust

In the moment: If you feel yourself bristle as your boss oversees and corrects your every move, try not to shut down and resist all instruction. Instead, listen carefully and do your best to follow orders.

Behind the scenes: Acknowledge that you are in a trust-building process with this individual. The scrutiny you experience isn't meant to disparage your work. Give this boss time to trust your capabilities.

Deal with Love-Struck

Overarching approach: Restraint

In the moment: If you notice that your boss seems enthralled with your stories and wants to get closer on a personal level, pull back. Share less about yourself—especially your private life.

Behind the scenes: Shift your association from friendly and chatty to professional. Focus on listening rather than speaking, and save your storytelling for safer audiences.

Deal with a Calculating Confidant

Overarching approach: Minimal communication

In the moment: If you sense that your boss has little patience for your stories and discounts your input, keep conversations and meetings with him or her short and to the point. Be especially careful not to divulge personal information.

Behind the scenes: Aim for a professional yet cordial relationship. Treat your boss in a friendly manner, but minimize unnecessary communication. If this individual continues to treat you poorly, look for greener employment pastures with a trustworthy employer.

Deal with a Tell-All

Overarching approach: Don't get roped in

In the moment: As your Tell-All boss unloads another personal drama while meeting with you, refrain from jumping in and adding your personal tale to the mix. Listen carefully, complete the meeting, and get back to work.

Behind the scenes: Because you're able to see through the Tell-All's ways, you'll find it challenging to work for this person. Start rekindling your professional relationships and look for work with a less manipulative boss.

Deal with a Liar, Liar

Overarching approach: Be true to yourself

In the moment: When you catch your boss lying, resist the impulse to correct this person or stage an intervention. Make a mental note and promise yourself that you'll address it later.

Behind the scenes: You have one of three options: meet with your boss in private and ask for an explanation of the behavior; don't do anything, and assume someone else will confront the issue; or gather your facts and go to someone with greater authority to report your findings.

Deal with a Sacred Cow

Overarching approach: Create alliances

In the moment: Should your Sacred Cow boss automatically reject your proposals without hearing your side of the story, do not attempt to convince him or her to do otherwise. Pull back and regroup.

Behind the scenes: Focus on quietly strengthening your alliances with the people within the company who can help turn your ideas into reality. Be sure to give your boss the unwarranted credit that he or she craves.

Checked Out

Overarching approach: Empathy

In the moment: You won't like it when your leader appears distant and disinterested. While you may want to scold your employer for being unavailable, try practicing patience. Ask your boss how you can be of assistance.

Behind the scenes: Understand that, for the time being, you have to manage yourself. See how you and your colleagues can band together to get the work done.

Deal with Spineless

Overarching approach: Work-around

In the moment: The next time you give your boss a detailed account of some workplace event, enjoy holding this person's attention, but don't expect any other outcome.

Behind the scenes: Make it your business to find the people in your company or department who actually get things done and work with them to create results.

Deal with an Artful Dodger

Overarching approach: Artful communication

In the moment: When an Artful Dodger asks you to deliver a tough message to another member of the staff, you may be uncomfortable with the thought of confronting a coworker on behalf of the boss. Trust your skills as a capable communicator and take on the task.

Behind the scenes: Take a serious look at whether you want to be your boss's verbal hit man. If you can handle it, working for an Artful Dodger could give you valuable skills for handling tough situations. If not, network for a better, less confrontational opportunity.

Deal with Junior

Overarching approach: Delayed gratification

In the moment: If your youthful boss cuts you off in the middle of a story, don't take offense and don't try to return to the tale. Instead, tune in to this new leader's priorities.

Behind the scenes: Take the time to learn the skills and procedures that your Junior boss feels are important. Once you've mastered his or her method of doing business, your detailed accounts may have more value.

Deal with a Former Colleague

Overarching approach: Acknowledge the loss

In the moment: If you find your former colleague cutting conversations short or limiting contact to scheduled meetings, you may feel slighted. Try to take your friend's professional distancing in stride.

Behind the scenes: See if your former colleague is interested in building a friendship outside of work while respecting his or her changed status on the job. Build other workplace relationships while you adjust to the loss.

Deal with an Unconscious Discriminator

Overarching approach: Educate, don't humiliate

In the moment: As you catch your boss inadvertently making a biased statement about some aspect of your age, gender, ethnicity, religion, sexual orientation, or nationality, take note. Use your quick-witted communication style to intercept and correct the faux pas as soon as possible.

Behind the scenes: Be careful not to embarrass your boss by educating and enlightening him or her in front of others. Instead, wait for a private moment to work your magic.

Deal with a Persecutor

Overarching approach: Expedient exit

In the moment: Should you become the target of this vengeful manager's attacks, avoid all temptation to defend yourself or attack back. Instead, keep quiet so that any assault can end quickly.

Behind the scenes: Jump ship as soon as you are able.

DEALING FOR DISARMERS

Deal with a Chronic Critic

Overarching approach: Lighten up

In the moment: As your hypercritical leader insists on pointing out the one error in any document you produce or task you perform, draw on your humor to lighten the severity of this minor infraction.

Behind the scenes: Understand that your sense of humor provides valuable relief to this kind of boss and to the people that he or she oversees. Use it to make your work environment a better place.

Deal with a Rule Changer

Overarching approach: Flexibility

In the moment: When your boss starts to rearrange the very plans that he or she made the day before, tap into your cooperative spirit. Shrug it off, make a joke, and incorporate the change.

Behind the scenes: Now that you know you work for a Rule Changer, adapt your repertoire accordingly. Use a pencil when writing down decisions, appointments, or plans. Brush up on your jokes about dealing with change.

Deal with a Yeller

Overarching approach: Tough audience

In the moment: Should your boss throw a temper tantrum in your direction, take a deep breath, watch the eruption, and refrain from making light of the situation. All you need to say is, "I hear you" or "Okay."

Behind the scenes: If you find that you're no longer interested in entertaining this hotheaded employer, circulate your résumé.

Deal with an Underminer

Overarching approach: Get serious

In the moment: If you discover that your boss has given you responsibility only to override your decision making, you won't be happy. No need to find the humor here. Instead, take on a serious tone and ask your employer to explain exactly what happened.

Behind the scenes: Consider this brand of leader a good teacher for you. You'll have many opportunities to confront your Underminer boss in a serious manner—without diluting your message with humor.

Deal with "I'm Always Right"

Overarching approach: Win-win

In the moment: When your boss insists that his or her way of handling a certain situation is the only way, you'll probably be able to agree and insert a little humor.

Behind the scenes: Your disarming attitude toward this heavy-handed leader will open the door for you to get your way much of the time. Just keep this boss laughing at him- or herself.

Deal with "You Threaten Me"

Overarching approach: Share the stage

In the moment: This boss may suddenly make sarcastic remarks or put you down if you accidentally steal the show by receiving too much attention for your performance or your winning personality. In those moments, it's best to downplay your popularity and remind the boss that you'd be nowhere without his or her guidance.

Behind the scenes: Make it your business to keep your boss in the spotlight by talking up his or her talents and achievements to coworkers, customers, and executives in high places.

Deal with Grandiose

Overarching approach: Give praise

In the moment: As your Grandiose boss winds up to retell a story regarding his or her glorious past, listen for a few minutes, then gently interrupt by saying, "You are amazing. Let me get back to work so I can keep your stellar reputation in the limelight."

Behind the scenes: Teach the rest of the staff how to incorporate your magical disarming ways so that they can handle this blustery boss with a minimum of agita.

Deal with a Control Freak

Overarching approach: Cut the tension

In the moment: On those days when you feel oppressed by your boss's heavy-handed management style, try cutting the tension with your humor.

Behind the scenes: Draw on your ability to follow directions while you keep this nervous leader posted regarding your daily activities. Employ your lighter side to lift your boss's spirits.

Deal with Love-Struck

Overarching approach: Pull back

In the moment: Should you sense that your boss has a crush on you, you can enjoy the attention, but keep your behavior cool and professional.

Behind the scenes: You may need to temper your normally familiar, jovial demeanor in this relationship. Until the crush passes, keep the jokes to a minimum.

Deal with a Calculating Confidant

Overarching approach: Don't ask, don't tell

In the moment: As you notice your boss digging for juicy tidbits—about you or your colleagues—use your impostor detector and avoid revealing anything of substance.

Behind the scenes: Trust your instincts and keep your distance. Continue to be cordial and productive. Don't engage in any form of gossip.

Deal with a Tell-All

Overarching approach: Set limits

In the moment: When this leader comes to you with another personal drama or trauma, you can derail his or her woeful outlook by finding the humor in the situation. The Tell-All will appreciate it.

Behind the scenes: Your can-do attitude may be tested as the Tell-All attempts to dump much of his or her workload in your lap. Decide how much overtime you're willing to put in and communicate it clearly to your boss.

Deal with a Liar, Liar

Overarching approach: Discernment

In the moment: When you catch your boss stretching the truth or lying to you about a specific topic, you can apply humor to the situation and gently expose the falsehood. If, however, the lie takes place in a public setting, you'll have to let it slide until you have a private moment with your manager.

Behind the scenes: You'll have to determine how dishonest this person is and whether you can live with it. If it gets too uncomfortable, seek a more trustworthy manager.

Deal with a Sacred Cow

Overarching approach: Keep all doors open

In the moment: You'll feel frustrated when this boss hedges on making decisions and blocks your ability to move forward on projects. Bring in your humor to lighten the moment and retreat so that you can regroup.

Behind the scenes: To get things done, figure out how to work around the Sacred Cow. If you can continue to humor this leader as you build the interdepartmental alliances you need to accomplish your goals, fine. Ultimately, however, this kind of work environment is too confining for your independent and efficient spirit. Ride it out as long as you can, but keep networking for better opportunities.

Deal with Checked Out

Overarching approach: Temporary loss

In the moment: If your boss is physically present but mentally and emotionally Checked Out, you may feel hurt by his or her lackluster responses to your humor. Try not to show your disappointment.

Behind the scenes: Focus on doing your job well, despite the lack of leadership. Share comic relief with your coworkers and trust that your boss will eventually return.

Deal with Spineless

Overarching approach: Respected spokesperson

In the moment: If your boss starts to waiver about taking a stand—whether it's clarifying policy with customers or settling a dispute between coworkers—offer to step in and take charge. A Spineless boss will trust you to use humor and a light touch to settle the matter without causing casualties.

Behind the scenes: Realize that because of your nonthreatening style, you'll probably become the spokesperson for your colleagues both within and outside of your department. Enjoy the role as long as it works for you.

Deal with an Artful Dodger

Overarching approach: Artful negotiation

In the moment: When an Artful Dodger boss asks you to be the bearer of bad news to a customer or member of the staff, clarify the message and say, "Let me think about the right way to say this."

Behind the scenes: Decide whether you feel comfortable acting as the bad cop for this image-conscious leader. If you don't agree with the overall message or fear that it won't carry the necessary weight coming from you, go back to the boss and say, "I'd be happy to deliver this message, but I need you to back me up. Can you be on the phone or in the room when I say it?" If the boss says no, complete the task at hand. Then decide how long you want to be put in the bad-cop position.

Deal with Junior

Overarching approach: Fountain of youth

In the moment: If your boss makes an off-putting statement—"Don't you think your way of handling this is a bit outdated?"—look for the funny side of the situation. Respond with something like this: "You're right. You're my ticket into the future."

Behind the scenes: Do your homework to keep your skills and information current.

Deal with a Former Colleague

Overarching approach: Observe and adapt

In the moment: The first time you receive orders from your fomer colleague, you may be tempted to make a funny retort such as "Yes, Master," which could be experienced as a sarcastic comment. Refrain from saying anything funny and simply follow your new boss's command.

Behind the scenes: Find time outside of the workplace to check in with your friend. At work, look for ways to support your former coworker's new leadership.

Deal with an Unconscious Discriminator

Overarching approach: Guided intervention

In the moment: If your boss inadvertently makes a derisive remark regarding your gender, age, appearance, ethnic background, religion, or sexual orientation, it will hurt. Don't react. Buy some time to think your response through.

Behind the scenes: Run the situation by a trusted friend or adviser. See whether you want to address the incident with your boss and what you might say that will help this individual avoid future offense.

Deal with a Persecutor

Overarching approach: Immediate egress

In the moment: As your boss goes on the attack, your best tactic is to listen without absorbing the rage. Don't try to defend or make light of the accusations.

Behind the scenes: Start packing your bags and exit as soon as possible.

CHAPTER 12

Medicine for Mellows: Dealing with Twenty Boss Behaviors

COASTERS AND LOW BEAMERS are staunch advocates for reasonable hours and manageable responsibilities at work. While these individuals are willing to do their jobs, they seek out situations that involve minimal stress and very little pressure. The Mellows have full lives outside of the office and encourage others to do the same. These employees know how to pace themselves and leave time for extracurricular activities.

Should you work for an authority figure who's demanding or critical, *dealing* will involve making a decision: either adjust your expectations and rise to meet your manager's demands, or get used to falling short and weathering the criticism.

To alleviate your fear of being ridiculed or making the wrong decision, practice two things. First, participate fully in meetings, projects, and company initiatives. Raise your hand and offer ideas. Ask questions when you don't understand. Second, practice making small decisions on your own at work.

In the pages that follow, you'll find concrete suggestions for dealing with each of the twenty difficult boss behaviors that we've covered throughout the book. Each Deal remedy includes:

1. An overarching approach—a quality or attitude that you should embody when interacting with this individual.
2. A tactic for handling the boss's behavior "in the moment" (as your boss criticizes you, undermines you, or begins to yell).
3. A strategy for managing the situation "behind the scenes" (actions that will lead to a better outcome in the long run).

Go to your profile category—whether you are a Coaster (page 128) or a Low Beamer (page 129). Find the boss behaviors that drive you bonkers at work. Read the Deal remedies below and practice applying them to your circumstances.

DEALING FOR COASTERS

Deal with a Chronic Critic

Overarching approach: Stress reduction

In the moment: When your chronically critical boss points out the myriad mistakes that you made during the day, you'll feel increasingly uncomfortable. As your stress level rises, take a few deep breaths and try to calm yourself down.

Behind the scenes: If you like the work environment and don't want to lose your job, you'll need to create a stress-management routine and engage in confidence-building activities (see Chapter 3).

Deal with a Rule Changer

Overarching approach: No sweat

In the moment: Every time your boss revises a plan or rearranges scheduled meetings, you'll be better equipped than most to adjust to the new reality.

Behind the scenes: Let this leader know that you can go with the flow. Check in on a daily basis to find out what decisions, policies, or events may be revamped and how you can help.

Deal with a Yeller

Overarching approach: Get out of the fire

In the moment: When you see your boss winding up for an explosion, brace yourself and try to watch the event like a spectator at a horror film. The more you can distance yourself mentally from your boss's anger, the better off you'll be.

Behind the scenes: This kind of situation is very destructive for most Coasters. The smartest strategy is to quietly seek safer employment under a less volatile leader.

Deal with an Underminer

Overarching approach: Cover your tracks

In the moment: The next time you discover that your boss has given the same assignment to you and a colleague, you'll know not to waste your energy on completing the task.

Behind the scenes: Make sure that you don't underestimate your boss's ability to dish out the same assignment to more than one person. Instead, when your boss asks you to perform a task, do some behind-the-scenes investigating to make sure you're the only one entrusted with this responsibility.

Deal with "I'm Always Right"

Overarching approach: Doing it their way

In the moment: When your boss insists that his or her outlook on any issue is the correct one, you won't mind agreeing with that perspective. Use your easygoing nature to say, "You're right," whenever necessary.

Behind the scenes: Try to perform your job in a way that fulfills your boss's requirements.

Deal with "You Threaten Me"

Overarching approach: Pump them up

In the moment: Because you do not seek the limelight at work, this boss is unlikely to feel threatened by you.

Behind the scenes: You can build goodwill by acting as your boss's best advocate. Acknowledge your boss and recognize his or her many successes.

Deal with Grandiose

Overarching approach: Meet the standard

In the moment: If your Grandiose boss takes issue with the quality of your work, complaining that you fail to meet his or her high standards, you may feel like running. Instead, try to apologize and say, "I'll work on it."

Behind the scenes: If you want to continue to work under this authority figure's guidance, apply yourself. Try exerting just 10 percent more effort to live up to your boss's standards.

Deal with a Control Freak

Overarching approach: Focus on details

In the moment: You aren't going to like being scrutinized and micromanaged by this brand of boss. If you want to save your job, attempt to listen carefully and follow instructions.

Behind the scenes: The pressure of working for a Control Freak won't work well with your easygoing nature. Start looking for another, less rigid work environment.

Deal with Love-Struck

Overarching approach: Proceed with caution

In the moment: If you notice that your boss would rather chat and take you out for long lunches than get down to work, you can enjoy the attention. Just don't let the relationship extend beyond work hours.

Behind the scenes: To ensure that your job will outlast your boss's crush, be sure that you continue to bring some professional value to the relationship beyond your charming personality.

Deal with a Calculating Confidant

Overarching approach: Careful communication

In the moment: When this cagey manager extends a meeting in order to "dish" about other employees, do not take the bait. Use such phrases as "I wouldn't know" or "I must have missed that."

Behind the scenes: If you're ever confronted by a coworker because you accidentally leaked personal information about him or her, own up to the mistake and apologize. Warn your colleagues about this dangerous boss's seductive ways.

Deal with a Tell-All

Overarching approach: Tea and sympathy

In the moment: If this kind of boss needs to share a personal story, pull up a chair and relax. Let your leader offload his or her problems and lend a sympathetic ear.

Behind the scenes: Your easygoing manner will be a source of comfort and support for this person. Use your charm to avoid taking on additional responsibilities.

Deal with a Liar, Liar

Overarching approach: Self-protection

In the moment: If you catch your boss in a lie, make a mental note, but don't let on that you're aware of the untruth.

Behind the scenes: Take a serious look at the character of this person and how his or her deceptive behavior may tarnish your reputation. If you decide to stay, carefully document your actions under the Liar, Liar's management so that you aren't falsely accused of wrongdoing.

Deal with a Sacred Cow

Overarching approach: Safe, but stagnant

In the moment: You'll be able to follow this cautious manager's lead.

Behind the scenes: Working for a Sacred Cow may work for you on many levels. Just make sure that you don't miss out on opportunities for advancement by hiding behind your boss.

Deal with Checked Out

Overarching approach: Self-management

In the moment: If you notice that your boss seems Checked Out and inattentive, quietly attend to your job.

Behind the scenes: Since no one is watching, this is an opportunity to shine. Do your job so that your manager can express appreciation upon his or her return.

Deal with Spineless

Overarching approach: Self-advocacy

In the moment: If your Spineless boss isn't able to come to your defense when a customer or coworker complains about you, try rescuing yourself.

Present the facts of the situation to the complaining party and work out a solution that everyone can live with.

Behind the scenes: It's important to be more proactive with this kind of boss. Keep clear records of your work and any exchanges that could lead to trouble. Also build alliances with the natural leaders in your department.

Deal with an Artful Dodger

Overarching approach: Artfully dodge the Artful Dodger

In the moment: When you walk out of a meeting where your boss just praised you, only to be told by a third party that you're underperforming, you'll feel confused. Clarify the situation by describing your bewilderment to the third party. "I don't understand. The boss just told me that I'm doing a great job, and you just told me the opposite. Which should I believe?"

Behind the scenes: Acknowledge the truth to yourself regarding your boss's two-faced ways. Be careful not to buy into the nice-guy image. Do your job and stay out of harm's way.

Deal with Junior

Overarching approach: Get smart

In the moment: As your boss ushers in new software and expects you to get it after a three-minute tutorial, say, "Thanks. I can work with that."

Behind the scenes: Use your charming ways to get your coworkers to teach you whatever new skills are required. You can learn at your own pace, but make sure to take advantage of this opportunity to stay current.

Deal with a Former Colleague

Overarching approach: Meet the challenge

In the moment: You won't like it when your Fomer Colleague boss says, "You're not applying yourself. I need to see more results in less time." Resist shutting down. Instead, respond with, "I can work harder for you."

Behind the scenes: Try to give your friend who is now your manager what he or she is requesting. You might succeed and enjoy it!

Deal with an Unconscious Discriminator

Overarching approach: Don't let it get you down

In the moment: It may sting when this brand of boss reveals some form of prejudice regarding your appearance, gender, race, ethnic background, religion, or sexual orientation. Your best defense is to stay neutral.

Behind the scenes: Think about your options. If the discrimination makes it difficult for you to do your job, you may have to seek employment elsewhere. Otherwise, shake it off and don't let this person's crude remarks ruin your day.

Deal with a Persecutor

Overarching approach: Survival

In the moment: When a persecuting boss singles you out and attacks your performance, try to look right through this person and fend off the toxic energy.

Behind the scenes: Do not accept this kind of treatment. Reach out to your friends and colleagues and jump ship.

DEALING FOR LOW BEAMERS

Deal with a Chronic Critic

Overarching approach: Make a critical choice

In the moment: This person's compulsion to find fault with every document you produce will get under your skin. Instead of defending yourself, thank your boss for the corrections and return to your workstation.

Behind the scenes: Decide whether you can tolerate an employer whose professional style includes finding the flaw in everything you do. If not, seek a more positive, supportive work environment.

Deal with a Rule Changer

Overarching approach: Flexibility

In the moment: If a rule-changing supervisor informs you that the project you just completed has taken a different direction, resist the urge to stomp off in disgust. Instead, take a deep breath and ask your manager, "Should I be checking in with you more often to stay abreast of these changes?"

Behind the scenes: If you decide that you can tolerate this kind of leader, make it your business to constantly check in. Find out daily what adjustments need to be made to existing plans.

Deal with a Yeller

Overarching approach: Weather the storm

In the moment: If your boss becomes irate over something that you failed to do or a mistake that you inadvertently made, you can weather the storm by listening without defending yourself. When the verbal tornado passes, excuse yourself with a reassuring statement such as "I'll take care of that" or "I'll attend to the problem right away."

Behind the scenes: Decide if this is a situation you can withstand. If not, focus your energies on finding a safer, less volatile environment.

Deal with an Underminer

Overarching approach: Step up and stand up for yourself

In the moment: Should you discover that your boss has given you responsibility, only to dish the same assignment out to someone else, you may take it as an insult to your intelligence. Rather than stew in silence, ask your boss for clarity regarding whom he or she would like to complete the project at hand.

Behind the scenes: Try keeping in close touch with your manager, letting him or her know what kinds of projects you'd be willing to tackle.

Deal with "I'm Always Right"

Overarching approach: I'm okay, you're okay

In the moment: When your righteous leader insists that you perform a certain task his or her way, refrain from arguing. It's best to say, "I'll try it your way."

Behind the scenes: See if you can appreciate the fact that you're working for someone who is willing to clearly state what he or she expects of you. Do your best to carry out the orders. If problems arise, report them as facts—not proof that this employer is wrong.

Deal with "You Threaten Me"

Overarching approach: Standing ovation

In the moment: It's unlikely that you'll do or say anything to threaten this recognition-seeking leader. If by chance you do receive public acclaim, make sure to give your boss credit for your success.

Behind the scenes: Now that you know your boss is easily threatened, be sure to offer constant praise and verbal recognition of this individual's status and accomplishments within the industry.

Deal with Grandiose

Overarching approach: Appreciative audience

In the moment: You're likely to appreciate the clear instructions and exacting approach toward any task that this boss offers. Should you get tired of listening to your big boss's war stories, politely excuse yourself with a statement like this: "Let me get back to that project you gave me earlier."

Behind the scenes: Find ways to rejuvenate. Get plenty of rest and build in vacations to recharge your energy and refresh your mind.

Deal with a Control Freak

Overarching approach: Follow instructions

In the moment: As your boss carefully explains what he or she wants, enjoy the clarity and ask questions to make sure you understand what's expected of you.

Behind the scenes: Be willing to do things according to the Control Freak's code. Keep your boss informed and you'll have this job for a while.

Deal with Love-Struck

Overarching approach: Careful consideration.

In the moment: Should you sense that your boss's amorous attention is focused on you, keep cool and stick to the business topic at hand.

Behind the scenes: If you're considering crossing the line with your manager, take it very slowly. You want to make sure this is a love connection, not an easy conquest for your boss. If you're not interested, trust that playing it cool will quell the crush.

Deal with a Calculating Confidant

Overarching approach: Silence is golden

In the moment: If your boss seems overly interested in your personal life or the private lives of your coworkers, use your innate ability to detect invasive personal questioning. Give polite, short answers such as "I have a great home life" or "I'm not really up to date on that person."

Behind the scenes: Stay focused on delivering a solid work product and remaining uninterested in any conversation that leads to gossip or confiding private information. You'll be fine.

Deal with a Tell-All

Overarching approach: Carry a heavier load

In the moment: If your boss starts whining or going into a long, melodramatic story about how difficult his or her life is, resist your desire to shut down. Instead, try asking, "What is it you'd like me to do?" If the response is "Just listen," follow that lead. If your boss wants you to take on his or her responsibilities, you'll have to determine how much you can shoulder.

Behind the scenes: Tell-All bosses lean heavily on their employees. Holding this person's hand emotionally and literally may not be something you're willing to do. If this emotionally draining leader doesn't work for you, seek employment elsewhere.

Deal with a Liar, Liar

Overarching approach: Turn 'em in or let it go

In the moment: You'll probably be surprised and outraged when you first discover that your boss has lied to you. Refrain from obsessing about the injustice or confronting the boss. Instead, document the infraction.

Behind the scenes: If your boss's lying is of a heinous nature, consider reporting it to HR or hiring a labor attorney. Otherwise, you'll have to decide if you can stomach this person's inability to tell you (and others) the truth.

Deal with a Sacred Cow

Overarching approach: Secure, but boring

In the moment: You should be able to work with a Sacred Cow with very little trouble.

Behind the scenes: Just make sure that you find out how your cautious leader wants you to perform the job. If you start to get bored, you may have to move on.

Deal with Checked Out

Overarching approach: Seek direction

In the moment: If your boss seems preoccupied and inattentive, you may want to lodge a complaint. Instead, look for someone else in authority to give you direction.

Behind the scenes: Do not give in to the urge simply to sit around and wait. You will improve your reputation and your mood by finding projects to fill the time until your boss returns to the helm.

Deal with Spineless

Overarching approach: Strategic alliances

In the moment: If your boss fails to stand up for you when a customer or coworker complains about your performance, try not to feel betrayed. Instead, seek the counsel of a strong colleague who may be able to argue on your behalf.

Behind the scenes: Create alliances with individuals who know how to take a stand and can assist in protecting you at work.

Deal with an Artful Dodger

Overarching approach: Personal decision

In the moment: The first time you discover that the boss who praises you in a staff meeting has criticized you behind your back, you'll want to protest. You'll be tempted to confront this person and ask for clarification. Don't do it. Instead, retreat and regroup.

Behind the scenes: You have a tough decision to make. Either you agree to work for someone who will never tell you directly when he or she is unhappy with your performance or you look for a more direct and honest manager.

Deal with Junior

Overarching approach: Stay ahead of the curve

In the moment: As your youthful leader introduces a number of technological advances and procedural changes, you may want to oppose these time-consuming adjustments. Try to keep an open attitude and participate in the process.

Behind the scenes: Understand that updating your skills is key to remaining employable. Enlist the assistance of your colleagues or take a class to learn how to integrate the changes.

Deal with a Former Colleague

Overarching approach: Redefining roles

In the moment: You may flinch the first time your fomer colleague orders you to carry out a task or responsibility that the two of you used to do together. While you may feel that he or she is being a bit rude, zip your lip and carry out the directive.

Behind the scenes: It may take a while, but you can adjust to this shift in power. Study your new boss and find out what he or she expects of you. A slightly different relationship will emerge.

Deal with an Unconscious Discriminator

Overarching approach: Second chances

In the moment: If your supervisor makes a statement that you find discriminatory or offensive, don't react. Instead, take a time-out.

Behind the scenes: Before reporting the incident to human resources, go back to the boss at a quiet time and say, "Can you clarify this statement for me?" Give your manager a chance to mend his or her ways.

Deal with a Persecutor

Overarching approach: Don't resent, document

In the moment: When you become the target of a Persecutor's unfair treatment, lie low and wait for the moment to pass.

Behind the scenes: Keep a record of each exchange with this unkind manager. If necessary, take your incriminating evidence to HR. In the mean time, polish up your résumé and get out.

Final Thoughts

CONGRATULATIONS. YOU'VE JUST made a valuable investment in your own personal and professional development. You've taken control of the most important relationship at work—the one between you and the person you call boss. Taking responsibility for the outcome of this association isn't easy. It takes courage to see how your behavior is influencing the situation. It takes commitment to change your reactions.

You could easily wallow in the blame game: complain about your boss; seek sympathy from friends, family, and colleagues. But you know that complaining does nothing to improve your circumstances. You may be right about your boss's obnoxious actions, but you're also stuck in a workplace dynamic that zaps your energy and limits your professional growth. By reading this book, you've changed the game.

Understand that building a better relationship with any authority figure is a process. We suggest that you read and reread about each of the Four D's. You'll want to become very clear about your automatic responses when interactions with the boss rattle your nerves. As soon as you catch yourself engaging in any of the ten coping tactics (obsessing, bad-mouthing, retaliating, shutting out, sulking, or others), *stop!* Find out where you are in the cycle of a toxic boss/employee relationship, and begin applying the Four D's.

Remember that true change takes time. While you may feel immediate relief because of your heightened awareness about the boss and what you can do to improve the relationship, it usually takes at least three months of diligent work to implement these tools fully.

You'll know that you've integrated this material into your daily life when . . .

- You no longer have to resort to counterproductive coping tactics.
- You can accept the boss for who he or she is.
- You no longer have adverse emotional or physical reactions to the boss's behavior.
- You know how to take back your personal power.
- You've found ways to adjust your expectations, fulfill your unmet needs, and alleviate your fears at work.

It's important to appreciate the courage it takes to look at yourself and identify how you may be helping or hurting yourself when it comes to the boss. Be patient with your process. Test out our techniques and allow time for lasting change to settle in.

Acknowledgments

HIS BOOK WOULD not have been possible (or as much fun) without the exceptional help of the following people:

Rob Gilpatrick, Judy Lang, Niamh Van Meines, Reverend Will Purdy, Jane Sandlar, Naomi Rosenblatt, Gwen Eyster, Rosamond Vernon, and Dick Hinchliffe. Thank you for taking your precious time to read an unfinished chapter or two and offering your observations, corrections, revisions, criticisms, and compliments. You do not know how helpful your comments were. *Thank you.* We incorporated everything you said.

Dan Mulhern and Carolyn Cassin, thank you for being our cheerleaders. Your faith, trust, and belief in us keep us going. Denyse Thompson, thank you for being our office manager/office mother; you know our needs before we are even aware of them.

Our agent, Elaine Markson, and her assistant, Gary Johnson, deserve a special thank-you for their industry knowledge and relationships. Mark Chimsky, we thank you for providing your wise counsel and invaluable support once again. Donna Ratajczak, you make our lives so much easier. Thank you for your insight, mastery of wordsmithing, and brilliant sense of humor. Adrian Zackheim and Adrienne Schultz, we are grateful for this opportunity. Your vision, business acumen, and editorial expertise inspire us to do our best work.

And now for the home teams:

David Winkler, we thank you for your unending patience and willingness to read everything we sent your way. We appreciate your humor and insight.

Nicole Winkler, thank you for listening to our stories and keeping us humble.

Clif Eddens, thank you for your absolute faith in the power of our message and your insistence that we provide concrete solutions for our readers. Without your love and support we would not have as much to give. So thank you for cooking, shopping, and reading from time to time. We love you.

Index